Adventures of a Curious Traveler

"Twenty years from now you will be more disappointed by the things you didn't do than by the ones you did do. So throw off the bowlines, sail away from the safe harbor. Catch the trade winds in your sails. Explore. Dream. Discover."

Mark Twain

"We speak of stories ending, when in truth it is we who end. The stories go on and on. "

Jacqueline Carey

Adventures of a Curious Traveler

Being the accumulated diaries, stories and
memories of a self-confessed travel addict

Leslie Ross

To friends and family who listened to me fuss and fume, to the kind folks who gave "another set of eyes" before this manuscript went out into the world, to readers who encouraged me to put all my stories together, and to Michael, my husband and editor, whose steady compass has always kept me on course and brought me safely home, this book is gratefully dedicated.

ISBN 13-97814-78385-851

Table of Contents

Table of Contents

Table of Contents

Introduction: To Begin

Walking in the rain in Beaune, France

"Once the travel bug bites there is no known antidote and I know that I shall be happily infected until the end of my life."
Michael Palin

Of course, there are better things to do than travel. And if you give me a year or two, I'm sure I'll think of some.

I was fortunate to have been raised in Nebraska, a land of lovely people and lousy weather. One advantage of growing up in the Midwest is that everywhere else looks so exotic. I'm still thrilled by mountains and pine trees, which makes living in northern Arizona a constant delight.

I didn't start out to be a traveler, but after college I left my ivory-towered grad school and went to Europe with a friend and a backpack, intending to stay for a few weeks. Instead, we were there for five months until the money ran out, and we were down to one meal a day. We bought a little VW in Athens and drove where the mood took us. We had adventures, we met people, we saw so much, and I decided that traveling was much more fun than anything else I could do. Discussing the niceties of Troilus and Criseyde or reading Beowulf for the third time paled in comparison to catching trains in Italy.

The lessons I learned on that first trip have influenced just about everything else I have ever done. Leaving a precise, academic life and getting lost in the world gave me the foundation for the life I love now and has enriched me in ways I am still discovering. I can still see every one of those days in Greece and Italy when we were drifters, following the weather and the legends to Delphi and Capri and Mystra.

While I've traveled, I've become a little evangelical about the whole process of travel and strongly recommend it as a cure for almost everything. It may not cure the common cold, but it will help you forget you have one. It may not mend a broken heart, but it will get you by until a new love comes along.

The time before a trip is full of planning. You have to decide where to go, how long to spend and what to see. Set yourself to learn about your destination, the history, the religion, the food, the wine, the language, the geography, so you will know just what you are looking at. Then you have the trip itself, where the whole world is open to you. Afterwards, you will have the time to remember and those memories will last for the rest of your life.

I couldn't tell you what I did last May, but I can tell you in precise detail what the sky was like, how the roses smelled, what the sounds were when the imam gave the call to prayer as I walked between Topkapi and the Blue Mosque on the Golden Horn. I can still taste the tea I had in Darjeeling with an Indian tea-planter and his wife and still remember the strong discussion I had with a young father in Athens about his little girl getting to play soccer. Walking down the causeway into Seti's tomb in the Valley of the Kings, smelling the lilacs at Chenonceau, going right into the middle of the Sistine Chapel, looking up to see God's hand outstretched toward Adam's and then not being able to see a darn thing because my eyes were full of tears, these will all stay with me for the rest of my life.

Travel encourages tolerance and appreciation of other cultures. It gets rid of stereotypes. Once you put faces on people, you can't say, "All Frenchmen are rude," "All Arabs are radicals," "All the people in Belfast carry guns." I can still remember being in the spice market in Istanbul and hunting for the bathroom. I finally ended up in a little restroom where there was a group of other women all wearing headscarves, waiting. And all I could think of was, "I'm in the Spice Market – in Istanbul, and I'm in a lady-line for the bathroom!" See, we're not so different after all. Travel is about leaving your comfort zone, giving yourself new worlds to look at and new ideas to consider. Be curious. Stretch yourself. The whole world is there just waiting for you. All you have to do is go explore it.

A lot of people have asked me where my ideas come from, and the only thing I'm really sure of is that they always seem to arrive at inconvenient times. I try to keep pen and paper in the car so I can pull over while I'm driving, but still a lot of scribbled notes seem to show up on the odd bit of paper, in the margins of newspaper articles, the bottoms of grocery lists or the back of a dry cleaner receipt. And since being upside down while washing my hair in the shower appears to be an exceptionally creative angle, I try to keep paper in the bathroom too. There seemed to be a lot of leaping in and out of the water while I was writing the piece about shopping. Since my stories are primarily arranged by country, this book can be read in stops and starts, and works perfectly, for example while waiting for the plumber to come or when you can't quite get to sleep.

I should mention that these stories I'm telling truly happened. Every now and then I've changed a name, either to shield someone or because it wasn't in my notes. I may have glossed over the crummy weather or a bad hotel because it wasn't relevant to my piece, but basically this is all genuine. Some of my stories are humorous because there is a lot of funny stuff out there. Others are "preachy" about the joys of travel because I'm passionate about its importance. Most involve some history because that is one of my favorite things. I find historical complexities fascinating, and I hope to make you curious too. I've tried very hard to be histori-cally accurate, but I'm covering a lot of territory here so please be tolerant of any errors. Also, there are no tales about exciting things that happened late at night because I never seem to be able to stay up that late.

I'm intimidated by the thought that somewhere out there people I don't know are reading my stuff, so I pretend that each essay is just a letter to a friend. And as I am devastated by criticism, I always assume my friend is very simpatico and non-judgmental. So, welcome to my travels, thank you for coming along.

The Logistics of Travel

Prep work is never much fun. The list making, the shopping, the information gathering and so forth are never as marvelous as the activity itself. But they do have their own particular charm; they are all indicators that something extremely special is going to happen. Travel has its own set of preliminary steps, the logistics of trip organization as you move from your base to an unfamiliar destination. While the suitcase-shopping or the map-reading or the weather-checking may not be your cup of tea, they do suggest that you are going to have an adventure. Good planning can make for a good trip so let me give you some thoughts I've had, some things I do. Please feel free to ignore or disagree with anything that doesn't suit your fancy.

Getting Ready to Go

"Sometimes you have to say goodbye to the things you know and hello to the things you don't!"
William Faulkner

A lot of my decisions to go traveling seem to come in the middle of the winter. It's cold, it's dark, and the sun is showing up way too late in the morning and going down way too early in the afternoon. I don't think spring is ever going to come, and while I don't know where I'm headed, I know I need to go traveling. I need to think about places where the oceans roar, the palm trees sway and there is a new vista around every corner. But while I figure out how to go about getting there, I can think about packing. That always cheers me up.

Planning Your Trip:

Deciding to travel is a little like falling in love. First there is the hesitation, then the preoccupation, the focus and finally the endorphin rush. All of these moods will seem familiar. It's when you get to your destination that you will know if it is only a one-night romance and you will not be returning, or if it is true love and you'll come back as often as possible.

Travel lures us away from our normal routine and places us in situations where we just might take a chance. I sat down near a line of Irish school children queuing up for entrance into a history park, chatted with their teacher and ended up surrounded by red heads and questions. I spent an entire morning meandering down the banks of the Seine and munching on crepes and drinking cheap wine.

I shopped for galabeyas in a Luxor market and discussed the pros and cons of headscarves with passing

With the whole world in your hand

Egyptian ladies. I would never have the courage to do any of these at home. But I've picked myself up from one world and plunked myself down in another, and I seem to have become a braver person in the process.

Deciding When and Where to Go:

Obviously whenever you can - grab it. But if you have your choice about the time of the year, look at the weather first and then decide what will affect your travel and what you can live with. Mid-winter in Europe is also mid-dark, and if you travel at that time of year you will cut yourself out of daylight hours strolling around the old part of town or having coffee on the piazza. In tropical countries, search for the driest season. I also try to avoid the hot weather in third world countries because things seem so much funkier. I'm afraid that my biggest criterion is when the tourists are NOT going to be there. I can put up with dark and cold and funky, but hordes of tourists milling around the Acropolis hill complaining about their feet, or a little lady in a bright pink hat yelling at her husband n the middle of the sacred sanctuary at Delphi, make me very grumpy. Besides, I think that the locals of any spot are much nicer if they haven't been overwhelmed by tourists for the last few months. They are much more willing to chat and to see you as a real person. Personally, I like off-season the best. The rates are lower, streets are quieter, the museums and cafes emptier, and the waiters in Paris almost human. But whether you are going to Tucumcari or the Taj Mahal, getting ready to travel is always fun. And the most important things to take always remain the same, humor, curiosity and an open mind.

Once that decision is made, I try to do as much reading as I can. Travel books give me an idea of where I'm headed, so I know what something is when I'm looking at it. They also keep me from making disastrous mistakes and skipping something I would have loved. (See "I Need to Go Back to Sparta," p.84.) But non-traditional reading--cookbooks, newspapers, historical novels, non-fiction accounts or diaries--help me know a little bit more about my destination too.

Choosing Your Luggage:

There's an awful lot of fussing about bags anymore – what is too heavy, too bulky or just too much. But if you pack well, you really don't have to worry about the airlines' rules. I can't tell you exactly what to take or how to pack it. If I describe how I get ready for a trip and what I take along, perhaps it will help you when you're standing in front of that empty suitcase with a pile of clothes next to it. Packing is a small matter when compared to the pleasures of travel, but luggage is what you live out of, and lug after you, for the entire trip so it needs to be considered carefully. That bag is going to have to go into the trunk of the car (or shuttle van) and out, through airport security, off the luggage carousel, through customs, onto the tour or cruise or hotel shuttle bus and follow you to your room or cabin. And unless you're on a cruise, the whole process will be repeated in a day or two.

As you are known by the company you keep, so you'll be known by the luggage you take. Keep your bags lightweight and mobile. The durable nylon used now is fabulous, and I love recessed roller wheels. If you've ever had to argue with a heavy case about going through a turnstile or up a curb, you'll find those wheels invaluable. And if your case has two handles, one on top and one on the side so you can put it up on the counter or grab it from the luggage carousel, you'll find that feature extremely handy too. Find a bright color, even if it is obnoxious. In the middle of all those tasteful black and dark green bags on the luggage carousel, your bubble-gum pink suitcase will be easy to spot. To make the case even more obvious, use a bright, elastic strap around the center. The strap identifies the bag and holds it together if it is damaged. (Mine is a gruesome lime green.)

Your name and address should be on a piece of paper inside each bag while the luggage tags on the outside might carry the name and phone number of your cruise contact, your hotel or the friends you will be visiting. I've known of people who take photos of their suitcases to supply if the luggage gets lost, but that, I think, is pessimistically planning for disaster. Rather than brand-new, a much worn suitcase is a great and useful friend. Not only do you know where the pockets and zippers are, but the more scratched and stained it is, the less someone is likely to steal it. My dark green London Fog bag bears battle scars from many, many trips and the last time I had it patched, I felt as though I was awarding it a purple heart.

Packing, the Undiscovered Country

"I ain't takin' nothin' that'll slow down my travelin."
Johnny Cash

Packing is a personal procedure and my ideas certainly may not mesh with yours. There are things I insist on taking, and then there is the stuff I manage to do without. But I have done a little traveling, and I'd like to share some of the lessons I've learned.

In Your Purse & Carry-On:

I have an unattractive but effective purse that I pull out to take with me when I'm traveling. It's a kidney-shaped, back-healthy bag in an undistinguished blackish color which will hold a passport and boarding pass in one front pocket, dark glasses in another with room for 2 credit cards, some $1.00 bills and a book inside. That leaves my hands much freer to get through the

airport. When I'm sightseeing, that purse is just as handy for guide books, maps, water bottles, etc.

I'm pretty picky about what I take in my carry-on bag. It will comfort and entertain me during the flight and perhaps sustain me for a day or two after I land. Again, we are in the realm of personal preference, but I always pack a no-iron long-sleeved shirt, a dark-colored T-shirt (which can double as a night shirt) and a set of fast-drying under stuff. Also included are the paraphernalia I know I will need for sure. Irreplaceable bathroom equipment, prescriptions and vitamins, extra

Decisions, decisions

contacts, basic make-up and a curling iron (it's a girl thing) are all carried. On board the flight itself, I try to have flight socks, an empty water bottle that I can fill after I'm through security, trail mix, a notebook, pen, an e-book and a nice fat, junk book for back-up.

In Your Big Suitcase:

There seem to be two schools of thought in the science of packing the large bag. The "kitchen sink" theory takes everything for every eventuality. If one pair of shoes is good, ten pair are better. If one pair of pants may come in handy, let's throw in six more for good measure. This theory imagines an entirely new outfit for every day and all the accoutrements that need to go along – and extra for emergencies. The other side of the debate only takes a carry-on (small) with a clean shirt, a change of underwear (maybe), a little bathroom stuff plus a passport and figures that a credit card and a smile will take care of the rest.

My packing lies somewhere between the "shove everything in" philosophy and the "buy-it-there" plan. When going on a tour I try to pack lightly, to take no more than absolutely neces-sary, figuring that I can buy it or do without if I need to. You've heard the adage, "Take twice as much money and half as many clothes?" It's true. If you are disciplined and relatively ruthless, you can travel much more easily. Fortunately, this premise can be relaxed a little when cruising since you handle your baggage so rarely.

If you can, pack neutral colors that will all blend with each other. Black and khaki or gray seem to work well. Add a little bit of white or red for interest and you're all set. If every T-shirt or blouse can be worn with every pair of slacks or skirt, there will be a lot less to take along. Plan on layering. Three thin things will be easier to pack and more versatile than one bulky item. Depending on the climate where you are headed, simple slacks, knit tops and a jacket or two will take you through the cities while cotton khakis, T-shirts and skirts will be fine for warm, leisure spots.

With luck, you should be able to get along with two or three pairs of slacks, a blazer, a dress sweater and two or three T-shirts or turtlenecks depending on the temperature. I'll add a dress skirt if I think I'll be doing something fancy, but that's about it. The real secret is making sure everything works together and then you'll have a pretty good variety of outfits. (Especially if you don't mind doing a little bit of hand-laundry.)

Staying in the same color scheme also means fewer shoes, purses and belts. I wear my heavy walking shoes on the flight and pack a lighter pair plus some low evening heels. My billfold has a strap and doubles as my evening bag. My black leather belt goes with everything I take. Cheap costume jewelry and a few scarves pack light, take up no space and will vary your wardrobe a little if you get bored. The whole trick is the ability to use everything in multiple ways.

Travelers who wear shorts and fanny packs, white tennis shoes and baseball caps, stand out and are vulnerable to peddlers and taxi drivers. Try to blend a little more into what the locals are wearing and you're more likely to avoid some of that bother. (And maybe you too will be asked for directions on the streets of Dublin. I didn't say anything, I just smiled and pointed. I didn't want to spoil the moment.)

As to the extras, that's where individual preference comes in. If you are thinking, "I might need this," you probably won't. If you think, "I can't survive without this," you had better take it with you.

My extras include a small camera, batteries, my travel journal, maybe a small umbrella, a check register (which works well for keeping track of expenses), a small book-bag as a day pack, some medium Ziploc bags for whatever and a reading book. I used to take more books with me, but now I beg, borrow, or buy as I go, and I've done some unusual reading that way. And the e-reader, of course, is my best buddy. To help fight impersonal, sterile hotel rooms, I may break my own rules and take a few personal items to bring a little bit of home along with me. I pack a small CD player and a water heating coil and a travel mug to fix my morning tea. Travel candles, packets of bubble bath, a cozy throw and a photo from home don't take much room, but they help me feel more settled. But I don't take anything I don't want to lose. I leave the family bible at home, and if I take any good jewelry at all, it is the sort that I wear all the time.

My bathroom/makeup stuff goes in a Ziploc bag as does a small medicine supply. Aspirin, antihistamines, etc. are handy as are a small bathroom scrubbie and a drawstring trash sack for dirty clothes. I try to take an alarm clock; you can't always trust the front desk. I put the creamy sort of stuff in travel-safe bottles and wrap them in plastic as well. Finding out that your favorite sweater has been cream-rinsed when you're unpacking is particularly unpleasant. Once I had a little case sliced in Egypt by a hopeful thief, so I also carry a small roll of duct tape just in case.

Nothing is big, nothing is heavy. I know I can handle it all myself if I need to, and I won't be burdened or bothered by wading through the suitcases hunting for bits and pieces. You'll realize as you travel more and more that you will have to take less and less. My daughter and I spent a week in London for her graduation present with only carry-on. It was boring, but at least we didn't have to schlep luggage through Victoria Station. Just remember that what you take with you can help you make the most of your trip, or drag you down. Be practical with what you pack, be concise and realize that if necessary you can probably buy it there or do without. I've only arrived without my suitcase once. I'll tell you that story in the next section.

How to Get It All In:

Since you have hopefully lightened your load, what is the best way to get it all in your suitcase? Everyone has a personal method for packing a suitcase. Let me tell you please, how I handle it.

I put the heaviest items, shoes (toe tucked in the heel), hairdryer, electrical adaptor, etc. along the edge nearest the wheels, hoping they won't shift when the bag is moved. Miscellaneous small stuff (clock, small umbrella, etc.), which I won't need often, go in the interior pockets. Everything else I pack in two stacks, tops on one side and bottoms on the other, because that makes them easier to locate. Large mesh bags for underwear work well to keep suitcase clutter to a minimum. And all those little things that are not breakable? They can also go in one or two plastic bags to keep everything organized. I've tried all the elaborate packing tools and still come back to Ziploc bags. They're clear, smooshable and keep paraphernalia from getting lost in the innards of a suitcase.

If I have to take any formal clothes, I leave them in the rarely visited bottom of the bag, still in their wrapper from the cleaners as there are almost no wrinkles that way. I also try to remember to tuck in a pareo (sarong). Depending on what I have needed, it has doubled as a skirt, bathing suit cover-up, shawl, sheet, towel, tote, window curtain and tablecloth. And on the very top of my packing I put a trash bag to hold dirty clothes - last thing in, first thing out. This is not particularly dramatic, but you have to admit it is practical!

Now that packing is covered, let's get down to those last-minute essentials.

You're On Your Way

"It is no coincidence that in no known language
does the phrase 'as pretty as an airport' exist."
The Long, Dark Tea-Time of the Soul
Douglas Adams

Just Before You Leave:

The month or so before I leave is one of my favorite times. I like getting ready. I'm admittedly over-organized, but I label three 3x5 cards: "To Buy," "To Take," "To Do." I don't bother to include the obvious stuff, *"take your suitcase" or "find your passport."* But I do list all the things that will take time to get together or that I might forget in the last minute flurry of getting ready.

The "To Buy" card is probably my favorite. When else do you have a perfectly legitimate, guilt-free excuse to shop? An amazing number of the things I decide I need to take along are items I still use all the time, the walking shoes, the comfy khakis, that nice brown belt. Traveling used to be a terrific excuse to buy junk books that would keep me happy when I was travel-weary, and book buying was one of my last celebratory actions before I left. Now that the library will let me have 10 e-books to take with me in my Nook, I almost don't get to go book buying anymore. It's thrifty, and there is less to carry, but it's not as fun.

The "To Take" card includes an umbrella, a trash sack for dirty clothes, maybe a pillow if there is room, my journal, some extra pens, a travel hair dryer, my reading glasses and so forth. But I try hard to make this list as small as possible. After all, I'm the one who's going to have to lug it around.

The "To Do" card is sort of longish and may need to begin a little earlier than the other two. Make sure your passport is current, check to see if any visas or shots are required. I go looking at the weather forecasts, check the type of electrical plugs and find my city maps. (I have a talent for getting lost.) I make sure that my prescriptions are in order, and make a copy of my passport, credit cards (and the emergency numbers to call in case they are lost or stolen) and itinerary. Email this information to yourself and you'll be able to access it away from home.

Get your hair cut, get your nails done, stop the paper, board the dog, load up your Kindle and call your credit card company to tell them that you'll be traveling. I know this last bit may seem unnecessary, but I have friends who had a suspicious home bank cancel their credit card halfway through a month-long Italian driving vacation. It put a serious damper on the whole trip.

I get some foreign currency in small bills. I don't get a large amount because every time you exchange money, you lose a little. The creation of the bland Euro has made traveling to many parts of Europe a lot simpler. I suppose that wiping out all those intriguing European currencies with their variety of colors and sizes, monarchs and monuments has been extremely efficient. I still miss the lira, the franc, and the deutschmark, but then I'm a sentimentalist.

Request that the mail and the newspapers be held. Think about turning the water off. Set up a timer to turn on lights in the evening. Ask the neighbors to keep an eye on the house. And if travel jitters aren't too terrible, try to get some sleep the night before you leave.

Getting to the Airport:

For a domestic coach flight at a non-busy time of year, an arrival at the airport an hour and a half prior to departure should be just fine. For an international flight, you should allow two to three hours. You will need to adjust how much time you give yourself if there is anything at all out of the ordinary. A holiday, bad weather, a security alert and so forth can throw off a schedule. Personally, I like to be early; there is a luxury in being unhurried. I would rather sit and people-watch then worry about missing my plane and frankly, I like airports. Anywhere there are restaurants, bookstores, bathrooms, airplanes and strangers with stories to tell is a fun place to hang out. (Once you've spent 11 hours at the Kolkata (Calcutta) Airport, everything else looks easy.)

To avoid problems at the beginning of a trip which can doom the entire enterprise, and to really get rid of the worry, I like to get to the international airport a day ahead. I spend the night in an airport hotel in Chicago or New York or Los Angeles and don't have to worry about making the onward connection. If I'm going on a cruise or tour, I always go in one day ahead. You may miss your connection; your flight may be late on arrival; you can even run into trouble with an accident on the freeway. I can't think of anything sadder than standing on the dock waving bon voyage to my ship.

What to Wear on the Flight:

When picking out clothes to travel in, I try to keep it loose, pretty and a little formal. You are treated as you are dressed and I'm always foolishly optimistic about a seat upgrade. I usually wear a skirt, cotton top and a jacket, all in dark colors. I find a skirt easier to travel in, and the darker color will help to hide the spills I'm destined to make during the flight. Shoes should be slip-ons, easy to take off during security checks and easy to put on after the flight. I was convinced of that years ago when I watched an overly-accoutered lady from New York wrestle with pulling her fashionably high boots on over her swollen feet and ripping them in the process. She shuffled off the plane.

Checking in at the Airport:

Make sure your bags are tagged correctly before you leave the luggage check-in area. Strange things can happen to a mutinous suitcase. It is self evident, of course, but be sure to measure and weigh your luggage before you go the airport. Charges for overweight bags or the airline's insistence to check your carry-on can be a nasty surprise. I got caught last year at London's Heathrow Airport by an airport employee who didn't like the size of my carry-on and its wheels. I argued because I had taken that bag in cabin everywhere from Cairo to Klungkung. But that nasty, skinny, sneering kid wouldn't allow it in the cabin, and I'm obviously still carrying a grudge. The bag got to Venice just fine so I shouldn't have fussed, but I did go buy a new carry-on before the next trip. Try to speak softly and courteously when checking in. Those poor folks behind the counter have to deal with rude and stressed travelers all day and you will be a pleasant surprise. It also might help to improve your seat assignment.

Getting Through Security:

Resist the urge to blow up (probably an unfortunate choice of words) when going through security. Be sure your shoes slip off and your socks are thick and be glad someone is concerned about your safety. If you can, treat that element of travel as part of the adventure. I know you are mocking me, but the procedure can be interesting. I checked in once with Turkish Air at JFK, and Turkey, like Israel, takes its security extremely seriously. There was a crisp body pat-down and then a hand-held scanner around the edge of the suitcases. (I asked of course, and they were checking for drug residue.) There was a dope-sniffing beagle who was cute but solemn, and three guys on the ramp, also cute but solemn. They were inspecting everyone boarding, and one lady traveling alone and wearing a lot of costume jewelry was pulled out to chat with. I'm not quite sure why that was suspicious, but I did keep my eye on her for the rest of the flight.

Once I was body searched in India behind a modesty curtain. I didn't have to undress, but she sure patted all over. Recently I was pulled aside to go through a large, curtained step-in X-ray machine at London's Heathrow. They were courteous when they asked me for the additional safeguards, but I didn't mind as it was a remarkable contraption and I had plenty of extra time. We discussed it in some detail until they were forced to get back to their job and asked me to leave the machine. Almost everything is entertaining if you ask the right questions.

Spending Time at the Airport:

I love airports. I love the feeling of infinite possibilities. I can get on a plane and in five or ten hours be on a different continent, thinking new thoughts and seeing new sights. I like airports for their potential and I feel more secure just knowing I'm there. I know I have navigated the dangerous shoals of getting to them, and while I'm waiting, I think they can be entertaining. While they are designed to all look alike, bland sterile islands with sanitary bathrooms and those horrid hard plastic chairs, if I hunt thoroughly, there are usually enough unique spots to keep me amused until the flight departs.

I love people watching. In the big international airports, there are travelers from all over the world being forced to coexist in ways that seem unimaginable in daily life. There are the small family dramas, the sadness of departure or the giddy excitement of arrival, the kid leaving home with a backpack and not a clue, and the reserved and closed demeanor of the constantly flying business traveler. My destination may be terrific but just getting there can be fun too.

I like airport shops. I investigate the ridiculously priced makeup and examine the women who are buying it. I peruse the best-selling book shelves. I buy a local newspaper or two. If it's in English, it gives me a closer look at the politics, the weather and the gossip. If it's in another language, I can practice my limited vocabulary and look at the pictures. I store up on granola bars, packaged crackers and mints in case of famine while on the flight. But I don't need to stay at the airport forever, so I get to my gate early. If a gate has changed at the last minute, I need to know about it with plenty of time to get over there. However once I'm sure I'm at the right spot , and I have an assigned seat, small carry-on so I don't need space in an overhead bin, and since I don't enjoy watching people schlep their bags down the aisles, I wait to board. I'm going to be on that flight for a long enough time without volunteering for more.

On the Flight: Survival Techniques

"Airplane travel is nature's way of making you look like your passport photo."

Al Gore

Now I know what the airline advertisements show…..gently smiling hostesses offering steaming beverages, soft pillows and luxurious seats while you gaze dreamily off into the wild blue yonder. I don't know where that plane is, I've been searching for it all my life.

Living on a plane for 12 hours is what really divides civilized man from the barbarian, since there is no conceivable way that spending so many hours in a cramped metal tube hurtling through space can be deemed pleasant. But it can be endured. Sufficeth to say, the wary traveler knows what the journey will be like and prepares accordingly. (Remembering that a century ago it would have been riding by mule back, trudging on foot, or sailing in one of those nasty little bilgy ships, so any complaint about how we get around today is foolish.)

Where to sit on the plane: (A highly biased view)

The aisle/window decision is strictly personal. Some flyers prefer the window as they can curl up against the plane's wall and ignore the rest of the flight. However one of the dangers of flying is staying too long in one position, and an aisle seat will let you get up, stretch, move around and arrive in a little better shape. If the equipment offers a middle section with only four seats, I will try to get an aisle seat in that center area as I will have fewer people climbing over me. And unless it is a full flight I may have that holy grail of coach travel, a vacant seat next to me.

I would also rather be as forward as possible because I prefer to ignore the fact that I'm that high off the ground with that many people around me. But let's face it – long flights are not fun. They all last too long as you travel in the company of 300 or so other trapped and beleaguered souls, confined to your seat by a non-negotiating flight attendant while you share an armrest with a gimlet-eyed stranger.

Additionally, I try to stay away from the seats just ahead of the emergency exit because they usually won't recline. Also, the first row on an international flight may offer a bassinet built into the forward wall. So if you prefer not to travel with babies, it's best to take a seat a little farther back. Some of the larger international planes have several sections in the coach compartment and the first block of seats may only be six or seven rows deep. These are often reserved for frequent flyers. But if you make your reservation early enough and have a chance to grab one of these seats, you can pretend that those other 240 people on the flight are not up in the air with you. Also, it is best to keep away from the last rows of the plane. The bathrooms are back there, and when the line forms it can get kinda crowded in the rear.

The best seat to choose will depend on the equipment you use, and there are all-knowing websites that will help you make a choice. Especially on an international flight, you are going to be scrunched in those 17½ inches for a long time, so the location is vital.

Getting Comfy:

Once you've found your seat, grab your in-flight essentials (which hopefully are in the top of your carry-on) and put the rest in the overhead. Now what are the in-flight essentials? Again that is a matter of personal preference.

Some women like to carry their own shawl or pashmina. I've tried because I think it looks dramatic, but the darn thing won't stay up while I've got a purse and carry-on in tow. My essentials do include a small bag with lip balm, saline nasal spray, anti-gas pills (it's not polite to mention, but everything expands at altitude), hand and face cream because it is dry up there and a small bottle of hand sanitizer.

I carry a satin sleep mask given to me long ago on a Singapore Airlines flight and carefully preserved since then. Once I've got it on, I can pretend I'm not surrounded by all those extra people. I've also kept that airline's flight socks. Not only are they dark, a useful thing on a long flight, but they were made to fit small Oriental feet. You might also consider a set of noise-cancelling headphones, an IPod and an e-reader loaded with hopefully riveting books.

Coping:

Drink as much water as you can, slather cream whenever possible and if you don't care about looking silly – practice some seated calisthenics. Avoid protein and alcohol as neither travel well. Skip the movie and use the darkness to nap. Encourage yourself to get up and walk around every two hours and do a few stretches. Once the doors have closed it's every man for himself, so grab a pillow and blanket, head for a center row and hopefully you'll be able to stretch out.

I look for any excuse to get up. A baby? I'll hold it. A child traveling alone? I'll entertain it. Someone finishing a book that looks good? I'll ask to borrow it for a little while when they're through. I take sponge baths in the bathroom when it is empty and offer hand cream and mints to everyone in my vicinity. When I can't nap, I walk around where I can. And I'm as charming to the stewards as possible and stay out of their way.

 Keep your meals light and remember that carbohydrates digest better than proteins. Stick with the veggies, salad and bread, skip the mystery meats and again, drink lots of water. No, it won't be exciting, but you didn't get on the plane for a gourmet meal anyway. And pass on the soda. (It's that gas thing again.)

Go ahead and set your watch to the new time zone and begin to adjust your sleeping and eating patterns to match. The earlier you start getting used to it, the easier the transition will be. Stow your shoes away, put on your flight socks, get out your book and crossword puzzle, open your trail mix, sip on your spring water and take advantage of the peaceful time on the flight.

It isn't often that you can be left all by yourself. Figure that a few hours in quiet meditation never hurt anybody.

An hour or so prior to landing and before everyone else thinks of getting things together, go ahead and get ready to deplane. Find your shoes, use the restroom, wash your face and redo your makeup if you need to. And then read or look out the window and watch yourself fly over the Pyramids or across the Irish Sea.

Changing Planes:

Somewhere between here and there it is entirely possible that you will have to change planes. Unfortunately, even the best laid travel plans can be imperfect, and irritatingly there are not non-stops to the all the places we want to see.

First find your next gate, double-check the departure time of the connecting flight and then go exploring. If your wait is long, you might see if there is an airport rest stop which offers a shower, a manicure or perhaps a massage. You may not actually need such services, but the self indulgence will be good entertainment. (I had my nails done at the Bangkok Airport which was fun.) Once I was stuck at LAX for six hours. (See what I mean by the best-laid plans getting messed up?) I considered a shoe shine which my tennis shoes made impractical and found the international bank to exchange some dollars. I am not a patient person, so I divided the wait into half-hour increments. I would walk one-half hour, sit one-half hour and repeat and repeat, etc.

People-watching is a fabulous way to pass the time. Airports are microcosms of the world with different languages, clothes and customs, but in this one instance everyone there has a common goal - to get through the traveling process as pleasantly and quickly as possible. You may never have another chance to see someone from Somalia or Katmandu or Kansas. Take advantage of it. And if you can get them to chat, all the better. (Admiring a child or pulling out family pictures can be an excellent ice breaker.)

If you are forced to hang out, some airports are better than others. Walking London Heathrow's Terminal 5 is a good long hike and an excellent way to stretch your airplane-stiffened legs. If you have to spend time, T5 is a terrific place to be. There are lots of fabulous shops to meander through, Harrods, Cartier, Bulgari, Burberry, Tiffany, Prada, Dior, Gucci and even a contest for a Ferrari or BMW. Heathrow handles more international passengers than anywhere else in the world and is the best spot for people watching I've ever found.

Even Frankfurt's international terminal was a joy on my way back from Calcutta. After three weeks in the north of India, the Germanic cleanliness of the bathroom floor was a religious experience. I did not kiss the ground, but I felt like it. Curiously the deli shop with its cheeses, crackers, meats and wine was right next to a sex shop with its appropriate merchandise. I stood there all by my jet-lagged self and snickered for a very long time.

And then I got on another plane.

Handling Arrival

"I can't think of anything that excites a greater sense of childlike wonder than to be in a country where you are ignorant of almost everything."

Bill Bryson

Landing:

You've begun to set up a home in your seat. Blanket on your lap, flight socks on your feet, water bottle tucked in the pocket in front of you, a civil if not amicable relationship with the person next to you. Cramped though it may be, you've grown accustomed to your nest. Then all of a sudden you begin to descend. The small objects on the ground become real again, trees, houses, cars and finally people. You land with a jolt, gather your world's belongings, the plane door is thrown open, and you step into exhaust fumes, humidity and a whole new place to explore and cope with. You know how smells will trigger memories? Exhaust fumes make me think of arriving.

If you only have carry-on, then getting off the plane quickly but politely is a good idea. You'll get to the transfer bus and in the terminal, through customs and immigration before the rest of the crowd gets there. Unless, of course, another 747 has landed about the same time, disgorged its passengers too, and then you needn't have bothered to rush.

If you have checked luggage, you might as well take your own sweet time leaving the aircraft. You can help other passengers with carry-on, coats and cameras and be courteous and relaxed. Pushing your way to stand in the aisle early won't get your bags onto the carousel any quicker. Rarely have my bags arrived at the luggage delivery before I do.

If you are frail or walk with difficulty, requesting a wheelchair from the airline to meet you upon arrival will be an enormous help. The porters know all sorts of interesting subterranean ways of getting around an airport and can also whisk you through customs. Once you have arrived in baggage claim and while you're waiting, grab a grocery cart. Some have a small fee and only take local coins, so it is smart to have a few on hand. Getting your case without hurting yourself or the person standing next to you is a talent, and as travelers tend to cluster around the front delivery chute, I head for the back. It doesn't make the process a lot longer, and it is easier to pull the suitcase off. Grabbing that bag off the belt is when you'll be especially happy you have packed lightly. Spotting my suitcase with its garish green strip is always a relief. I don't know where else it could have gone, but I feel better having it in hand.

Years ago we knew a very large, very nice man who worked as a bouncer in a local tavern. At one time he had been a baggage supervisor for United at Chicago's O'Hare Airport. Also based at O'Hare was an international pilot for United who was universally detested. And when that pilot checked in for his flight, no matter if he was going to Paris or Moscow or Hong Kong – his bags went to Rio.

If disastrously your suitcase doesn't show up, most major airports will have a lost luggage office close to baggage claim. Go visit them, explain your plight, describe the bag and tell them how you can be reached. If you can get the name of the person helping and a direct line to that office, the personal connection may help. I've only arrived at my destination once without my bags, and I've told that story a little later.

Feet on the Ground (Sort of):

Arrival is always a little difficult. Everything has changed, and a sleepless night on the plane makes it harder to cope. Combine that with jet lag and even an experienced traveler will wonder why in the heck she is doing this to herself. The exhaust fumes alone are enough to knock your socks off, and the difference in language is somehow a surprise

This is all part of the process of plucking yourself up from one world and plunking yourself down in another. You've left the old and familiar and are about to embrace the strange and wondrous. Getting away from familiar surroundings will allow you to see everything with fresh eyes. Traveling is a privilege, a chance to go out and see a new part of the world. (Not that I always remember that as I'm staggering through customs.)

The First Day or Two:

Try not to nap when you get to your destination or you will be doomed for days. The best thing you can do after a hot shower is to walk forever. My whole world tends to tilt a bit when I have jet lag, but I still think getting out is healthy. You may fall face down in the mashed potatoes at dinner, but staying up until evening is the smart thing to do. Walking will stretch your legs, will keep you awake and will let you begin to acquaint yourself with your new world. Those first impressions will be the clearest memories you will take home with you. The scents, the colors, the accents are all new and should be treasured. They will become recognizable and ordinary soon enough.

I've found that there are a few phrases that will get you through almost everything. I once spent two months in Greece with just "thank you," "you're welcome," "how much is it?" and "hot water?" Figuring out how to say "I'm sorry" in Italian got me out of several traffic tickets. If you haven't learned any other words, be sure you know how to say, "Please," "Thank you" and "Where is the bathroom?" And as I've said before, courtesy and a smile are universal.

While you are adjusting to your new world, remember that whatever you say, say it quietly. Americans, while wonderfully friendly the world over, are also known for their loud voices and carrying conversations. Most of the world dislikes being overheard; we don't seem to have that problem. The locals really don't want to know that Vienna's St. Stephen's Cathedral looks just like the Corn Palace in Mitchell, South Dakota, nor do they want to hear how uncomfortable your hotel bed was. As unusual as your surroundings may be, in this part of the world you are the stranger and should behave as a polite and soft-spoken guest.

Coming Home and Re-entry:

I'm sentimental. I love it when the immigration man says "Welcome home" as I go through his line. As you return to the rhythms of home, there is always some degree of "travel withdrawal." You're thrown back into the real world with a sense of dislocation, and as you adjust again to another time zone it is easy to wonder why in the heck you've put yourself through all this. That's simple. After bravely enduring bad hotel mattresses, bad coffee and living out of a suitcase for weeks, you are home, and you have brought back priceless memories.

Travel is priceless because you will never unpack, launder and put away those memories. And they will never leave. I can still see my husband's hand as he reached out for mine, and we swam in a sea of yellow tangs off the Kona coast. I can still see the little Turkish girl's grin as she practiced her English and I answered her properly. I can still see the rogue elephant crashing through the trees in an Indian game preserve. And I can still see the face of the little Egyptian man who showed me a photo of his small daughter as I showed him a photo of mine.

Travel broadens the mind, dissolves stereotypes, rids you of preconceived notions and lets you know there are whole other ways to see the world and to handle its problems. Travel teaches us patience and forbearance, pity and awe. I've written a lot about travel, what I saw, what I thought, when I saw beauty and when I got lost in the rain. The following stories are what have happened to me when I've been out in the wide world and the memories and lessons I've brought home with me.

The Vagaries of Travel

Travel brings with it its own small set of idiocies, irritations and issues. These are problems and situations not normally encountered in daily life, and they tend to be the sort of occurrence that are much more enjoyable "recollected in tranquility" then during the experience itself. In other words, stuff happens, and it is a lot more fun to talk about it once you're home and safe rather than while you're going through it. In the middle of the muddle, it's hard to realize that you'll have a story to tell. But they do deserve telling.

Hiking in Montenegro

Celebrating Jet Lag

"Seize the moment. Remember all those women on the Titanic who waived off the dessert cart."

Erma Bombeck

The word "travel" comes from "travail," a disconcerting factoid not normally shared. It originates with the early pilgrims to San Juan de Compostela in northwest Spain who had to tramp across France, clamber over the Pyrenees and trudge to the Atlantic coast to do homage to the saint. Sometimes they got back home, sometimes not.

Since then, our travel methods have become much less taxing. We have cars, trains and for long distances, the miraculous airplane. Although it doesn't equate to the problems early travelers faced, happily enduring jet lag is the greatest burden we must bear. I know I am truly traveling when the jet lag sets in. My equilibrium goes off kilter, my nose stuffs up, my eyes are full of sand, and my brain goes on disconnect.

I have three levels of jet lag. The first is the domestic East Coast type which occurs on a four-hour flight with three time zone changes. It's inconvenient but handleable. The second is the European variety. This is when you've spent the night on a plane instead of in a bed, and then when you arrive the next morning attempt the hard job of convincing yourself to stay conscious until that evening. The other sort is the Indian/Asian jet lag where the flight is so long that the plane becomes your home, and eventually you do sleep. And having been unconscious for awhile, when you arrive it is a whole new world of smells and sights. The language has changed, the air feels different, and over the trees there is the roof of a pagoda gleaming in the sun.

Dealing with this cross between an inconvenience and the flu, there is a whole list of remedies offered. Over the years, I've tried most of them. I've taken melatonin capsules and herbal valerian, switched my sleep patterns counterclockwise, twisted my body around yoga positions, deep breathed, shallow breathed, increased my carbs, decreased my proteins and insisted on sunshine when what I actually wanted was a long nap. Frankly, none of them actually work. Although a lot of water, a Benadryl and some earplugs do make the trip easier to handle.

I know I'm not suffering the way early travelers did, crossing the vast oceans in little boats, enduring hard rides and cold inns, but I'm still doing the same sort of thing. I'm separating myself from the comfortable and the familiar and launching myself out into the different and wonderful. There is a point in the flight when it's all worth it, when you climb out of your seat, step over the blanket-wrapped, outstretched legs of other travelers, and go to peer out the window to watch the sun rise on Mt. Fuji or the Irish cliffs. It's surreal and glorious.

Anymore I've learned to accept jet lag and kind of enjoy it. It becomes part of a big trip. Like the greeting aroma of airplane exhaust when you deplane, it means that I'm traveling, and I'm about to have an adventure. Still groggy from the plane flight, I've gotten to negotiate my way with humor through children and backstreets in Bangkok. I've peacefully endured an interminable bus ride to the Black Pagoda on the sultry Bay of Bengal. I've watched the gothic ceiling of the Cathedral in Toledo whirl around me, and (don't tell anybody) but I've fallen asleep leaning against a massive pillar in Karnak's Hypostyle Hall. Full of jet lag, I am content to sit at a café table with a warm cup of something and smile at the world because I've gotten just where I want to be. Now I can soak it in.

On my first trip to Dublin, I struggled with the grocery-luggage carts they offer near the baggage carousels. I finally got one pulled away, and although the dumb thing was heavy and awkward, I wrestled it toward customs. A sweet Irish porter took pity on me. The reason I couldn't navigate the darn thing was because I'd pulled out two of the silly trolleys stuck together. He pulled the two apart, patted me on the shoulder and sent me off. "Sure and it's the wrong time of day for you entirely. Go and have a nice cup of tea and you'll come around in no time."

Jet lag is like that.

Back in my own clothes again

Traveling Light

"The scientific theory I like best is that the rings of Saturn are composed entirely of lost airline luggage."

Mark Russell

When I was young and the world was new, I went to India for the very first time. Lack of experience and an exotically distant destination encouraged me to pack heavily. I think I did include the kitchen sink. I also had innumerable pairs of shoes, slacks, blouses, sweaters, dresses, etc., for we would be in the steamy tropics as well as the high Himalayas, and I wanted to be prepared for anything. It was organized by color, type, weight and probably alphabetically as well.

It was a long flight, 36 hours bed-to-bed and I was numb when we got to New Delhi. My suitcase did not roll off the conveyer belt. "It is not here," shrugged the nice little man at the customer service desk, in a massive case of understatement. "It will come." But he didn't know when. Obviously my clothes did not have the travel stamina I had and had stopped in Paris for a breather on the way to Mumbai (Bombay).

There was no way to know how long I would be "suitcase-less." We got to the hotel and showered. Wearing a towel wrapped around me, I wondered how it would look for dinner? I eyed my roommate, a cold-eyed stranger, wondering about her nobility of spirit and her size. Would her clothes fit? Would she share?

Like Robinson Crusoe stranded on that island, I took stock of my possessions. Luckily I had a carry-on bag with one extra outfit and my bathroom stuff and makeup. So I could be clean and pretty. I just couldn't change my clothes very often.

I faced dinner with trepidation. Instead, I became the center of care and solicitation from the strangers who made up my travel group. One kindly and fortunately largish man gave me a tee shirt as a nightgown. A little old lady loaned me a sweater she had knitted herself. A nice teenage guy had an Oxford shirt for me. They called themselves "Leslie's Closet" and went from being strangers to sympathetic friends in a matter of minutes. They were kind-hearted and generous, and I was overwhelmed. During the days that followed, I found that to be possessionless was extremely liberating. While my roommate was pulling out and repacking her clothes (nothing she had fit me, and she had a certain meanness of spirit), I would wash and hang out my other outfit and go out for a walk. India is the most diverse place I have ever visited with an overwhelming variety of faces and smells and sights. I like everything foreign and being "suitcase-less" gave me more opportunity to explore.

I shopped for all sorts of things that I normally would have brought with me and found out how interesting foreign drugstores are. Hunting for toothpaste, for example, became an adventure. The varieties of shampoos were entrancing, and I smelled like sandalwood for the whole trip. Shopping for underwear was challenging, and I bought exotic and unnecessary sandals just because I had an excuse.

We were in the country as guests of the Indian government, and when we were in Hyderabad were invited to dinner at the Nijam's palace. Obviously neither of my well-washed, but well-worn, outfits would do. Our hostess, hearing of my plight, sent a sari to me to wear as well as a lady to help do the tucking and wrapping. I spent the entire evening dining in the center courtyard of a palace, clad in silk, afraid to move for fear the whole shebang would slide off. It was marvelous.

Eventually my suitcase did show up, each compartment tidily packed and full of now unnecessary clothes. I was thrilled at the variety but was almost sorry to get back to normal travel. For several days, I had been footloose and fancy free. I had relied on the kindness of strangers, been given a chance to explore, and discovered what was important and what was merely convenient. It was a good lesson, learned early.

I need to take humor, patience, courtesy and curiosity when I travel. Everything else is secondary.

My new friend and I

Useful Phrases

"In Paris they simply stared when I spoke to them in French; I never did succeed in making those idiots understand their own language."

Mark Twain

What, you may ask yourself, could she possibly say to this old Greek gentleman? He said, "Good Morning," I replied, "Hello," He said, "Alpha, beta, gamma, delta, epsilon," (or something that sounded like that) and I replied, "Thank you." I was waiting in line to climb the well-worn marble path to Athens' Acropolis, and he was standing picturesquely by the side. Then he took my hand and held it and someone took our picture. It wasn't a particularly long conversation, but isn't he just the cutest thing?

You don't actually need a lot of vocabulary to get by in a foreign country. I have a friend who was going to spend several months in Italy on a research sabbatical and asked me for any language suggestions that I might have to help him ease into the country. Assuming his sense of humor was still intact, and after much careful consideration, I sent him the following phrases to help him along:

"Good Morning.": "Buona Mattina."
"Italy is a beautiful country.": "L'Italia e un paese bellissimo."
"I love Italy.": "Lo amo l'Italia."
"Could I have directions to the Coliseum?": "Potrei avere indicazioni per il Colosseo?"
"Could I have directions to the Duomo?": "Potrei avere indicazioni per el Duomo?"
"Could I have directions to St. Mark's Square?": "Potrei avere indicazioni per Piazza San Marco?"
"I think I am lost.": "Penso di essere perso."
"May I buy you a glass of wine?": "Posso acquistare un bicchiere di vino?"
"Do you know Elisaetta Conalis?": "Sai Elisabetta Conalis?"
"You are very beautiful.": "Sei molto bella."
"Is that your father?": "E che tuo padre?"
"I'm afraid it is time for me to leave.": "Le mie scuse ma esso sono tempo affinchè me vadano."

Seriously, when I am out of the country, I am always pleasantly surprised at the few essential words it takes to get by. A great many people in other countries have been taught English in school (that's always embarrassing when you don't know their language at all; it makes us seem so provincial and arrogant), or they are good-natured enough to put up with my small phrases. Granted you can't get into any deep discussions about the nature of existence, but it is quite possible to make do with the bare necessities.

I spent my first month in Greece singing the Greek alphabet in front of street signs to figure out the letters (that amused the locals), and accumulating the phrases "Thank you," "How much does this cost?" "Where is the restroom, please?" and "Hot water?" This last phrase was particularly helpful as it was winter time and the cheap hotels I was using only offered hot water for a few hours a day.

Sometimes just entertaining the locals is a worthy endeavor. My father used to tell travel stories on himself, and one of his favorites was about standing on the beach in Mazatlan, lost, thinking that the name of his hotel was "The Playa." Asking several exasperated people who passed where "la playa" was, one kind man eventually bent over, scooped up some sand, poured it in his hand and explained, "aqui, senor, aqui es la playa." It was a vocabulary lesson he always remembered.

Practicing your Italian (or Indonesian or Turkish) on the forbearing natives can be just as much fun as letting them practice their English on you. I once spent a tremendous afternoon on a train with two Italian high school students and their grandfather and two dictionaries, one Italian-French and one French-Spanish. It took us several hours, but we finally established that they loved soccer, he had been in a builder in Pisa, and that I was related to every famous American they could think of. (I stretched the truth a little there.)

Asking directions can be an adventure all by itself. Instead of smugly traveling the familiar way between your home and the office, school or airport, eyes practically closed because you know the highway so well, a new road and an unknown language will make you much more aware of just how vulnerable we all are. Pulling out a map, pointing and looking perplexed will open you to the kindness of strangers. I've always been thrilled at how considerate most of them are. Granted when asking for help, you have to have some sense. People in little towns are more helpful than folks in big cities; inhabitants of non-tourist spots are usually kinder than those who have been buffeted by tourists, and if you ask street directions of the street urchins of Calcutta or Rio, you'll be lucky not to lose your watch, your wallet and the gold in your teeth.

But I have had an elderly lady in Vienna walk me several blocks to the museum I was hunting for, a little boy in Bali take me by the hand to show me his school, and two busy (and heavy laden) lady shoppers in Stockholm take the time to get me to the right bank.

Communicating is what it is all about. Throw yourself on the mercy of the world. The world will catch you. And you will come back with terrific stories to tell.

Louis Vuitton and Me

So there I was - standing in the custom's line at New York's Kennedy Airport. I had just finished a long flight home, staggered through immigration, grabbed my battered and bruised suitcase from the carousel, heaved it onto the cart, rolled it to the customs area and was listing slightly as I waited to have my bag and passport examined.

I always hunt for the shortest line that has the least stressed, most amiable looking official. Do you feel vaguely guilty while you are waiting for customs? I do. It's silly, because I rarely smuggle emeralds, but they're checking me over, and I guess it is always possible that they could not like something about me or my bag. Perhaps it's just because it's the federal government who is doing the looking-over. (Did you know that most people would rather deal with the Mafia than the IRS?) I found a medium-short line with a nice-looking young guy who was getting people through quickly. "Thank you, ma'am," he would say, stamp the passport, and send that traveler on her way. While waiting and leaning on my luggage pushcart, I glanced at a central open space between the custom's checkpoints.

There was a small melodrama going on as a couple had been pulled aside to have their luggage minutely inspected. A large, uniformed and ferocious looking man was painstakingly going through the contents of all the suitcases of an obviously affluent American couple. Why affluent? They had tons of matched Louis Vuitton luggage. I have never seen so many expensive suitcases outside a store. And it was all open. All the haphazardly packed shoes, all the dirty underwear, all the wrinkled slacks, all were out for inspection at Kennedy Airport. The obvious owners of the examined cases were both affluently heavyset, in their 60's, well-heeled and well-padded and all of their chins were shaking. They were not happy campers.

As I stood there securely waiting for my cheerful skinny inspector, the heavy-set scary guy finished up with the rich folks, came over to my line and replaced my friendly immigration man. He brought with him all my unrealized fears of being suspected, stopped, searched. He looked me up, he looked me down, he looked at my passport, he looked at my face, he looked at my passport again. "Where did you go?" "Where do you live?" "What do you do for a living?" "Why were you traveling?" I was in a pure panic. This guy was a customs terminator. I could tell I was going to be in that landing area too, my dirty clothes spread all over the counter.

I decided it couldn't get any worse and asked him why the questions. "Oh," he said, "I was just curious, you look like an actress on *General Hospital*." I wasn't sure if he meant a Florence Nightingale or a Nurse Ratched, so I smiled at him, grabbed my passport and told him, "Not fair, you scared the heck out of me." And then my battered old suitcase and I rushed off to catch our flight home.

Now, why did the couple with the chins catch the eye of the customs guy and get their stuff inspected? I think it was probably the luggage. If you have the budget to afford Louis Vuitton, you also have the funds to buy enough overseas to pique the interest of the Customs Inspectors. Lovely luggage such as Coach, Tumi, Prada and Louis Vuitton all indicate that here is a person traveling with a healthy bank account and expensive tastes. This makes the traveler vulnerable to thieves as well as suspicious officials. At any rate, choose your luggage carefully. Far away from home it can either be your downfall or your lifesaver.

On Being Sick and Lost, Cold and Worried

Fortunately, I'm still not at the level of Isabel Allende who writes, "I travel in spite of myself. I'm not a good traveler or a happy one. Travel requires a disproportionate effort, especially when it's to places with no room service." But lest you imagine that my travels are always worry-free, and explorations are done under a constant, problem-less, sunny sky, I have several confessions to make.

I have been lost practically everywhere. Sometimes it is fun. The Vatican was fun, Salzburg was fun, Bangkok was fun. Sometimes it is a little cold and scary. I've been alone and tired, trudging in a pouring rain back to the hotel in Stockholm, on foot and walking back to a distant pier in Venice (which is in the canal-less and not so pretty part of the city) and totally turned around in Cairo's Khan el-Khalili Bazaar with absolutely no one to ask for directions.

I have been sick more times than I can count. Amoebic dysentery in Sikkim forty years ago gave me with a fragile tummy, and I have been cursed ever since. The night train to Assam lacks romance and color when you are quite ill. I have had food poisoning on the Amalfi Drive. (Never believe anybody on Capri when they tell you that fresh-picked grapes still warm from the sun have been washed in sterile water.) Flu kept me in bed so long in Antalya that the tour left without me, and I began to recognize the imam's calls to prayer. There was that sneaky ice cube during a Nile cruise that made Abu Simbel horrid, and the only place I really got to visit in Bruges was the local lavatory. I have been so sick that I have sworn – several times – never to go traveling again if only I can feel well enough to get home.

I've spent too many hours in airport terminals waiting for delayed flights, crossing my fingers that the next plane would land and then take me on with it. And I've spent too much time squashed in coach next to the chatty lady in the pink boa who is doused in cologne and whose mission it is to keep me awake for the entire flight.

I've been miserable and clueless in a car, in an airport or in my hotel room, and wished more than anything that I could go home. But I'm getting much better. I'm getting more careful than I used to be. I carry umbrellas and maps, sometimes only eat bananas and local breads, never order ice cubes and stop and ask directions constantly.

In *Hold the Enlightenment*, renowned travel writer Tim Cahill declares, "Adventure is physical or emotional discomfort recollected in tranquility." I have tried to give you the tranquil recollections without the discomfort.

The real lesson learned is that I did get through the horrid problems. I did get over the sickness; I did finally find my way back to the hotel or the car; the plane did finally take off. There was light at the end although that is darned hard to remember when you are panicking. Everything is handleable eventually. And the memories of morning light over Cheops' pyramid, the scent of lilacs at Chenonceau, the serious discussions with Turkish children, make everything completely worthwhile - even that big lady with the pink boa.

A Traveler's Tales

The following pages are a compilation of my journals, memories, musings and newspaper articles. It is by no means complete and as with most intensely personal things, full of my own opinions and faulty recollections. To paraphrase Disraeli, "Like all great travelers, I've seen more than I remember and remember more than I have seen. "

   I've worn out a lot of shoes, broken my share of suitcases, gone through several passports and managed to get lost in almost every major city in the wide world. I hope that the stories of my misadventures may help you to leave the old and familiar and embrace the strange and wondrous. Travel is a privilege, a chance to go see a new part of the world and in the process, discover a new part of yourself.

Bali, the Land Beneath the Rainbow

The Dancers of Bali

The night was black and the noises coming from the surrounding jungle certainly weren't made by any critters we have in my little mountain town. A huge bonfire in the middle of the clearing gave a reassuring center of light but did little to brighten the dark forest surrounding us. The wind blew, trees rustled, strange animals made night cries. It was all dark, all foreign, all a little frightening. And it was obvious that Bali was a heck of a long way from home.

Then out of the blackness came the sound of hand clapping and then rhythmic chanting that grew louder and louder. Dressed in black and white checked sarongs, first one man then another came leaping out of the trees toward the blaze. The firelight gleamed on bare chests as by the dozens they came chanting and clapping into the circle.

Coiling into concentric rings around the fire, fifty or so men began one of the most famous of the dances of Bali, the *Kecak*. Hands rose to the sky and then pulled in. With arms extended, bodies swayed to the left and the right. Moving in unison, the only music was the complex interlocking patterns of their chant and the rhythmic beat of palms against bare chests and thighs. Lit only by flickering firelight, the performance was evocative and exotic, a fascinating introduction to the dances of Bali. Especially as I had been traveling for the last 32 hours, that evening around the fire was quite a culture shock.

Its people believe that Bali is the island of the Gods, the island of the arts. On this small lush Indonesian island east of Java, art is so much a part of life that there is no specific word for it. Everyone is simply an artist.   Painting and sculpture are a part of everyday life.   Dance accompanies every festival with performances for the pleasure of the gods, for status and prestige and for the entertainment of family and friends.

 I was fortunate enough to see several different types of dance during my stay. The *Kecak*, which was so startling (especially with a bad case of jet lag) is recent, only appearing in the early 1900's. The dance describes an episode from a story in the *Ramayana* in which an army of monkeys helps Rama rescue his wife Sita from a king who has abducted her. The dancers around the fire provide the rhythm of the dance, shouting "tchac-tchac-tchac" to imitate the

The "Barong," magical protector of the Balinese

A Balinese gemelan orchestra at full din

sounds of monkeys and to give the dance its name – the *Kecak*. To be honest, they didn't sound like monkeys to me, but who am I to argue with fifty half-clothed men in the middle of the jungle?

After that dark, late night, I had a chance the next afternoon to sit in a sunny courtyard and see a performance of the *Barong Dance*. "Lord of the Forest" and magical protector of Balinese villages, the Barong is a mythical, shaggy creature with a lion's face, a broad clacking jaw, bulging eyes and a long flowing white mane. Two men, one in the head and one in the hind parts, operate the creature which was costumed in gold-painted leather and gilt mirrors that caught the afternoon sun. Amazingly balanced (especially the fellow at the rear), the beast whirled around, swished its tail, snapped its jaws at the orchestra and danced around the courtyard.

Everything was silent as the Barong finished his dance. Then from behind the temple gate came the monster, the evil witch Rangda who rules over the spirits of Darkness. Dressed in red and black, she is a child-eater who haunts the graveyards. The dancer wore a long shock of straggly white hair; from her mouth hung a flaming tongue and around her neck was a grue-some necklace of human hands. With threatening fangs and bulging, bloodshot eyes, she attacked the gentle Barong. (I use the term "she" in the theatrical sense; the witch was played by a man.) The duel represents the never-ending fight between good and evil as each tried to overcome the other with magical powers. The witch stalked the dragon with screams and curses. The Barong had helpers, knife-wielding men who lunged at Rangda to weaken her, and who she then enchanted to turn the knives upon themselves.

As the gamelan orchestra played loudly, a deafening combination of gongs, xylophones, drums and flutes, the men ran back and forth waiving their knives, and several threw them-selves rolling on the ground in a desperate attempt to escape the witch. I was seated in the first row, and the knife-wielding magical frenzy being performed right in front of me was quite convincing. It took all the magic powers of the Barong to rescue his men and to overcome the evil witch. But eventually Rangda was defeated and once again good triumphed over evil. The Balinese natural world was restored. The good guys won.

Dance in Bali celebrates the cycle of life and death, the struggle of good and evil. It is one thing to read about it in a travel book. It is quite another to sit in a dark jungle or in the sunny courtyard of a Hindu temple and join in the experience.

A Balinese artisan carving my crane

The Wood Carver's Story

I tried to whittle once when I was young. After an hour's hard work sitting on the back porch, I ended up with a lumpy piece of wood, a dull knife and splinters in my fingers. So I gave up the hobby as a bad idea. And then 30 years later I went to Bali and saw just what could be done with time, patience, skill and imagination.

This legendary Indonesian island is one of the most lovely and peaceful places I've ever visited. Mist rises from the rivers and the rice paddies gleam emerald in the soft sun. I walked past blooming jasmine and hibiscus, through carved stone arches mossy with age to a sacred banyan tree with its altar holding offerings of fresh fruit and flowers. The Balinese don't own this beautiful place; they feel that they only look after it for the gods.

Entire towns focus on one type of craft from wood carvings and stone figures to jewelry and furniture. We spent a little time in the village of Mas, the wood carvers' village. Located just south of Ubud, this is a village famous for its wood carvers, mask makers, antiques and furniture. Surrounded by lush green rice paddies, this important Balinese area is quietly serene and idyllic. Life is easy and slow moving, and the little town is rich in fishponds, crimson flowers, soaring palms, bamboo forests, thatch-roofed cottages and talented craftsmen.

I followed a winding alleyway to a studio in a family compound, where the carvers lived along with their extended family and various dogs, chickens, ducks and pigs. The man's name in the photo is Wayan, the traditional name of all first-born sons. (Also, fifth-born and ninth-born because the Balinese have just four names each for boys and girls). He was working with his brother Nyoman (third-born) and had just recently been married. He hoped for many children. His English wasn't good enough for me to ask what would happen if he had five children and had to start over with names. (Just as well, humor doesn't always translate well.)

31

Wayan was carving a small crane. Sitting on a raised platform or "bale," barefoot on a small woven mat and wearing the traditional batik sarong, he held an 8-inch block of light capaka wood between his calloused feet and roughed out a basic shape with a small axe. With infinite patience and skill, he removed the bulk parts of the wood and then chose more and more delicate chisels as he defined and shaped the fragile piece.

The original Balinese carvings were of gods, heroes and demons on a grand scale for temples and palaces. I am happy that they are now also carving smaller pieces for the tourist trade as getting one of those huge and ornately carved columns through U.S. customs would have been a little tricky. I bought the lovely bird of course and carried it all the way home on my lap. I hope I paid too much for it.

The rest of my time on the island I spent in frivolous pursuits. I had tea at the base of sacred Mount Agung. I searched for the most picturesque and perfectly terraced rice field. I tried to keep track of the hibiscus, bougainvillea, jasmine, water lilies, magnolia, frangipani and orchids but I lost count. I met gentle children with disarming smiles and bought every banana they offered for sale.

The Balinese feel that there are good spirits in the world but also evil spirits. These cannot be defeated but only kept in harmony as symbolized by the black and white checked poleng cloths you see everywhere. To keep the universe in balance, it is necessary to hold on to both day and night, bitter and sweet, wet and dry, because these opposing forces depend on each other to exist. There is no good without evil, no light without dark, no birth without death.

It is a whole different way of looking at the world. I don't know if smiling at children or sipping ginger tea or watching a man create a delicate bird from a piece of log actually helped the balance of the world. But it felt like it.

The walled city of Dubrovnik

A monastery courtyard

"Pearl of the Adriatic," the ancient city of Dubrovnik, Croatia

"Those who seek Paradise on earth should come to Dubrovnik."
George Bernard Shaw (who rarely had a nice thing to say about anything)

My hands smelled of lemon cream one morning. Not so unusual, you might think. Except the lemons were picked in this sunny and tranquil courtyard of a Franciscan monastery in Dubrovnik, and the cream was bought in a pharmacy inside these monastery walls which dates back to 1317. By bringing this little jar back home, I am holding both history and fragrance in one bottle to remember Dubrovnik.

Dubrovnik, Croatia is on the eastern side of the Adriatic Sea, on the way sailing to or from Venice. The Croatian coast of the Adriatic has been luring travelers for centuries. In the 10th century, the Byzantine Emperor wrote of the "city on the cliffs" to his son. Lord Byron called it the "pearl of the Adriatic," Bernard Shaw named it "paradise on earth." Shakespeare's magical *Twelfth Night* is set there. Richard the Lion-Heart and Jacques Cousteau explored, Agatha Christy honeymooned, Edward Windsor and Wallis Simpson escaped and Isadora Duncan was inspired. Artists and kings came here for beauty. And I wouldn't want to argue.

The city's setting gave it the same sort of popularity crisis that all good locations have, everyone wanted it. At one time or another, it has been the turbulent property of practically anyone in the area with power. The Byzantines, Venetians, Hungarians, Ottomans, French, Austrians, Germans, Serbs, you name it, they've fought over it. (Having a strategic location and an excellent harbor can be both a blessing and a curse.) Throw in a devastating earthquake or two, and it's a miracle there is anything left at all.

Leaving Venice and sailing south down the rugged Dalmatian coast, we drifted past limestone cliffs and green mountains, through coastal islands blanketed with forests, fields of lavender and the occasional tiny monastery. When the ship docked at Dubrovnik, the city looked just as prosperous and peaceful as it did 500 years ago when it was the trading rival of Venice.

Pass through a massive gate and over the drawbridge and come take a walk with me around the perfectly preserved Old Town. In this jewel of a city, we can walk through marble-paved squares, narrow streets and stairways, convents, gilded churches, baroque palaces, fountains and museums. We can peek into the tranquil 14th century Franciscan Monastery complex with Gothic relics and manuscripts, the Church of St. Blaise with its magnificent baroque interior or the Rector's Palace with its impressive collection of Venetian paintings.

When we were there, we walked down the Stradun, a limestone street which bisects the city and is polished to a silky smoothness by centuries of foot traffic. It is lined with open-air cafes and designer shops and runs tidily between the towering west gate (the Pile) and the east gate (the Ploce). (At night, this perambulation is a citywide ritual called "the dijr.") The street ends at a high, round 15th century fountain, the Onofrio. Locals and tourists were splashing their faces. This was the spring-fed water source for the city. With the high medieval walls surrounding it and a fresh water supply, Dubrovnik could withstand quite a siege.

We hiked up a lane into the higher parts of the town where the air carried the scent of jasmine and lemon trees. The large, formal squares gave way to smaller ones, and the side streets were filled with fresh seafood restaurants, bakeries with crispy, fresh baked goods and the smell of the sea. Farther up, the narrow streets were barely wide enough for a cart, laundry was hung out and neighbors leaned out their windows to talk to friends across the way. It was late in the day and some ladies were sitting on the steps, catching up with the news. There were a few cushions on the stairs, probably permanent furniture for the chatty group.

At the southeast corner of the city walls, we climbed the steps of St. John's Fortress which has stood guard over Dubrovnik's harbor since the 14th century. Today, it is home to a Maritime Museum which is full of plunder from Greek amphora to 19th century wreckage, all from shipwrecks off the Dalmatian coast. There are scale models of famous ships, surprisingly accurate ancient maps, knives, dueling pistols, antique coins and other booty. Tucked in a corner is a fabulous old chest with a "do not open" card on top. Okay, I confess, I opened it. Absolutely no pirate treasure, but I bet there was some once upon a time.

Hiking around the two-mile medieval ramparts that encircled the city involved a little puffing, but I consoled myself with the thought that I was working off the fresh baked bread I had at my last stop. I was fortunate to be there late in the day when the narrow medieval streets were in shadows; the red terracotta rooftops were gently lit by the setting sun; the green hills were full of wildflowers and the gray limestone mountains and the blue Adriatic cradled the city. It was one of those lyrical places again.

In Dubrovnik, you can walk along a seaside path fragrant with flowers and lavender. Sit down at an open-air café and order a platter of just-caught mussels in tomato sauce with a glass of Croatian wine to wash them down. Watch the fishing boats come into harbor, the sun set on the sea and realize that this is a very perfect place.

In the fall of 1991, the world watched as the red-tile roofs were shelled during the Balkan War. Now this ancient and historic site has been meticulously repaired. The only real reminders of the war are the unrepaired shell holes in the monastery courtyard and the bright orange roof tiles that have replaced the softer sienna ones broken by the shelling. Beauty is fragile but in Dubrovnik, it still triumphs.

Copenhagen's Little Mermaid

Copenhagen, Denmark

"Copenhagen: a city that exists primarily to inspire a deep regret among those cursed to live elsewhere."

Peter Jon Lindberg

Of Mermaids and Men

The mermaid sits small and forlorn at the edge of the sea, lovely and wistful. She is a beautifully bittersweet figure, doomed by unrequited love to live in a friendless land, giving up her immortal soul for a pair of feet. Although visited each year by thousands of tourists, she is essentially alone and lonely. She is forever separated from the things she loves, a stranger in a strange land.

Hans Christian Anderson, (the middle name is always included to distinguish him from that other well-known Danish author, Hans Moslem Anderson), was a writer of extraordinary poignancy and beauty whose creations are painfully lovely. The statue of the Little Mermaid at the edge of Copenhagen's harbor is the symbol not only of his genius but also of the many exquisite treasures that this perfect city offers.

Although Copenhagen is quite large and very modern, the old part of the city still feels like a small town. There is no glittering skyline and only a few skyscrapers. The first things you may notice are the green roofs of the weathered copper-clad churches and the countless bicycles alongside the car traffic. My first morning there, I threw on a pair of jeans, grabbed my tennies and went out for an early morning walk. It was lovely. There was a lake next to the hotel and pedestrian streets and cobbled squares were quite close. Everywhere there was the smell of fresh-baked bread and soap-scrubbed front steps.

The city was only a tiny fishing village until the warrior Bishop Absalon (love the name) built a fortress there in the 12th century, and it was trade and the toll of passing ships that made Copenhagen the principle harbor in the Baltic. The Danish royal family has been reigning for more than 1000 years, and Copenhagen has been the royal capital since 1416.

I confess for a love for all things Danish. I grew up in a Danish town in Nebraska among Johannsens, Sorensens and Jensens, and you will never find a kinder or more hard-working people. Although they were all so tall that it wasn't until I got out in the wide world that I found out that I was a normal height and not seriously stunted, which was a great relief. Copenhagen is full of the same sort of people, kind, hardworking and tall.

The old section of the city is user-friendly and compact, and most of the main sights and attractions can be reached on foot. It is supposed to take only 25 minutes to walk across the old part of the city, but of course that doesn't take into account stopping, shopping or getting lost.

However, even in the heart of the busy, summer season there is always a lakeside bench or a quiet café to sit and watch the world go by. If you wanted to sightsee a little, you could walk from the Little Mermaid south along the water, past the Old Citadel and the Gifion Fountain and then stroll through the small cobbled lanes of the Nyboder district. Originally built for Danish Naval personnel, these 17th century homes have slanted gables, low doors and are painted a cheerful sunflower yellow.

Then on to the Amalienborg Slot. The Palace consists of four 18th century French-style rococo mansions built around a cobbled courtyard. When the swallowtail flag is out, the queen is home if you would care to go for tea. Some of the rooms are open to the public, and they are perfectly lovely, all golds and blues and ready for a Hans Christian Anderson story. Keep an eye out and you may see the very tall, very disciplined Royal Life Guards in black bearskin busbies accompanied by their band, marching down the street to Rosenborg Castle and its marvelous gardens.

Follow those Royal Life Guards, and you can visit the Rosenborg Slot, a 17th century castle which has been lovingly restored and has a grand Knights' Hall, as well as a Princess's precious lacquered chamber. The Danish crown jewels are tucked away in the basement, and you should also take a few minutes to explore the elaborate gardens surrounding the building which are the country's oldest.

If you're not "castled out," there are also tours of the gilded interior of Christiansborg Slot. The Danish Parliament meets here, and there is an interesting self-guided tour of the ruins of the original castle built by the enterprising Bishop Absalon in the 12th century. Near the Christiansborg, which dominates the heart of the city, be sure to notice the pastel rows of 300 houses along the Nyhavn, the oldest part of Copenhagen Harbor. The canal is packed with old wooden ships, and its dockside is now called the "longest bar in Scandinavia." Apparently ancient sailors and modern tourists have similar propensities.

Along one of the city's lovely canals

Then there is the fabulous National Museum which covers 14,000 years of Danish history from the Ice Age to the Vikings and the Middle Ages. There are golden horns, Bronze Age Viking helmets, the coffin of a Viking girl and a miniature sun chariot drawn by horses. Obviously peat bogs and barrows are excellent preservatives. The full and lengthy timeline of Danish history is presented with stories of daily life. Prehistoric, Medieval, the Renaissance, the 18th century, take your pleasure.

 And of course, try to spend some time at the Tivoli Gardens. They cover about 20 acres and are perfect for people watching. There is an outdoor amusement park, restaurants, a fabulous carousel, concerts and fountains. Just the gardens alone are worth the visit so be sure to take a camera and try to catch the colors of the flowers and the smiles of the children.

Finally, if you haven't walked your legs off already, try a climb up the Rundetarn (Round Tower), a 17th century observatory. The view of the twisted streets and crooked roofs of old Copenhagen from the top of the tower is worth the climb. It was built in 1642 and is still maintained. Peter the Great of Russia, never a subtle fellow and in Denmark for a state visit, galloped up the ramp on horseback.

I bet the Danes were extremely polite to him. They are a gracious people and should be visited whenever possible.

The funerary temple of Hatshepsut at Deir-el-Bahri

Egypt, the Mother of the World

A Walk in the Valley of the Pharaoh Queen

Come for a walk with me. In the early morning the air is crisp, the sky is blue, the desert is blooming; it could be our Great Southwest. However, to the north you can see the pyramid-shaped peak of the goddess Metsegar, "she who loves silence." The mountain rises up over the Valley of the Kings and guards the tombs of the pharaohs. You are walking along the Nile in the fabled land of Egypt.

Over the mountain spine from the Valley of the Kings, where explorers and thieves have found so many treasures, lies another valley with another famous temple. But this one is not hidden underground. Instead, it stands uniquely and proudly in its own valley. Its appearance echoes the uniqueness and greatness of the lady for whom it was built, Hatshepsut, Egypt's only woman pharaoh.

Let me tell you the story as it was told to me. It's about eternal beauty, lust, greed, power and blind ambition, all the makings of a Hollywood movie. But it all happened once....in ancient Egypt. The favorite daughter of a popular pharaoh, Hatshepsut was vital and vain, ambitious and compelling. When the king died in 1492 B.C. (yes, this is an extremely old story), she declared herself pharaoh, the first woman to reign in a country which never, ever, changed anything.

For a few years she ruled with her half brother, and on his death declared herself regent for her young nephew and became absolute monarch. And no, she didn't share.

She was a master politician and an elegant stateswoman who successfully controlled the most powerful and advanced civilization in the world for twenty years and left behind more monuments and works of art than any other Egyptian queen. At the peak of her power, she constructed a fabulous funerary temple across the Nile from Thebes, near the Valley of the Kings and the soaring plateau at Deir-el-Bahri. This is where we are walking this morning.

In the cool clarity of the Egyptian morning, in the stillness of the desert, look around you at this breathtaking monument which is carved from the living rock of the mountain. Built by her lover, Senmut (I picture him looking a little like Daniel Craig), the architecture is original and bold, and after 3500 years is still considered one of the finest buildings in the world. Predating the Parthenon by 1000 years, it is built into the limestone cliffs of the Theban Mountain and rises out of the desert in three huge terraces which are approached by a massive causeway. The temple faces east toward the rising sun, and the warm golden glow of the stone seems to hold the morning light a little longer than the surrounding cliffs. It was called Djeser Djeseru or "the most magnificent of the magnificent" by the ancient Egyptians, and I won't argue. The building is severe and spare, and the blending of the monument with the cliffs rising behind it is not something you will ever forget. Rather as if Frank Lloyd Wright had helped in the design. Although much has been lost, the valley temple, lush green gardens, small chapels and the avenue of sphinxes are all gone, much remains. And it will leave you breathless.

Walking up the ramps into the Temple itself, there are rich and fabulous reliefs of two ships transporting obelisks from the granite quarries at Aswan. There is a scene of the queen in a fishing boat and carvings showing her birth from the god Amun. Carved on the walls are details of expeditions sent to the mysterious land of Punt returning with ivory, exotic animals, spices, gold and incense. There are detailed descriptions of the sea journey (led by the chancellor, lover, architect Senmut), and even the reception offered him by a bearded African chief and his very hefty wife.

After 4500 years, the colors are still there; there are the reds and yellows of a sacred cow, the turquoise of an ibis in flight, the blues, reds and yellows of pharaoh offering gifts to a hawk-headed god. If you can imagine that once you came up a causeway lined by sphinxes, lush gardens, trees and flowers all in the middle of the stern and forbidding desert, it must have seemed like paradise.

In one chapel the words are inscribed, "I will make you to be the first of all living creatures, you will rise as king of Upper and Lower Egypt, as your father Amun, who loves you, did ordain." After her death, Hatshepsut's name was removed from the obelisks, her face obliterated from the statues. They attempted to erase her from history. But her temple still remains and will stop your heart with its beauty.

Camel Riding at Giza

"A camel is a horse designed by committee."
Alec Issigonis

I have a confession to make, I've never met a camel I was genuinely fond of. Oh, sometimes they have a noble stance, their gait is truly majestic and hypnotic, and of course those beautiful brown eyes and huge eyelashes are beguiling. But I've never been introduced to one that I would like to take home to meet the family. They tend to sneer, and they all have an attitude problem, a haughty, arrogant approach to life. There is that distinctive fragrance, "eau de camel."

Ambling with my new friend, the Camel

There is the way they stand up hind-end first after you've clambered on so that you feel as though you're doing a nosedive off the deep end. And then there is the spitting issue.

Arriving in Egypt exhausted and funky, there are bags to claim and Cairo customs to endure. Outside the airport, there are importuning guides clustered around the doors. Then the blessed car and driver will be waiting for you, hopefully with blessed air conditioning.

Driving into Cairo, you pass through a vast area ominously called the "City of the Dead." Filled with the tombs of sultans, these Islamic cemeteries date back to the 7th century A.D. Cairo's population is now so enormous that this "city" is also filled with hundreds of thousands of living residents, camping out in the tombs and monuments. It is less a "city of the dead" and more a "city of the impoverished." From the tomb of a beloved 12th century sultana, there is laundry hanging to dry. In front of the gravesite of a mystic Islamic cleric, there are shoes on a doormat. This "city" is horribly poor, but it's alive and coping.

A long drive through overwhelming traffic, deafening car horns and a maze of streets eventually brings you to the Mena House on the Giza Plateau. Almost at the base of the Great Pyramids, the hotel is set on 40 acres of jasmine-scented gardens. Built as a royal hunting lodge for the Khedive, it was converted into a hotel in 1869. The original Moorish, Coptic, Ottoman arabesques are now combined with all the attributes of a modern luxury hotel. You can't beat the location, half a mile away from the Great Pyramid of Cheops. There is a used-camel lot located conveniently close to the hotel as well. At dawn the next morning the staff took us to the camel yard for the short ride to the Giza Plateau where the pyramids and the Great Sphinx are located. It's a touristy thing of course, but in the early morning before the hoards descend, going by camelback is a fabulous way to get your first close look at the pyramids.

As I mentioned, despite the movies' romantic attachment to the "ships of the desert," I find camels to be unpleasant and sneaky animals. Luckily they are handled by ambitious and hard-working camel boys who grin as they help silly American tourist ladies mount.

The camel handler gave a sharp tug on the reins, and the animal I was to ride gave out a roar, which is not a good way to begin a relationship. Ungainly and clumsy, the camel folded her legs and dropped heavily to the ground. Not knowing what else to do, I made a major error and tried to mount the camel as you would a horse. Future note: camels and horses are not at all alike. Camels stand up backwards, their rear ends going high in the air. The camel fellow smirked as I fell forward, ineptly grabbing the camel's neck. She looked condescendingly back at me, since bedeviling lady tourists is obviously a favorite pastime. Apparently the correct way is to "step lightly onto the camel's neck and spring into position on the saddle as the beast lifts her head." Yah, not in this lifetime. Once aboard, we lumbered toward the Giza Plateau, looking un-Lawrence-of-Arabia like, but feeling marvelous.

Aren't they fabulous!

We undulated up the hill, those huge camel feet thudding in the sand. Trust me, approaching the pyramids especially from the additional altitude of camelback, is an incredibly overwhelming and humbling experience. The pyramids are every bit as breathtaking, enormous and ancient as you would expect. Built at the very dawn of time, they are the only marvel of the Seven Wonders of the Ancient World that are still standing today.

I've seen the Great Pyramid of Khufu many times in movies and on TV, but I wasn't prepared for the real thing. Let me be numerical for a minute. Begun in about 2550 B.C., it is still one of the largest buildings ever erected, incorporating two million stone blocks, each weighing 2½ to 15 tons. It is roughly 450 feet high, each side is 750 feet in length, and the base covers 13 acres. If those dimensions are monumental to us who are accustomed to the mass of skyscrapers and coliseums, imagine how the Pyramid must have appeared, covered in gleaming white limestone, to villagers who had never seen anything taller than their own mud huts. The engineering is equally monumental, but there's no need right now to go into the method of construction (although personally I lean toward the ramp theory).

I couldn't pass up an opportunity to go inside the Great Pyramid, after all Belzoni had done it. It was early morning, and the plateau was relatively empty. Dismounting gingerly from my camel, I was invited inside. Hunching over, I first went down and then climbed up the narrow stairs, obviously chiseled by short and sadistic tomb robbers. This small tunnel was far away from the 20th century, dark, dank and air-deprived, and there was no way not to be aware of the weight of the rock above me. The 1908 edition of Baedeker's *Egypt* warns "Travelers who are in the slightest degree predisposed to apoplectic or fainting fits, and ladies traveling alone, should not attempt to penetrate into these stifling recesses."

Stooped and shuffling up past the small, simple Queen's Chamber and then through the narrow confines of another passage, I could finally stand up. I had arrived at the incredible Grand Gallery, the famous and immense passageway which continues steeply upward all the way to the entrance of the King's Chamber. I can only hope the tomb robbers were as impressed as I was.

The King's Chamber is the pink granite room where King Khufu was buried. Now barren and empty, all that is left is the king's immense sarcophagus of red granite from Aswan. The king's mummy and whatever treasures accompanied him were looted long ago. Some of the colossal ceiling stones for the King's Chamber weigh as much as nine tons, which is better not to think about while you are standing under them. Placed below the apex of the Great Pyramid, this room is a remarkable place to be. There is a small, mysterious shaft going up from the ceiling to the outside that points to the circumpolar stars which never disappear in the sky. Although unexplained, I like the theory that it may have been put there to help the pharaoh find his way to the heavens.

After a while, we retraced our path back down through the small passageways and back to our own century. It is disconcerting to come out of the darkness into the harsh sunlight and from 4000-year-old ancient stones into the 20th century. Once outside in the beautifully fresh air, I chatted with little Egyptian boys, a couple of goats and I had my picture taken by innumerable Japanese tourists. Somewhere in Yokohama there is proof of my adventure.

There are several ways to see the Great Pyramid. You can stay safe and clean on your couch and watch a *National Geographic* special, you can read a travel book or see it in a movie, or you can go to Egypt and crouch your way through dark and narrow tunnels to search for the heart of the Great Pyramid of Giza.

Oh, and the camel? I told the driver, "No, thank you," and walked back to the hotel.

Feluccas still sail the waters of the Nile

Aswan

Once I met a boy whose village had drowned.

In the upper part of Egypt, just south of the Nile's first cataract, lies the Nubian frontier. The city of Aswan marks the ancient southern boundary and the classical point where civilization ended. It is an exquisite place with the town on the east bank of the river and the desert coming right up to the water's edge on the west bank. The idyllic area is dotted with green and perfumed islands, storied hotels and small, elegant boats called "feluccas" which drift along the shore. Nearby are Ramses' arrogant temple of Abu Simbel and the equally arrogant and massive concrete Aswan High Dam.

In 1970, the Aswan High Dam was built with a great deal of Russian assistance. Its purpose was to provide hydroelectric power, control the Nile flooding and maintain President Nasser's prestige and ego. Its result was to create an artificial lake, Lake Nasser (remember the ego?), and to flood large areas of Nubian territory in the Sudan.

The grandiose and beautiful Temple of Abu Simbel was threatened by the rising water of the dam and rescued through the heroic efforts of an international group. The entire mountainside was cut into pieces, taken apart and moved to higher ground where it was reconstructed into a man-made mountain. The lovely little Temple of Philae, with its beautiful relief work paying tribute to the Egyptian goddess Isis, was also nearly lost under the water, but a joint operation between the Egyptian government and UNESCO rescued the site. In an immensely complicated engineering project, the shrine was surrounded by a cofferdam and the inside pumped dry.

Then every stone block of the temple complex was labeled and removed to be reassembled later on higher ground. Millions of dollars were spent and precious, irreplaceable monuments were saved.

The boy's village? It is under water. An enormous lake covers the Nubian Sudan. His grandparents have died; his parents live and work in the town of Aswan, and his brothers and sister do not remember their village. We managed to save the monuments, but lost this boy his home. Dressed in a flowing galabaya and looking like a drawing from a Victorian travel diary, he sails his felucca on the blue waters of the Nile between the yellow desert sands and the palm-lined banks. He seems content, but he has lost his home and his culture and doesn't know or care.

Most visitors use Aswan only as a jumping off spot for Abu Simbel, but we were able to spend a few days in the town. We stayed at the Old Cataract Hotel, a legendary and luxurious Victorian hotel built of redbrick with Moorish flourishes. It's horrid, I love it. You can sit outside on the terrace and have tea, little sandwiches and cakes or inside at the Terrace Bar in a rattan chair with a cocktail. Either spot comes with a view of the Nile and Elephantine Island. It is the place to feel like a traveler, not a tourist. Czar Nicholas, Winston Churchill, the Aga Khan and Agatha Christie have also been guests. As Christie wrote part of *Death on the Nile* while staying in the hotel, she's probably still lurking in one of those rattan chairs.

The little Temple of Philae is beautiful to visit. Although if you've gone to Luxor first, you may be such a history snob that it will be hard to spend time looking at something that is only Ptolemaic. But after the grandiosity of the Hypostyle Hall, the small island with its small temple is a delight. Granite quarries in the area supplied much of the red granite used for the tombs and monuments. Nearby, in the Northern Quarry, the "Unfinished Obelisk" is a monument in stone to some poor fellow who probably lost his job 3000 years ago when the 2.3 million pound column developed cracks and had to be abandoned in its bed.

We sailed on a felucca to Kitchener's Island where the British general took a break from Khartoum and India, and created a botanical paradise on an island given him by a grateful Egyptian government. There are proper English walkways, exotic trees and flowers everywhere. I bought a sandalwood bead necklace from a vendor, and the fragrance scented my closet for months, reminding me of the lovely island. After the crowded rush of Cairo and Luxor, it was a blissful to stroll down the "Corniche," Aswan's broad promenade, watch the river flow by, inhale the perfumes and spices, look for the ghosts of Victorian travelers and step back to a quieter, gentler time.

"Outed" in the Valley of the Kings

At first glance, the Valley of the Kings is pretty disappointing, and I had a better view than most. Early in the morning when it was still cool in the Theban Hills, I hiked over the mountain spine that separates Hatshepsut's valley of Deir el-Bahri, from Biban el-Muluk, the Valley of the Kings. This one single gorge holds the magnificent tombs of 63 pharaohs, the greatest archaeological treasures in the world.

It's not a long hike, an hour at most. The first part of the climb was steepish as it took me to a high spot on the cliff above the temple. Looking down over the Hatshepsut complex, I was happy I'd made the effort. The breath-taking view was worth the climb. The queen's magnificent three-tier temple was below me and in the distance was the desert and then the sharp green line of the Nile and its flood plain. Over the ridge, the steep trail descends down to the Valley floor.

All along the climb it was easy to see I wasn't the first person to walk there. Bored temple guards had scratched graffiti in the caves above the temple. And for 400 years the well-traveled path along the cliffs was used by the artisans who built the tombs. They walked from their mud-brick village of Deir el Medina down to work in the Valley of the Kings 3500 years ago. I've walked in history's footsteps before but never had quite so memorable or intimate a climb.

Over the Pharaohs' Valley broods the mountain of the goddess Meretseger, "she who loves silence." The mountain's pyramid-shape may be one of the reasons for the re-location of the burials. It was hoped that the sacred form might help to protect the kings of Egypt since the size, complexity and devious tunnels of their mighty pyramids had been no defense against talented and ambitious thieves. The pharaohs left their vulnerable pyramids for more subtle and secret burials in the Valley which were hard to get to, easy to defend and had a strong limestone bedrock. These were extremely practical people.

Tourist in front of King Tut's tomb. (The loose scree behind me hides the entrance to the magnificent tomb of Seti I.)

The Valley of the Kings itself is quite long, thin and barren, and there were few signs of life. Dotting the hillsides were open trenches which my guide said had been dug by Howard Carter during his fruitless years prior to the Tut discovery. But even in Egypt, where the weather is so dry that nothing changes, that seemed a stretch. That early in the morning the large bus parking lot was still empty, but they had opened the refreshment stand and the restrooms. (Please do not forget the restrooms.) The view got more disappointing as we hiked down and the refreshment stand was the only bright spot. It had already been a warm and thirsty day, and my water bottle was empty. Stopping at the stand, I got soda and water, used the restroom, the normal stuff. But it was standing and waiting for my friends to do the same that got me into trouble.

Have you seen an old hidden treasure movie called *The Sphinx*? It is a terrifically corny film that is redeemed by its location in Egypt. It tells the classic story of lost Egyptian tombs, ancient curses and buried treasure, starring the beautifully vapid Leslie-Anne Down and the handsomely brooding Frank Langella ...who does look entirely satisfactory in a galabaya. At the end of the movie (spoiler alert), the treasure room is found. It is also satisfactory, full of gold, ivory and alabaster, sarcophagi, mummies, all the stuff you would expect from a professional family of tomb robbers who had been using it as their own private vault for the last 3000 years. "Everywhere the gleam of gold." And where was the entrance to this mythical treasure trove? The men's restroom in the Valley of the Kings.

So after a while, bored from waiting and mulling over the movie, I meandered toward the bathroom's entrance to take a quick look inside. I watched and I waited, and no one went into the men's restroom. I watched and I waited, and no one came out of the men's restroom. So figuring I was safe, I walked in to look at the crawl space over the urinals, where the entrance to the treasure tunnel was supposed to be. At the same time, a little old man in a white cap and immaculate galabaya was leaving a stall, looking down as he arranged the folds in his robe. And there I was, meandering around the men's john. After a startled glance at me, he fled the scene. Somewhere in Luxor there is a nice little old man who is convinced that red-haired, lady tourists from Arizona are perverted.

Disappointed by the men's bathroom, my next letdown was Tut's tomb. No wonder Howard Carter couldn't find it. As you can see by the obligatory photo, "Tourist standing next to tomb," there was not much there and inside it was just as disillusioning. There were only two real rooms, empty now since all the treasure, except for the bits and pieces purloined by Carnarvon, is in the Egyptian museum. The actual burial chamber had a strange row of 12 baboons looking down at the huge stone sarcophagus which held the boy king's mummy.

It was small and bleak. I wasn't expecting Frank Langella, but it would have been nice to have had a few gold figurines lying around. (There is gossip that his intended tomb was stolen by his successor, the evil and conniving chancellor Ay, but that is another story.) After the grandeur and Cecile B. DeMille scale of Karnak and the Hypostyle Hall, Tutankhamen's little tomb was disillusioning. I have no idea how they crammed all that exquisite treasure in there, but I think that it was pure luck and stubbornness that led Carter to it.

Seti's tomb next door, however, was another matter.

The Extraordinary Belzoni

At the outset, I should disclose that I am the founder, president and currently the only member of the Northern Arizona Chapter of the Giovanni Belzoni Fan Club. It is at present a solitary organization, but I expect that once my petition to have Belzoni made the patron saint of amateur archaeologists is approved by Rome, the faithful will flock to meetings. Then we shall establish the United Pot Hunter's Union and so forth.

Two famous profiles, I'm the one with the nose

"The Great Belzoni" was a circus strongman, an actor, a hydraulic engineer and most of all an adventurer. He was an authentic Indiana Jones, albeit an Italian one, with a story too strange for the movies.

Born in Padua Italy in 1778, the boy fled to England at the age of 16 to avoid political imprisonment. Because of his gigantic build, he earned a living for the next 12 years in circuses in England, Spain and Portugal where he was billed as "The Great Belzoni, the Patagonian Samson." After a period in Amsterdam learning to be a hydraulic engineer, Belzoni heard that the Pasha of Egypt wanted to build a "water-lifting device." Lured by tales of treasure and adventure, Belzoni, his Irish wife Sarah and his manservant, James Curtis, left for Egypt in 1815. His invention failed to please the Pasha and the trio was left stranded and penniless in Cairo. However, Belzoni met the British Consul, Henry Salt, who offered him a job - to recover the giant seven-ton head of Ramses II buried in the sand in Thebes and send it home to the British Museum. (Shopping for souvenirs was more ambitious then.)

Armed with only four poles and some rope, Belzoni sailed down the Nile to the ancient city of Luxor. After shifting gigantic columns which had the temerity to be in his way, Belzoni had the 9-foot statue on a boat for England. Johann Burckhardt (another European adventurer of the period) described the feat this way, "He handles masses of this kind with as much facility as others handle pebbles, and the Egyptians, who see him a giant in figure for he is over six feet and a half tall, believe him to be a sorcerer." A story, violently denied by the French, suggests that Belzoni was there just in time to prevent the French from making the Ramses head smaller and more handleable by drilling into it and using a stick of dynamite to reduce the size.

Belzoni had the perfect skills for the job - vast strength, engineering knowledge, bravery, cunning and an inventive disregard for authority. During the next seven years, he swashbuckled his way down the Nile Valley, making discoveries no one thought possible. He discovered, and uncovered, the huge temple of Ramses the Great at Abu Simbel, was the first to penetrate into the Great Pyramid at Giza, excavated at Karnak and discovered eight unknown tombs in the Valley of the Kings, the royal burial ground.

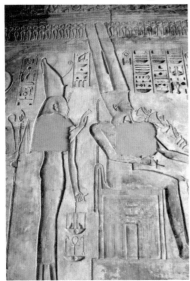

Interior of a royal tomb in the Valley of the Kings

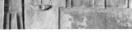

The gods Isis and Amun Ra

One of these tombs was that of Seti I. I have been to Giza and Karnak, seen Abu Simbel and the head of Ramses, but nothing is as marvelous as Seti's lost tomb, hidden for 3000 years until Belzoni broke through into the secret chambers. Come exploring with me. It's early in the morning; it's still cool and the other tourists haven't had a chance to arrive and stir up the fine dust in the tombs.

As I have mentioned, the Valley of the Kings is located in a long and desolate "wadi" on the West Bank of the Nile. The tomb entrance to Seti's burial is an unimpressive rectangular open-ing. However once you are inside, it is literally a whole other world, an underworld. Walking down, the tunnel is unexpectedly wide and the grade is gentle. On either side walls are elabo-rately decorated with paintings of the gods, the pharaoh, his family and fawning courtiers. The sumptuous colors of red and green, blue and gold are still fresh and vivid; it looks as though a great, brightly-colored papyrus was unrolled around the walls. Deep in the center of the earth, the ancients painted a road map for their king to the Blessed Land. The ancient Egyptians were very methodical people, and they were insuring that their pharaoh knew the way to the afterlife.

A wide stairway leads to the first corridor and then a second stairway and a second corridor, and then 11 pillared rooms which go deep into the mountain. Everywhere there are splendid bas-reliefs showing the pharaoh Seti praying to the sun god-Ra, making offerings to Anubis, the god of the underworld, the mother goddess Isis and Osiris, god of the afterlife. Here the King stands, broad shouldered and proud, locking arms with the falcon-headed Horus. In the hundreds of beautiful paintings which surround you are representations of the Queen, the royal children, hundreds of servants and worshippers. They all bring offerings to the god-pharaoh. Imagine Belzoni, the first man in 3,000 years, interrupting that procession as he walked down that same corridor. He must have felt like a ghost.

Finally descending through many corridors and rooms, you reach the vaulted burial chamber. This is where Belzoni found the elegant, translucent alabaster sarcophagus (which he "borrowed" and sent to London). This is the heart of the tomb and looking up high above, the ceiling is painted a lovely, deep azure blue. The familiar constellations of the Egyptian night cover it and the stars shine down on the dead king as the goddess Isis stretches out her arms to protect him.

And then there is Abu Simbel. You must remember that by the time I was there I was a monument snob. I had seen so many incredibly ancient things, walked through such ageless ruins (try visiting the Hypostyle Hall at Karnak sometime if you want to feel insignificant), that it was taking a lot to inspire me. I remember stopping at the temple of Philae on its own little island in the upper Nile and being disappointed because it was only 2000 years old. Egypt can do that to you.

Carved into the face of a mountain on Egypt's southernmost border, Abu Simbel was meant to impress and intimidate Egypt's enemy and sometime trading rival, Nubia. Ramses II never did anything by halves and this colossal monument to "The Great Bull, Beloved of Maat, Protector of Egypt, Conqueror of Foreign Lands, Rich in Years, Great in Victories, Lord of the Two Lands, etc." is worthy of the god-king who dominates the history of Egypt. He left his name, his face, his exploits and his DNA permanently imprinted on his country.

When Belzoni visited the monuments, 40 feet of sand covered the entrance and the debris in some spots was up to Ramses' chin. Neither the local officials nor the villagers were particularly interested in hard labor or ancient Egyptian archaeology, and so most of the digging was done by Belzoni and his five companions. Eventually excavating the interior of the 54-foot temple carved into the living rock, he found a series of halls extending into the sandstone.

The Great Temple of Ramses II at Abu Simbel

In the enormous first room, eight colossal statues of the pharaoh served as pillars. As you went farther back, the floors rose and the chambers became smaller. Until, in the deepest part of the sanctuary, you would reach the "holy of holies," with the seated gods themselves including the deified Ramses II. Considering Belzoni's sticky fingers, it's fortunate that he didn't attempt to send one of the giant statues back to London with the rest of the booty.

The walls illustrated scenes which showed Ramses' prowess in battle. He was especially fond of the battle of Kadesh against the Hittite Empire, and this relief is also one of my favorites. It illustrates the largest chariot battle ever fought - perhaps 5,000-6,000 chariots; it ended in a tie; Ramses declared a victory, came home and had a parade. He carved the erroneous propaganda all over the Egypt, and this is how the battle is remembered – he won.

Twice a year on February 2 and Oct 22, the rising sun shines all the way into the temple and illuminates the gods in the deepest sanctuary. These may be the dates of Ramses' birthday and coronation, but no one is quite sure. At any rate, twice a year the sun's rays go all the way to the back and the gods shine.

Ramses' construction of Abu Simbel in the 13th century B.C. is not the only miraculous event. There is also the recent incredible salvage operation to consider. The building of the Aswan High Dam in 1959 and the resulting rising waters of Lake Nasser threatened to drown the monuments under 20 feet of water. Between 1964-68, a multinational team of archaeologists, engineers and heavy equipment operators combined to cut and dismantle the complex into 20-30 ton blocks, raise them to a bluff overlooking the lake and reconstruct the entire temple complex.

The chief miracle, of course, is the raising and precise repositioning of such an enormous and ancient monument. The other wonder is that so many countries in the Middle East could agree to get anything worthwhile accomplished.

We were at Abu Simbel during the midday. I'd like to go back at dawn, perhaps when the morning sunrise goes all the way to the back and lights the faces of the ancient Egyptian gods, and pretend I was Belzoni, seeing it for the very first time.

If you wish to join the Belzoni Fan Club, I am taking subscriptions.

London England, Big Ben from Westminster Bridge

England, Centre of the Universe

"This royal throne of kings, this sceptred isle, This earth of majesty, this seat of Mars, This other Eden, demi-paradise...This blessed plot, this earth, this realm, this England."
W. Shakespeare

I confess to loving practically all things British. Now that they've given the Stone of Scone back to Scotland, I have difficulty finding any fault with them at all. Even with the soggy weather and even soggier vegetables, it is impossible not to be happy in England.

Just look at the place names, Baker Street means Sherlock Holmes, Wimpole Street would be the Barretts, Abbey Road for the Beatles, Saville Row for a suit, Downing Street for a prime minister. England is full of all the stories we grew up with, Paddington Bear and Alice, Robin Hood and Bilbo Baggins. And there is the countryside with legendary names, Stonehenge, Stratford, Land's End, Tintagel. What is there not to love in this strong, green land?

There are the myths, Boadicea and Alfred, Arthur and Mordred. There are the writers, Chaucer and Shakespeare, Austen, Keats, Dickens, Kipling, Christie and Tolkien. The explorers, Drake, Cook, Livingstone and Burton, the incredible heroes, Wellington, Nelson, Churchill. There are the statesmen, the composers, the artists. You see, we really have no choice, it's a wonderful country.

Walk this Way: London, the Heart of the City

Where do you find streets with single syllable names? Bread Street, Beer Street, Lud's Gate? Names so uncomplicated that you know they came from a simpler time, before kings and churches, before artificial developers and land-grabbers. You find these streets in the oldest parts, in the roots, in the heart of the great city of London. This is not an urban center of asphalt and faceless skyscrapers with sterile shopping malls and identical shops. This is where the City was born, the old Roman wall, the narrow streets where the Great Fire began, the embryonic beginnings of one of the world's most fascinating capitals. The cobblestones speak and voices of long ago tell their stories on the wind. Let me take you for a small stroll around the beginnings of the great City.

If you have the courage, begin near Pudding Lane at the massive "Monument to the Survivors of the Great Fire and the Plague." This first story will not be a pretty one, so you may want to move on quickly. In 1665-1666, the Black Death killed 20% of the population while the Great Fire of London gutted 80% of their homes. This giant column was designed by Christopher Wren and erected in 1677, commemorating "London rises again." The cobblestones worn smooth speak of agony.

Around the next corner, a cheeky Cockney voice will wish you "Top of the mornin' Guv'ner," as Albert Doolittle or a companion will tell you that a true Cockney is born within the sound of the Bow Bells from the church of nearby St. Mary-le-Bow. Down the narrow cobblestone street, listen for the raucous voices of hawkers, bawling their wares from trays or carts, "Pans, Pans to Mend," "Cockles and whelks, soles and eels for the old man's meals," "Needles and Pins, needles and pins? When a man marries, his trouble begins."

In this part of the City, you could wake early to the muffin man's bell and watch modest maids scurrying on errands for their mistresses. Or see grandly dressed footmen, letters in hand, striding amid the flower girls, chestnut sellers and barrel-organ grinders to deliver

And the cobblestones tell their story

messages from their masters. Later there would be the chaos of carriages and grooms, sedan chairs and porters, Londoners on their own important business or pleasure.

Down Bread Street, we hear the rumbling and tireless voice of that devotee of gambling, gossip and pretty serving maids, the Surveyor-General of the Royal Navy and blessedly inexhaustible diarist, Samuel Pepys. Pepys lived, worked and wrote his private diary during the Restoration. His bluntness, whether he is trying to seduce his wife's maid or complaining about the court, "Every one about the Court is mad," is a charmingly honest mix of lust and insight.

Turning the corner up Cheapside Street, the magnificent and ancient Guildhall presents a silent and imposing facade, until we hear the thin mew of a cat. Dick Whittington was a poor boy who traveled to London with his cat in 1364 to seek his fortune. After spending miserable days and nights starving there, Dick despondently set out to return home. But as he rested his weary legs on Highgate Hill, he heard the sound of Bow Bells ringing out, "Turn again Whittington, thrice Mayor of London." He returned to London where he made his fortune and was Lord Mayor of London three times. There is a statue of the cat at the foot of Highgate Hill. (The cat, of course, claimed all the credit for this rags-to-riches story.)

We might not want to stroll down Love Street (draw your own conclusions) as the stories we may overhear would be a little racy. But in Pudding Lane, there are the kingly tones of charismatic young Charles II fighting the flames of the Great Fire himself, lifting buckets of water and calling for buildings to be pulled down to stop the blaze that was to engulfed the City. Stop for a pint at Williamson's Tavern off Bow Lane and listen carefully. Do you hear roaring, genial laughter? That's Shakespeare's Falstaff or rather his inspiration, Sir John Oldcastle, full of wine and women and an overwhelming love of life.

Finally, listen for Latin oaths at the Roman wall and Latin prayers at the Temple of Mithras, the soldiers' temple. The nondescript set of steps you are climbing, the old pile of stones you are inspecting, are relics of a mysterious temple of Mithras, the soldiers' deity. You can still see the grooves which were made in the stone by the opening of the heavy temple doors. Imagine Roman soldiers praying for truth, honor and courage in this lonely gray post so far from their warm Italian sun.

Meandering anywhere is intriguing, but exploring the heart of an old city, a great city, may be the most gratifying stroll of all.

Looking for Peter Pan

There was a time before Walt Disney and his cartoonists found Peter Pan. Before Mary Martin and Cathy Rigby and even Robin Williams, took the boy and changed him into an adult parody of a child. Before Peter Pan even went to Never Never Land.

And where was he then? He lived in the heart of London. In Kensington Gardens.

J.M. Barrie, who wrote *Peter Pan and Wendy* in 1911, told the story this way, "All children are birds before they are humans, they are naturally a little wild during the first weeks, and very itchy at the shoulders, where their wings used to be....The moment Peter saw the trees of Kensington Gardens far way, he entirely forgot that he was now a little boy in a nightgown, and away he flew right over the houses to the Gardens. It is wonderful that he could fly without wings, but the place itched tremendously, and perhaps we could all fly if we were as dead-confident-sure of our capacity to do it as was bold Peter Pan that evening....The reason birds can fly and we can't is simply that they have perfect faith, for to have faith is to have wings."

Peter Pan and the children
in Kensington Gardens

Peter talks to a wise old crow in the Gardens who explains that he is not a bird, but rather a baby. "And the birds taught him the bird ways, to be easily pleased, and always to be really doing something and to think that whatever he was doing was a thing of vast importance." Once he reached Kensington Gardens he could never be a real person again, nor could he go back to being a bird. He was the boy who refused to grow up. And one summer morning my daughter and I went to find him.

First you take the tube to Lancaster Gate on the Central Line. When you come up and cross the street, be sure to look in the wrong direction because that is where the London traffic comes from. Once you've reached the safety of the other side, you walk along an iron fence where street artists have pinned up their wares. Some of them are quite good and it's tempting to stop, but the Gardens are waiting for you.

In Barrie's day, there was a balloon lady who sat just along the railing. She had to stay by the fence and hold on because if she let go her hold for just one moment, the balloons would lift her up and she would float away. She sat very still and had quite a red face from the strain. We looked for her, but apparently the balloons had finally won because she was nowhere to be seen.

Once you reach the gate, turn right and go down the path. Past the ice cream seller, past the precise Italian fountains, past picnickers on blankets, mothers chasing children, children chasing dogs, dogs chasing each other, all into the vast rolling park. Walk down the path by the Serpentine, the long green lake in this heart of London. Past birds, each one on its own piling in the lake. (I did wonder how they decide who gets to sit where. Do they dibs the night before? Do they flip a fish for it? Is it first come, first perch?) Past the mothers pushing prams and the little girls tugging. And there is Peter Pan.

It's been called "the most beloved statue in the world," and I'm not sure that is an exaggeration. Barrie commissioned the piece in 1912 and kept the project a secret with only George Frampton, the sculptor, and Lewis Harcourt, the commissioner of works, aware of the plan. He arranged for the bronze sculpture to be erected overnight so that children visiting Kensington Gardens the next day would think that it had appeared by magic. And so on May Day, 1912, Peter Pan returned to the Gardens.

The boy stands with his pipe on the top of a tall tree stump, never growing old, never growing sad. Look carefully and you'll see the girl Wendy and several exquisite, life-sized fairies, rabbits, mice and squirrels carved all around. You'll also see real children looking and touching and climbing. They can't resist him.

Pan left to live with the Lost Boys, but a little bit of him stayed in the Gardens. And there is whimsy and pluck and magic and a little bit of childhood for each of us as long as he is there.

A Tourist Visits the Tower – a Complete Fabrication

There I was in London on a little shopping vacation. I had been to all the really important sites, Harrods, Selfridges, the Liberty Emporium and so forth and I still had a free afternoon before I went home. There was not much time; there were a lot of options; I needed advice.

Because I knew I needed help, I did the only logical thing I could think of, I asked my concierge for advice. He joked and said, "Well, you could always call the Palace." Even if he wasn't serious, I thought that was a good idea. After all, I met Queen Elizabeth's second cousin's husband's sister on the Cape two years ago. So I phoned the Palace. Phillip answered, and I said, "Hullo, is the Queen there?" He went and found her, and she got on the phone and I asked "Hi Elizabeth, how are you?" And explained about meeting her second cousin's husband's sister. We chatted about the kids and the dogs and the weather, and then she asked if there was anything she could do for me.

In Arizona, our ravens can fly

I explained about my unexpected free time and asked a favor. Would it be possible for her to recommend a guide? With only a short time to sight-see, I didn't want to waste any of it. Did she suppose she might know someone to show me around? I needed someone who was knowledgeable and experienced, and I knew she had connections. She thought for a few minutes, I could hear her twirling her tiara, and then she said that she had just person for me, and that I should meet him at the Tower of London in 30 minutes or so.

So I grabbed a cab and raced over to the Tower. A small warning for you. That is certainly not a correct name. It is not a tower; it is a lot of buildings. I suspect it is so old that nobody wanted to be insulting and tell the English they have it misnamed. The gentleman at the front gate did put me off a little since he was dressed in a very fancy red and blue number. He said he was called a "Beefeater," and I guess considering the price of a steak over there that a man might put up with wearing almost anything for a decent meal.

He sent me down a road made of cobblestones (which does explain why their cars don't last). When we reached some stairs coming up from the river, the red and blue hamburger man stopped. He said that some princess or other was climbing up those steps because her sister, the queen, was sending her to prison, and she just sat down in the rain and wouldn't go any farther. Well, I can tell you, I certainly did sympathize. Even if you have a really good lawyer, that's a bad spot to be in. I don't know what would have happened to my cousin Herman if he hadn't had a good attorney. But apparently the girl was released eventually and did well.

Then I got to go under one of those portcullis things (the movie people would love all these set decorations), and I was asked to wait by the big building in the middle of the yard. The sign in front said it's the "White Tower", only it certainly could have used a fresh coat of paint and maybe some new window treatments. I was standing there waiting for Elizabeth's special guide, and some man went running past, holding his hand out after a big black bird that was just hopping along on the ground. He was calling, "Here Cedric, here Cedric, be a good bird and let me put you to bed for the night." But the bird wasn't having anything to do with it. He kept just ahead of his birdman as though he were teasing him and playing a kid's game. And of course, he reminded me of little Herman, Jr. His parents can't control him either.

I don't know what the heck they were up to, but I should tell you, in Arizona our ravens can fly.

While I was stopped there, all sorts of tourist people went by. I knew that they didn't know anymore than I did about the Tower, but I did notice that they were headed for some sort of lovely, high-end jewelry store, called "The Crown Jewels." Now I like pretty things as much as the next woman, so I walked over and peeked in the shop. There were the loveliest things, although I do think that some of the necklaces would be a little garish to wear. There really wasn't time to take anything outside and see it in proper light or to try anything on. As I'm Elizabeth's guest right now, I didn't think it would be polite to go shopping. But when I get to come back again, I am so taking my credit card with me and spending some time.

Poor, poor man

And then while I was looking at a particularly nice dinner ring that would go beautifully with my new silk suit, a very strange man approached me. Now I've read all about travel in foreign parts and being careful of strangers, but this fellow was a dozzie. He was wearing tights and a cape and earrings. I really don't know how he made it this far without getting mugged; he wouldn't have gotten around the block in my neighborhood. I pretended not to notice his outfit and turned my back to try to ignore him. The way you do with strange men. Then he gave me quite a start. He put one hand over his heart and the other on the top of the grip of his sword and bowed and said that he's been sent by the Queen to show me around the White Tower.

Even for an Englishman he had a horrid accent, and you know how they mispronounce so many of their words. He said he was Welsh, and then he started on his lecture, so you will need to pretend that what I tell you about next is coming directly from his mouth. But it certainly seemed very peculiar there by this old building with this man in tights and slippers, and I didn't want to interrupt or make fun of him for fear of making him feel bad. But I wish you good luck trying to figure out what he was saying half the time.

"This great building behind you is the White Tower. It was built of stone in 1078 by William the Conqueror in the corner of the old Roman walls to protect his Normans. With great turrets on each corner, it has served as fortress, armory, treasury, mint, palace, refuge and prison. It has had many noble and illustrious guests held by command of the throne. One such was a heroic and treasured prince of Wales.

"Now Llywelyn the Great ruled Wales against the vicious and invading English until 1237. But even his noble heart finally broke under the English onslaught. He left two sons behind him, Dafydd who was half English and lived to become the curse of his country, and Gruffydd, a giant of a man who had a Welsh mother.

"Now Llywelyn had weighed his two sons in his mind as to which would be the better ruler for the land. Dafydd's mother was sister of the English king and surely the king would think kindly of his nephew. So thought Llywelyn and accordingly he made Dafydd his heir, the one tragic mistake which undid all that he had accomplished in his own brave life. Dafydd reigned six years only, but in those six years he brought to the ground the strong Wales which his great father had built. His weakness and cowardice led him to turn over his half-brother to the English tyrant.

"Gruffydd was a grand, handsome prince, full of turbulent valor and so the English feared him and put him in the White Tower as a prisoner. Many years they kept him idle and well fed until finally this headstrong and impatient man yearned for freedom. He made a rope from his own bedclothes and began to let himself out of his high window. But many years of soft living had made him too heavy. The rope broke and he plunged to his death.

"And thus died the last great hope of the Welsh people." And then this poor man put his head down and looked as though he might begin to cry. But he was obviously a sensitive soul, and I guess that goes with the territory along with the stockings and the cape and such. Now, I'll be honest. That accent of his was so heavy, and he got so excited talking about his prince that I missed half of what he said. But it did seem to be a weight/sheet quality problem. I bet they bought them on sale.

Then it started to rain. To be polite, I suggested we visit a lovely tea room I had noticed when the cabbie brought me. But he asked if we could go to his favorite pub around the corner. Perhaps they didn't object to swords and capes as much. I said, "Of course," and he cheered up quite a bit. So we sat down in a little warm nook while he had a pint and I had a sherry. He told me more stories about the Tower and I asked him about the lovely jewelry store there.

I will need to remember to write a thank-you note to Elizabeth.

Walk this Way: London, the Inns of Court

London is one of those marvelous cities where it is possible to spend an entire day happily exploring just one small area. The city is so rich in history that a single square block may hold 2000 years of legend and enough stories to satisfy even the greediest history junkie.

Come take a walk with me around one such neighborhood. The Inns of Court occupy a compact district just west of the City (London's financial district) extending northward from the Thames. This is the home of the four ancient societies that have the exclusive right to admit and confer the title of "barrister," entitling the anointed to practice before the Bar. For hundreds of years, this has been the professional center of England's bewigged and gowned profession. (FYI, solicitors, who don't get to wear the wigs, provide legal advice, while barristers actually take the cases to court.)

Ede & Ravencroft, England's leading wig makers

The architecture of the four Inns of Court, the Inner Temple, the Middle Temple, Lincoln's Inn and Gray's Inn, mirrors the cloisters and squares of Cambridge and Oxford as it was those graduates that first formed the Inns of Court. There are passageways, court-yards and lanes through beautiful gardens. And in the middle of the greenery and the benches are stories of life and death, full of high drama and colorful characters.

The tale begins, strangely enough, in Jerusalem in the early 12th century. The Knights Templar were charged by the pope with protecting pilgrims to the holy sites. As they became wealthy and powerful, the Knights estab-lished themselves throughout Europe. Equal to kings and answerable only to the pope, the arrogant order fell from power in 1308. In London, as elsewhere (memo, becoming wealthier and more powerful than any pope or king is a really bad idea) their treasures were seized and property taken by the crown. About the same time, the lawyers of London were looking for a spot close to the Royal Courts at Westminster. So the Crusaders moved out and the lawyers moved in. The Inns became places to live, worship and learn the law. Today each Inn is a series of quadrangles with working spaces, a communal dining hall and a chapel, a calm oasis right in the middle of the City.

Strolling down a lane toward the Inns, on your right is a tavern, the "Cittie of Yorke." There has been a pub on this site since 1430 for the care and coddling of lawyers, and the large back bar is the longest in the city. A little farther down is a shop that sells wigs for the barristers and judges. Some of the chambers have the barristers' names listed outside. The author John Mortimer was among the members, and on the directory for the "Ground Floor, South" some clever person has put the "Erskine-Browns" and "Horace Rumpole" on the list.

See the round building in front of us? That is worth a stop. This is the Knights Templar Church that was built in 1100 and the unusual shape was inspired by the Church of the Holy Sepulcher in Jerusalem. The interior is pure and elegant Gothic architecture with nine recumbent figures frozen in stone, once and future knights poised to spring again to war.

The historic buildings of Lincoln's Inn are set in beautifully maintained private gardens. There is a story that the Old Hall, begun in 1490, was partially funded by fines levied on its members if they were caught "having or enjoying a woman in the garden or in Chancery Lane." The Inn finally insisted on old laundresses so as not to tempt the lads. Those who have studied law at Lincoln's Inn include Sir Thomas Moore, John Donne, William Penn and 16 prime ministers including Benjamin Disraeli, Margaret Thatcher and Tony Blair. (Don't you love the continuity?) In the 18th century, poor mothers would sometimes abandon their newborn babies in Lincoln Inn's Chapel. When left there, the Chapel would adopt the baby and care for it and then provide either an apprenticeship or a marriage dowry. It was the custom to give these foundlings the last name of "Lincoln."

Of all the Inns of Court, probably the best preserved is Middle Temple. Set on a wide expanse of green, to visit there seems like stepping back in time. Middle Temple Hall is at the heart of the Inn and to walk into a building that has remained unchanged for 400 years is a fairly amazing moment. From the balcony, lift your eyes to the open timbered ceiling. It's called a "hammer beam" roof and 400 years ago it looked down on Queen Elizabeth I. In 1602, London's leading band of players was invited to give a Christmas play before the Queen and so the Chamberlain's men (perhaps including Will Shakespeare) gave the first performance of *Twelfth Night.*

At the head of the Hall is the Bench Table. Twenty-nine feet of continuous plank, it came from a giant oak felled in Windsor Park and given to the Inn by Queen Elizabeth, whose portrait stands behind. Look over to the left and you'll see a little battered table, hardly worth a glance. It is to this table that a lawyer steps when he is "called to the bar" to sign the Roll. The oak that forms the top was given to the Inn by Sir Francis Drake. It's the hatch cover from his ship, the *Golden Hinde* (goosebump moment). They're setting up for a banquet tonight and as you watch, one of the waiters drops a fork, picks it up, looks around, surreptitiously wipes it on his jacket and replaces it on the table. So much for fame and glory.

The United States is a nation of immigrants with many excellent examples of people who have had the good sense to move here from many other countries. However, we are all bound by the ideals, ethics and craft of British Common Law, and the Inns of Court are our foundation for a legal and just society. When you know someone who has "passed the Bar" it originates from passing Temple Bar on the way to Court. When someone "approaches the bench," it comes from going toward the long, high table in the Middle Temple. And when "the bell tolls, it tolls for thee," it is the grave and solemn bell of Lincoln Inn.

Stonehenge, the Ultimate "Honey-Do"

We're spring-cleaning at my house. We're clearing out clutter, rearranging, painting, etc. In a job of this magnitude, I see myself more as the job supervisor than the actual manual laborer. I pick out wall colors, he does the painting. I go shopping for the new kitchen hardware, he installs it. I think that maybe the couch would look better on the other side of the room, he moves it over there. Men are certainly handy to have around, even if you don't need to parallel park.

As he was shifting the solid walnut bureau (and it ain't light), I considered what it took to get things rearranged satisfactorily. It's not easy. Can you imagine what a chore getting Stonehenge just right must have been?

Beginning nearly 6,000 years ago and thousands of miles from the first stirrings of civilization in Egypt and Mesopotamia, stone-age villagers of Western Europe produced structures as remarkable as any pyramid or ziggurat. Using muscle, rope and logs plus incredible engineering skills and imagination, these Neolithic hunter-gathers and farmers created monuments to last for all time. Some 50,000 megaliths are found all over Western Europe, with some of the stones weighing 50 tons and more. If you search while you are traveling, you can find them on the island of Malta, in Spain and Portugal, in France and the British Isles and as far north as Denmark. Some are largely underground and covered over with earth, while others are above ground, built of upright stones.

In its beginning Stonehenge was a bank and ditch arrangement called a "henge." It was dug with tools made from red deer antler, hammer stones and wood. Everyone was quite happy with the effect. The little Neolithic couple is newly married, and they think everything looks great. She's got a place for her pots and pans; he has a comfortable spot to watch the bison races. Then around 2,000 B.C. rearranging began. Bluestones were brought from 240 miles away, from the Prescelly Mountains at the southwestern tip of Wales and arranged in the first stone circle. The bluestones weigh up to 4 tons each and about 80 were used. Can't you see the

Ancient Stonehenge on Salisbury Plain

61

discussion? They've been married a while, she's just back from visiting her sister in Wales. "Honey?" "Huh." "Do you love me?" "Huh?" "Boadicea has the most wonderful arrangement of blue standing stones. I think some would look very nice in the front yard."

So using roller and sledge from the inland mountains and barges and boats along the coast, the enormous blue stones were floated and dragged to Salisbury Plain. And everyone was quite happy with that.

The giant sarsen stones form the outer circle of Stonehenge and weigh as much as 50 tons each. The original 30 uprights were brought from the Marlborough Downs, 20 miles to the north. Once they were erected, continuous giant lintel stones were placed along the top surface. This is an incredibly complicated engineering feat, requiring skill, commitment, time and a vast amount of manual labor.

Can't you see what started it? They're about to celebrate their 25th anniversary, and she's just been to visit her mother in Marlborough. "Honey?" "Huh." "Do you still love me?" "Huh?" "Mother says that there is a new standing stone home décor we really need to look at. The shaman who lives next door to her has one."

So, using logs and levers, rope and sweat, the massive stones were brought into place. And everyone was quite happy with that.

Although Bronze Age builders left behind no written records to explain the purpose of the great stones and mounds, there are a lot of suggestions. A temple made for worship, an astronomical observatory, a sacred site for burial of powerful kings, are all popular suggestions. My own favorite is that Merlin called the stones to stand with magic and his harp.

While we can't say for sure what its intent was, as you approach Stonehenge on vast Salisbury Plain, the more impressive the site becomes. The ancient patterned stones stand their implacable guard. Only something tremendously important would have been worth 1,500 years of so much effort. It was built to last forever. So when you visit, treat it as a place of honor and realize that some poor guy gave his all in the ultimate "honey-do" to move that stone to just the right spot.

Walk this Way: London, Southwark

I came to Southwark by river, although now there are many ways to reach the south bank of the Thames. There is the ever-extending tube or a taxi or the fabulous pedestrian bridge they've built between St. Paul's and the Globe. But the river is the old way, the real way to get there. A hundred years ago, I would not have gone at all. A lady didn't venture into that notorious part of town with its disreputable businesses, brothels and bear gardens, taverns and theatres and even more scandalous inhabitants.

Building on the south side of the river began in the 1st century A.D. when the Romans used the mudflats and sandy islands to anchor the only bridge across the Thames to Londinium. Because it was a safe distance away from the regulations and restrictions of the Courts and the City, the lawless and rowdy area flourished as a haven for criminals and free traders.

Come walk with me through some of the legendary and notorious places on the "wrong side" of the river. In the unsavory world of Southwark, there were inns and alehouses, stews and thieves' dens, prisons, play houses and bear-baiting rings. Wandering bank-side at night you could not escape the howling of dogs and the roaring of chained bears. It was not a place to be if you were alone or vulnerable.

Begin, if you would like, at the faithfully reconstructed Globe Theatre. A perfect replica of Shakespeare's original timbered playhouse, the theater is open to the sky and has a thrust stage, a circular yard for the groundlings and three tiers of seats. When the weather was fine and there was no plague in the city, a new play by Shakespeare could bring 3000 people across the river, enough to fill the Globe. Groundlings would stand in the "yard" for three hours while the wealthier patrons would sit in the galleries.

It is not hard to imagine Hamlet striding there or Falstaff bellowing for ale. If you've the time and the inclination, there is a marvelous museum below which demonstrates the methods used to achieve special effects for Elizabethan theater, as well as the techniques used in the construction of the highly elaborate costumes required for the plays. There is also a detailed exhibit describing the rebuilding of the Globe, a 48-year labor of love. As no one was thoughtful enough to leave an architect's plans, the playhouse was rebuilt using clues from panoramas of the day, written descriptions, archaeological finds and hints in the plays themselves. All the traditional crafts and materials were used to build the new theater, lime plaster, oak laths and staves, reed thatch. I wonder how hard it was to find a "wattle and daub" man in modern London.

After you've torn yourself away from the Globe, be sure to notice the simple plaque nearby on Park Street which prosaically states, *Home of the original Globe Theatre*. "Soft, what light from yonder window breaks?" "My horse, my horse, my kingdom for a horse." "To be or not to be." Please pause for a moment and consider that the world first heard those words on this spot.

Stop for a pint at the Anchor Tavern where for 800 years sailors off the tea clippers, dockers and now office workers enjoy a pint and where Samuel Pepys watched the Great Fire of London burn across the river. The Tavern is located on Park Street, originally called "Maiden Lane" after the "maidens" who worked there. Then walk down the cobbled, echoing Clink Street threading between brick cliffs of warehouses and past the London jail so notorious that "Clink" is still slang for prison. You're in the London of Charles Dickens's nightmarish boyhood, the dark alleys of Oliver Twist and David Copperfield.

Past Clink Street, at St Mary Overie Dock, is a replica of Sir Francis Drake's *Golden Hinde* which set sail around the world in 1577. Then left onto Cathedral Street and there you will find Southwark Cathedral, optimistically sterilizing the goings-on in this corner of the City. There has been a church here for over 1000 years. The nearby streets housed the shops of glaziers, leather workers, printers, pottery makers and brewers who all settled here to avoid the strict rules established by the guilds of the City of London.

Tread carefully through the Borough Market, a vast open-air space under a Victorian-style warehouse roof, which has flourished there since the 1st century. It's the best food market in the country; it may be the best in the world. Straight from the sea and from the farms, the shops and stalls offer fresh fruits and vegetables, fish and fowl, cheese and bread. Everything appears much as it would have to Chaucer or Shakespeare, Pepys or Dickens.

We end at the George Inn in Borough High Street. This is London's only surviving coaching inn with its black and white half-timbered balconies surrounding a courtyard. If you listen, you can still hear the shouts of the drivers and hostlers, feel the crush of merchants, travelers and traders. If you glance just to the south, there is the Talbot Yard, home to the Tabard Inn where Chaucer's pilgrims began their epic journey to Canterbury. Have a glass of stout and a pasty sandwich and enjoy your own London pilgrimage.

Southwark has changed almost beyond recognition. You have to use your imagination now to feel the flavor that once was here. Spend some time in the Tate Modern, the largest modern art gallery in the world (the restaurant on the 7th floor has a nice lunch and a great view). Take a ride on the London Eye (a giant Ferris wheel), stroll along pedestrian-friendly sidewalks through green parks and past enough boutiques, shops and restaurants to keep everyone happy. After all, Southwark still has a reputation for entertainment to maintain. But in the middle of all the modern stuff, keep an eye out for Shakespeare's melancholy coward and hero, plump, drunk John Falstaff, and if you can, offer him a dram at the George Inn.

The Play's the Thing, London is Theater at its Finest

It was raining when we came out of Drury Lane Theatre, and it looked so much like the opening scene of *My Fair Lady* that I peeked around the column for Eliza and her flower basket. Do you remember the beginning of that marvelous musical? Having been to the theater, misogynist and linguistics expert Henry Higgins meets the Cockney flower girl taking shelter from the rain on the theater steps, and the whole lovely story begins.

Professor Higgins and his Eliza are long gone, but the Drury Lane Theatre is still there. Actually, the playhouse is properly called the "Theatre Royal Drury Lane." Built under a charter from Charles II, (getting rid of Puritan dourness as quickly as possible) it opened in May of 1663. Since then it has been visited by every British monarch, provided entertainment for the masses and has triumphed over tragedy, bankruptcy, fire and even a murder.

Theater doesn't get any better than this

The theater has two ornate royal boxes, and it was here that an orchestra first played Great Britain's "National Anthem" and "Rule Britannia." Name a musical and it's played here, *Camelot, My Fair Lady* and more recently *The Producers* and *The Lord of the Rings*. Name a great actor or playwright of the British stage and they have walked its boards, David Garrick, Richard Brinsley Sheridan, Sarah Siddons, Edmund Kean, John Gielgud, Laurence Olivier, Kenneth Branagh and my own personal favorite, Nell Gwyn.

Just in case Nell Gwyn isn't high on your list of interesting people, her's is a terrific Cinderella story. The illegitimate, illiterate daughter of a Cavalier captain and a "low woman," she began by selling oranges at the Drury Theatre and rose to become one of the most popular comic actresses of the age. Samuel Pepys, who knew a pretty ankle when he saw one, was quite taken and wrote, "…hath the notions and carriage of a spark the most that ever I saw…I confess, (I) admire her." Charles II agreed with Pepys and Nell Gwyn became his mistress and the mother of two of his children. She was lovely, generous, reckless and funny.

When an Oxford mob mistook her coach for that of the Louise de Kéroualle (Charles's unpopular French Catholic mistress) Nell famously called out smiling, "Pray, good people, be civil, I am the Protestant whore!" The crowd surrounded the coach and cheered her. So when you're at the Drury Lane, please imagine Nell there as well, capturing the heart of a king.

The theater even has great ghosts, and when one is seen it means good luck for the actor or the production. The "Man in Grey" is seen dressed as an 18th century nobleman with powdered hair, a cape, boots and a sword. Another actor haunts backstage where he killed a friend in an argument; the ghost of a famous comic guides nervous actors around the stage and the dancing of another can be heard in one of the dressing rooms. Finally, Charles Kean, the 19th century actor, has been seen sitting in the front row and then vanishing when the lights go up.

London has always been rich in theaters. Even in the days of Charles II, when the Drury Lane was built, there were playhouses all over the City. Not just for the elite or the overdressed, the theater was a place where a working man could relax for a few hours. Ordinary people could see anything from bawdy, music hall shows to full class productions. They would laugh, cry, shout, hiss and throw pennies on the stage in appreciation of a good performance.

The Theatre Royal has brilliant productions, a fabulous history, a great location, ice cream or a glass of wine during the interval, ghosts, a famous pub across the street and even its own restaurant where your table is reserved for the entire evening. You'll be happy you went.

France, Liberté, Egalité, Fraternité

Getting Lost and Found at Notre Dame

The first time I was in Paris I got lost. Unfortunately that isn't a bit unusual, but I am pretty sure that the fault wasn't really mine; it was more the City's responsibility. There are just too many enticing and beautiful things going on in Paris to bother to look at the street signs.

There is the fragrance of fresh bread baking which lures you into a little patisserie for a warm croissant. There is the little girl in braids holding a red balloon who stops and waives at you from the park across the street. There is the lined and weathered face of an old man as he sips his morning coffee in a little café, the wonderful bookstore with all its old leather-bound books (luckily, all very cheap, unfortunately all in French) and the flower seller on the corner offering bunches of lily-of-the-valley.

So when you are laden down with loaves of fresh bread, little leather books and bunches of flowers, who has time to notice precisely where your feet have taken you?

Luckily I ended up by the river. The Seine is an excellent landmark because it runs through the heart of the city so at least you can be pretty sure if you are on the left-bank or the right-bank. (As long as you notice when you cross large bridges.) But the river is not a bit straight, so it doesn't help as much as it ought.

As I walked down the river's promenade, there was a very huge, very old building on a tiny island on the right. This was a good thing. Old, large buildings tend to be important and might be on my map, that is if I could figure out just which monumental edifice it was. Paris has rather a lot of them.

Getting closer, looking up, there were marvelous flying buttresses on the building. Flying buttresses are a particular favorite of mine. They transfer the weight of the roof to the load-bearing walls so that it was possible to turn the old squat, barrel churches into the soaring anthems of the medieval cathedral. Then the music changed to accommodate the new architecture, trade increased to accommodate the building project, and then the towns enlarged to take care of the pilgrims and so forth. And all because of flying buttresses.

Closer still to the building, I could see marvelous carvings of fantastic and hideous creatures on rain spouts coming from the roof. So let's see, Paris – the Seine River – flying buttresses – gargoyles. Ha! I knew where I was. I didn't need a hunchback to tap me on the shoulder! I had accidentally stumbled on Notre Dame. How fortuitous.

I parked myself under a shady tree, pulled out my loaf of bread and sat down to munch and appreciate the view. Notre Dame is so familiar an icon that when I was actually in front of it, the first thing I thought of was that silly rhyme:

"The Gargoyle often makes his perch, On a cathedral or a church,

Where, mid ecclesiastic style, He smiles an early-Gothic smile."

That's not particularly respectful, but Notre Dame does look just exactly as it should, the soul of Paris, the heart of France. The artists of the time "dreamt in sculpture, dreamt in rhyme. And from nowhere came the age of the cathedrals where stone after stone man built with faith and love."

Granted it is just another big, old cathedral. I could give you all sorts of boring dimensions and a history of the towers, the arches, the naves, but it is the passion (and the engineering) of the building that matter to me. Even the most hardened anti-history buff would get goosebumps here. Two thousand years ago there was a Roman temple, then in the 4th century a basilica followed by a Romanesque church, and finally in the 12th century the Cathedral was begun. The Third Crusade was called from its uncompleted steps; in this ancient building, the mother of Joan of Arc pleaded with a papal delegation to save her daughter; Mary, Queen of Scots was married; Napoleon was crowned and the magnificent "Te Deum" was sung celebrating the liberation of Paris from the Nazis.

Inside the cathedral are exquisite rose windows which shine like jewels. Then a climb all the way up to the Hunchback's bells will give you fabulous views of the city. If you can manage to be there in mid-winter, the non-tourist season, there will be no lines, no wait and no crowds to come between you and all that Gothic beauty.

As I left, there was a street musician in the square playing the violin, so I put a few francs and some lily-of-the-valley in his open case. And finally I stopped at the bronze star, the "kilometre zero" marker set in the cobblestones in front of the Cathedral. Custom holds that if you stand on that reference point for all the highways in France, you will one day return to Paris. So far that tradition has worked quite well for me. (Please note that I've also thrown coins in the Trevi fountain in Rome and kissed the Blarney Stone in County Cork, I'm not taking any chances.)

Getting a little lost is part of the fun of travel because it's the serendipity that makes it all worthwhile. The French have a word for it, "flaneur" which seems to involve rising late, having hot chocolate and meandering. It is an excellent way to see the world even if you do get a little lost.

The River Cher glides under the arches of Chenonceau Chateau

Castles and Kings

The chateau was empty. Winter brings a time of quiet to the Loire Valley. The tourists are gone, life resumes its slow passage and the ghosts come back.

Several years ago we went south from Paris to Orleans, and then spent two weeks slowly driving along the little country roads that meander down the valley of the Loire River. We pointed our small rental car west from Orleans, Joan's city, down the southern bank of the Loire where the kings of France built their pleasure chateaus. Forests, little towns and smaller inns, mushroom caves and vineyards that have been there for hundreds of years dot that side of the river. Between the 11th and 18th centuries, the kings of France built their palaces there as well. There are over 120 castles and chateaux situated in a small area, and I don't think I have ever been in a lovelier spot. Of all the chateaux, the most beautiful is Chenonceau.

Chenonceau was built across the small Cher River in 1521, and the river flows through the graceful arches of the gallery so that the palace is mirrored in the water. It is often called the "Chateau of the Six Women" because it was owned by a series of famous ladies including the lovely Diane de Poitier to whom the delicate chateau was originally given. Upon the death of her lover, Henri II, she was driven out by his widow, Catherine de Medici. (Never underestimate the jealousy of an Italian Medici widow.) Strangely, Poitier and Medici each still have a garden there. Chenonceau was also home to the eternally mourning queen, "Louise the Inconsolable" and the foolish Mary, Queen of Scots.

In more recent history, Chenonceau has still played an interesting role. During the First World War, the owner of the chateau installed a hospital in the castle and the long gallery was used as a hospital ward. During World War II, the famous hall was used by French resistance fighters as an escape bridge across the River Cher. The chateau's main entrance was in occupied France while the southern door of the gallery opened onto the free zone

Inside the chateau, the rooms are filled with marvelous ribbed and vaulted ceilings, huge fireplaces, 15th and 16th century furniture, splendid Flemish tapestries and paintings by Rubens, del Sarto and Correggio. Some of the rooms have fresh bouquets from the 17th century gardens. It was off season when I was there so that I was about the only visitor. The day I visited, there was a fire built in every room and polished floors gleamed golden in the light. Bowls of lilacs stood on the tables, their scent filling the rooms. There was music playing and the entire castle stood waiting for Mary of Scotland to return.

The drama of the castle extends outside as well. Henry II's mistress, Diane Poitier, "the beautiful one," and Catherine de Medici, the king's wife, built "dueling" formal gardens at the entrance (imagine brocade in plant form). There are more gardens surrounding the Chateau, each reflecting the strict order and harmony of the French Renaissance. There is a water garden with a lake edged with lime trees. There are precisely arranged ornamental gardens with bright blocks of color symbolizing the themes of religion, love and music. There are even geometrically organized kitchen gardens, surrounded by apple trees espaliered on the walls. Vegetables were planted by texture, height and color. Broccoli, cauliflower and carrots have never looked so lovely.

There are more chateaux in the Valley, Amboise high on a hill that holds da Vinci's grave, Chambord the overwhelming jewel in Francois I's crown, Blois with its paneled room of secret compartments, Villandry with its spectacular gardens and so on. Each chateau has stories of passion and intrigue, love and war, death and defiance. There are secret passages, hidden staircases, moats, great walls, towers and tapestries, and while ghosts are outside my realm of expertise, there is a flavor, a hint, of passion and beauty from days gone by.

In the Loire Valley, Meeting Leonardo

I met Leonardo in France one fine spring day. No, no, not that one, wrong Leonardo. I meant da Vinci, not DiCaprio.

In the small town of Amboise in France's Loire Valley, there is a modest manor house. And in a little room looking out a tiny window, I came close to genius. Let me tell you the story.

Amboise is located in one of the most marvelous areas of France, the Loire Valley. Running through the heart of French history as well as the heart of the country, the Valley is full of historic towns, villages and world famous castles. The kings of France built their lovely chateaux along the river, and the area is rich with meandering streams, majestic forests and lush green countryside. It is easy to stop and look for Beauty and her Beast.

Amboise is a pretty little town that was built on a hill overlooking the Loire River. A 6th century fortress and later a monastery, the castle became royal in 1434 during the reign of "Charles, the Well-Served" (a great name). The great French king, Francois I spent his childhood here, and it is because of that king that Leonardo came to France.

da Vinci's only self portrait

I know that we are all familiar with da Vinci's brilliance as a scientist, inventor, painter, sculptor and engineer whose genius, perhaps more than anyone else, represents the Renaissance humanist ideal. His famous notebooks reveal a radical spirit of curiosity and creativity that were centuries ahead of his time. Not that it matters, I suppose, but Leonardo is said to have been a strong, extremely handsome man, blessed with a fine voice. Not bad qualities for the illegitimate, left-handed son of an Italian peasant woman.

But do you know how the world's most famous painting, the *Mona Lisa,* ended up at the Louvre? After the death of his Medici patron, Leonardo was offered the lovely job of "Premier Painter, Architect and Engineer" to the king of France which included a manor house near the royal chateau at Amboise. He was also offered something even more precious, the freedom to "dream, think and work" on anything he fancied. Accepting the offer, he left Italy carrying his sketches, notebooks and three paintings, including the *Mona Lisa*, strapped to his mule as he climbed over the Alps from Italy into France.

Da Vinci spent the last few years of his life living and working at the Renaissance manor of Clos Luce in Amboise and is buried on the terrace just outside the chateau in the small chapel of Saint-Hubert. At Clos Luce are models of machines that existed only in his notebooks and in the surrounding park are touchable models of more of his inventions.

Clos Luce is an interesting place to explore. The gardens are tiny and precise, filled with birds and the scent of roses. Nearby there is an underground passageway which leads from the manor to the chateau about four blocks away. Francois would use the tunnel to visit his remarkable guest, and in the kitchen is a huge hearth where they would chat, the 22-year-old king and the 64-year-old genius.

But it's Leonardo's bedroom that I found the most fascinating. Looking out a little window, the view was of steep slate roofs, people walking along narrow streets, the castle looming on the opposite hill. The scene looks much the same as it did when da Vinci was there. I know that because on the bedroom wall beside the window hangs a small sketch that shows almost an identical view, the roofs of Amboise and the walls of the chateau with its massive tower and fragile chapel spire. Leonardo made this drawing during the last years of his life. He slept in that bedroom and did the sketch from that very window. Even though separated by 500 years, it was unnerving to be that close to such genius.

Although supported and encouraged by the greatest of the Renaissance kings, after sunny Italy the bedroom and the view may have seemed cold and lonely. On his deathbed, the man who embodied the ideals of the Renaissance apologized to "God and Man for leaving so much undone.... And he wept that he had not accomplished more." Legend has it that the king was at his side when he died, cradling Leonardo's head in his arms.

To clear your mind after so much artistic intensity, you may want to stroll downhill to Amboise and have coffee and chocolates in the Pâtisserie Bigot, the famous shop that has been making cakes, chocolates and ice creams since 1913. You can have a chocolate, celebrate the man who epitomized the ideals of the Renaissance and feel blessed that he left us such a legacy of creativity and curiosity.

Up, Up and Away

I'm a traveler by nature, a curious searcher for serendipity in places far from home. I've "carred," "bussed" and "plane-ed". I've cruised, barged and boated. I've "elephanted" and "cameled."

Ballooning in Burgundy

But the best traveling I've ever done is by balloon. One spring several years ago, I spent some time in the Saone River Valley in France. It's some of the most beautiful country I've have ever seen with rolling hills and valleys, green pastures, fields of yellow flowers, white Charolais cattle, hawthorn in bloom and lots of little villages that didn't look as though they have changed since St. Joan rode through.

The balloon was a large one, tethered in a meadow, and six of us clambered into the basket. My fingers clenched the side, and I refused to look down for the first ten minutes because I'm not particularly good at heights. The ascent was slow and gradual, so it wasn't as frightening as I had feared. I felt a little like the Wizard of Oz waving good-bye to Dorothy as he floated away in the balloon. All those brave statements aside, I do have a photo of me inside the balloon, holding on to the basket for dear life, and saying through clenched teeth, "Take the darn picture."

The cows got smaller and the view got bigger as we kept going up. We floated this way and that forever, sailing over the river and the little towns on its bank, over meadows and parks, huge trees and hedgerows. It was a marvelous afternoon.

The descent at sunset was just as much fun. We landed near a small village, inadvertently causing a great deal of excitement. Children running and dogs barking, people coming out of their homes, and one fellow who was hopping around on one leg while standing in his doorway, trying to pull on his pants so he could come out and see what the fuss was all about.

Finally, the balloon landed in a field full of flowers and children. It was wonderful. There was a lot of commotion and hubbub as the little ones crowded around, giggling and pushing and trying to practice their English. Someone brought out the traditional champagne to celebrate a successful landing, and we toasted ballooning, France and the afternoon in general. It was a magic day.

Watermill cottage built for
Marie Antoinette at Versailles

The Ghosts of Versailles

*"Courage! I have shown it for years; think you I shall
lose it at the moment when my sufferings are to end?"*
Marie Antoinette, on her way to the guillotine.
(And no, she never said, "Let them eat cake".)

When we were little, we use to look for ghosts. (Which in Nebraska is pretty darn optimistic.) But try as we might, we never saw a single spirit. Grownups have always looked for ghosts too and sometimes they think they might have found them. While I frankly put no credence in the stories, I know that a place full of turmoil and strife can certainly seem haunted. One of the most valid of these stories has to do with the ghosts of Versailles, because if ghosts could walk anywhere, they would surely be there.

Although Louis XIV's palace at Versailles, 12 miles southeast of Paris, began as a simple hunting lodge, by the mid 17th century enlargement and remodeling had transformed it into an astronomically extravagant showcase and formal setting for the Sun King. There were palaces of glass, collections of porcelain, works of marble, gilt and crystal, monumental gardens, greenhouses, grottos, small lakes and dramatic water fountains There were fantastic fetes and galas, sumptuous dinners and balls, and 10,000 residents all revolving around Louis. It was the golden setting for the supreme power of the monarch and gave an undimmed glory to France. The "butcher's bill" came later.

The little chateau, the Petite Trianon, was built in the gardens of Versailles so that Louis XV could stroll through the gardens he loved, and it was given to his successor's queen, Marie-Antoinette so that she could escape from the "stifling etiquette of court life." She had musicals and tea parties and redecorated both inside and out, building a theater and creating an English garden. She was heedless, young, inexperienced and unprepared for the formality and intrigues of the French court.

Eventually, following the popular concept of going back to nature, she built an even more elaborate refuge, le Hameau. This was a little village with cottages, barns, stables, a dairy and was stocked with all the appropriate animals. For the 28-year-old naïve and childless Queen, it was both a diversion and amusement. Looking for privacy and "natural simplicity," she spent more time there than at the palace. She was only able to play there for six years, then the mob stormed the Bastille, and the games were over. Four years later, with her hands bound behind her, she went to the guillotine.

In August of 1901, two Victorian school teachers visited the gardens of the Petit Trianon. Exactly what they thought they saw there has always been rather murky. I'll give you the short version. "They began searching for the Petit Trianon but became lost. Two men dressed in long grayish-green coats with small three-cornered hats passed them. When asked the way, the ladies were directed down a path. Walking by a shaded gazebo, they arrived at the little palace where they found a woman sitting outside, sketching. She wore an old-fashioned dress, covered with a pale green scarf."

The date they visited was the anniversary of the sacking of the Tuileries, when a mob of thousands had stormed the palace, the Swiss guards had been chased through the gardens and massacred, and the royal couple had been imprisoned. The day that the queen learned that the mob from Paris was marching toward Versailles, she had been sitting at the Petit Trianon. The ladies then came across a painting of Marie Antoinette drawn by a contemporary artist. It was the same woman they had seen sketching, wearing the same dress and pale green scarf.

The two women wrote about their experience and spent the next 25 years being both praised for their adventure and criticized for their foolishness. I think that they both saw something mysterious and wanted so badly to believe what they had seen that they convinced both themselves and a lot of other people as well.

To be honest, I've always thought that Versailles was a bit much. The palace alone has something like 1300 rooms. Just one melted-down giant gold candlestick from the Hall of Mirrors was enough to finance a small French war. The Petit Trianon, however, is perfectly lovely. Its small but elegantly harmonious proportions make it one of the most flawless buildings in France.

The rustic buildings at le Hameau are still there too, the mill, the pigeon house and the dairy where Marie Antoinette could play at being a milkmaid before she was taken away by the mob. The lake is still full of carp who beg for the stale bread which the Queen included in her budget, so I threw them the last of my sandwich. If there were ghosts, they would be here where there was once great beauty and great loss. When you go to Versailles you can see for yourself.

Neuschwanstein Castle, Hohenschwangau, Germany

Germany, Simply Amazing

Neuschwanstein, Foolishness at Its Finest

I had my first view of the castle of Neuschwanstein over the south end of a northbound horse. Wrapped in scratchy, old wool blankets and perched on bales of hay, we rode in a little horse-drawn covered carriage up a long winding road to the castle. A bearded old man, his head sunk down between his shoulders and pipe permanently clenched between his teeth, clucked to the ponies as the cart lurched off, wheels creaking slightly.

Even though everything was covered with snow, the ponies knew just where to go, keeping to an invisible track as we rode up the mountain side. The morning was icy clear, and every bush, tree and boulder was edged with frost. The slopes and ridges sparkled, and the only sound was the "huffing" of the horses as they pulled the little wagon. None of it seemed real. It was one of those "travel moments" that you remember forever.

Traveling in the winter months lends an entirely new outlook to everything you see. The light is softer, more golden and all the more precious because it is so short. The people you meet are kinder and more solicitous, less buffeted by tourists. Some tourist destinations may be limited (try finding hotels with heat in the Peloponnese in mid-winter), but those you do visit will be blissfully empty of other travelers.

We had spent the night in the village of Fussen, a 700-year-old medieval town prettily nestled between two lakes in the Bavarian mountains. The old Roman road, the Via Claudia, passes through, and the region is rich in castles, cloisters and citadels, the most famous being Neuschwanstein, the castle of the "mad king," Ludwig II.

Ludwig was born in 1845, and became king of Bavaria when he was 18, the son of a stern father and a vague but beautiful mother. He had no budget; he had no common sense or restraints and he was a teenager. Things turned out pretty much as you would expect.

He created what he felt was a perfect castle, incorporating bits from different monarchs, different eras, different countries, with a little bit of fantasy thrown in for good measure. He was devoted to the composer Richard Wagner, and to his themes of knighthood, chivalry and the Teutonic gods. Ludwig's gradual retreat into fantasy and madness left his country bankrupt, but with a heritage of beautiful castles in the Bavarian Alps.

Neuschwanstein is a fairy tale castle. (Walt Disney took it as the model for Sleeping Beauty's Castle at Disneyland.) The castle was designed by Christian Jank, a theatrical set designer rather than an architect, which explains a lot. The palace complex has a gatehouse, a knight's house, a citadel, a bower and shining towers. The interior is even more fantastic.

In the winter there are very few tourists and we were the only visitors that morning. The castle guide was surprised and happy that we were there, and we were surprised and happy to have our own private tour. The seven-year-old daughter of our tour guide trooped along with us. When we reached the throne room, she took my hand and told me all about the decorations in great detail, including (I think) what had happened to the throne. But as neither my German nor her English were particularly good, I did miss a few of the finer points.

As castles go, Neuschwanstein is not large, but it makes up for its lack of size with flamboyance and fine detail. The entrance hall is Medieval while the two-story throne room is Byzantine complete with pillars of imitation porphyry, a little bit of Hagia Sophia in the middle of the Alps. The bedrooms are neo-Gothic filled with an overabundance of carving. Imagine what fourteen busy Bavarian woodcarvers could do in four years. The chapel is Louis IV and the dining room is straight out of Wagner's Ring Cycle. The lavish Minstrels' Gallery that takes up the entire fourth floor is copied from the 12th century Singer's Gallery at Wartburg Castle and comes complete with a full set of Parcival murals. Between the living room and the study, there is a grotto with stalactites and an artificial waterfall. The winter garden is from a fantasy story, and this entire hodgepodge is set in the scenic Bavarian Alps.

Ludwig's beautiful castle is well worth the visit. True, it is not old, there is no ghost of Richard the Lionheart or authentic tales of knightly valor, but its towers and spires are lovely none the less. It is what we all want a castle to be, the unobtainable, ivory Grail Castle. Ludwig was able to build whatever he could imagine, and his legacy is one of fantasy, of magic, of wonder.

Berlin, a House Divided

I know this photo doesn't look like much. It's only a brick line through some city pavement. But I realized when I saw it that it actually means the world. This line marks the spot where the Berlin Wall once stood. It's all that's left of that demarcation of bitterness and grief.

Think back. The Berlin Airlift. The dead zone between the rubble-filled East and the green, growing West. The cold war and JFK announcing, "Ich bin ein Berliner." And 24 years later, Ronald Reagan thundering, "Mr. Gorbachev, tear down this wall!"

Berlin was a grim spot during those years. The wall was a thick and ugly pile of concrete and stone, capped with barbed wire which divided the city at its heart and separated both families and friends. The city was "an island in the middle of a red sea," and it took 20 hours to cross to West Germany instead of the modern three hours. There were severe visa restrictions and "world tour" was not in an Eastern German dictionary.

Do you remember the jumps for freedom, that three-story leap across to the western sector? The "killing zone" between the barricades? Neighbors who were betrayed by their friends? When the Wall fell and the records were open, many decided not to look at the Secret Service files because they did not want to know who had betrayed them.

The "non-wall" of Berlin

And then after 28 years of frozen brotherhood, surprisingly, it crumbled. Do you remember the night you heard the Wall had fallen? Like watching the landing on the moon, for many it was a goosebump moment. On Nov. 9, 1989 the East German government announced that East Berliners were free to travel to the West. A few brave souls tested it and within hours thousands descended on the crossings and a freedom carnival began. Did you watch it on television? Right around the wall there was a strange sort of church-like quiet and later it got pretty rowdy with ecstatic celebrations in front and parties on top. It was a euphoric, heart-rending time.

Compared to the original 87-mile-long concrete barrier, there is not much left now. There is a memorial with a few pieces of show-cased, graffiti-covered concrete. Checkpoint Charlie, the small guard house that was the focal point of the Cold War, is now in a little museum and visiting the imitation one at the actual site with its fake M.P.'s is anti-climatic. Memories and the bricks in the pavement are about all that is there. And that is as it should be. Sometimes not seeing something is as satisfying as visiting it.

Greece, Cradle of Everything Interesting

Lost and in Love Again with Athens

"Not all who wander are lost."
J.R.R. Tolkien

Athens is full of flowers, kittens, friendly folks and lots of fabulous rubble.

The first time I was in Athens I wore a cowboy hat, which is not quite as silly as it seems. Even as far away as Greece, there isn't anyone who doesn't love a cowboy. As I poked around the maze of lanes and streets of that splendid and ancient city, little boys pretended to have gun fights with me, impassive black-clad little old ladies giggled, people who spoke no English would smile and say, "Ah, John Wayne!" and I beamed back at all of them. It was a silly but effective ice breaker.

I've been back several times since then, and every time I visit I find more to love. Athens is a sprawling, modern city with too many people, too much traffic and exhaust, and way too many concrete buildings. But shining above the city is the immovable grandeur of the Parthenon, reminding you of the riches all around. Ancient theaters, stadiums, cobble-stoned streets are all a testament to the fact that this is where man's quest for individual greatness began. This is where art, drama, science, mathematics, democracy, all had their beginnings. Wherever you are in the city, there is charm, humor and a sense of creative discovery.

Through the millennia, there has been much written about the beauty, antiquity and character of Athens. And this is all true, of course. But I have noticed that they have neglected to mention a thing or two.

Since the huge Acropolis Hill dominates the city, and the Parthenon can be seen from almost every neighborhood, tourists are drawn there as a moth to the flame. But it is possible to get lost trying to find it. This is not, however, an easy thing to do. The Acropolis sits majestically on a towering plateau high above the city of Athens. The ancient Greeks knew the value of a good location. Begun in 447 B.C. when Athens was at the height of its power, it symbolized the might, influence and religious zeal of the city. For the last 2500 years, pilgrims, politicians and tourists have been climbing the Sacred Way toward the hilltop temples. The road is wide and well-trodden.

With typically foolish optimism, I decided to walk from the main square, Syntagma, to the Acropolis. However, wandering through the rabbit warren of streets, I somehow managed to approach the "Sacred Rock" from the back of the hill. No problem; I'm from Arizona; I'm tough; I can certainly find my way around a mesa. It was not that simple. I clambered over ruins, climbed over columns, scrambled up hills and detoured around ancient foundations. However, getting lost always has its bright side. As I emerged, marble-scraped and bewildered from a grove of olive trees, I met a group of Greek school children in from the country on a field trip. They thought that a lost lady tourist was much more interesting than Greek ruins, and proceeded to practice their English on me as they showed me the way. So rather than the typical 15 minutes to reach the Parthenon, it took me an hour to get there, and I scraped both my knees in the process. But I had an adventure, saw the "untrodden path" and taught some nice Greek kids how to say, "Good morning, it's a beautiful day," in English.

The travel books have neglected some other things as well. Sometimes they don't mention the fake statue on the Acropolis Hill. One of the glorious temples there is the Erechtheion with six beautifully sculpted women who act as columns, the "Caryatids." However, only five of them are still in Athens. The other one was "liberated" by Lord Elgin when he took several tons of souvenirs home to England, and she is still held captive in the British Museum. On moonlit nights, you are supposed to be able to hear the marble women crying for their sister. I went one night when the moon was full, but it was all very silent. Perhaps you need to be Greek.

I'm sure they don't bring up getting lost in the Plaka. Below the Acropolis Hill, the Plaka was the old working-class district of Athens. It is now a labyrinth of alleys, winding streets and stairs, full of flea markets, taverns, tourist shops and small museums. Through the millennia, thousands of people have managed to find their way around, working, loving, fighting and drinking. I managed to get lost again. I stopped several times at t-shirt shops to ask directions. Everyone was very helpful in pointing me in the right direction, and so to be polite I bought a t-shirt each time. I finally found my way out of the maze, staggering under a load of Greek tourist t-shirts. Everyone I know got one for a Christmas present that year. Getting lost always has its rewards.

On one trip, I stayed at the Hotel Grande Bretagne. Impeccably located on Syntagma Square in the center of Athens, kitty-corner from the Parliament Building, it is the city's most legendary lodging. With silk ottomans, stained glass ceilings and opulent, mirrored rooms, it was originally built to house guests visiting the Palace. I'm sure that many of those who stay there are told that Winston Churchill was also a guest. In fact, Alexander's Bar with its tapestry, cigars, cognacs and brandies seems a perfect spot for him. But do you suppose the guests are told about a possible underground tunnel leading from the Parliament into the basement of the hotel? It was dug as an escape route should those in power become too uncomfortable in the official buildings and need to get out the back way.

Around the corner from Parliament, and across the street from the Grande Bretagne, are the National Gardens with Greek kittens who call it home. And around the corner from the kittens is a flower stall to buy a fresh bouquet every morning, and just down the street is an excellent art shop. In the evening, sit out in one of the many outdoor cafes on the Square and watch the world go by. Have a glass of Greek wine (avoiding retsina) and chat. There isn't a Greek who doesn't love to talk. "You're from the States? You been to Chicago? You must know my brother!" And feel very, very lucky that you're traveling and that you're in Greece.

The Temple of Apollo at Delphi, Greece

Delphi, Visiting the Center of the World

 I don't really know why, but in some places the distance between heaven and earth doesn't seem quite so vast. Kenneth Clarke, in his monumental documentary *Civilisation,* described the Scottish island of Iona in this way. "Some God is in this place….. (there is) a sense of peace and inner freedom. What does it? The light, which floods round on every side? The lie of the land? The combination of wine-dark sea, white sand and pink granite?"

   Delphi is in the same sort of setting, a spot with infinite boundaries.

   At the beginning of the world, Zeus loosed two eagles, one from where the sun rose, the other from where it set. They met in the center of Greece, and a stone was erected there to mark the omphalos, the very navel of the earth. Here Apollo, the god of light, harmony and order spoke through the oracle to man, and here beat the political heart of the ancient world. Sacred Delphi was revered by the ancients as the womb of the world as it nurtured religion, statecraft and the arts.

   To reach Delphi we drove north from Athens, past vineyards and olive groves and through dusty villages. We shared the potholed road with rattling trucks, tourist buses, donkeys, sputtering motorcycles and women trudging under heavy loads. Past Thebes where cursed Oedipus ruled, we began to climb through sparsely settled country until our tour bus stopped partway up the mountain. Far below, between the dry hills of pine and scrub, a small bridge could be seen at the junction of three dirt roads. Our guide pointed down and said with great authority, "That is where Oedipus killed his father." In Greece, history is not something in a dull and dreary book. You live it and breathe it; it is always with you.

Oedipus would come to Delphi.

Delphi sits on a small plateau carved into the side of Mount Parnassus, the home of the Muses. The view from the site is awe-inspiring. (And I'm not the only one to think so. There has been some sort of religious center there for the past 3000 years.) The springtime sun slants across the mountain highlighting the ruins of the ancient treasuries, the theater and the columns of the Temple of Apollo. Below the sanctuary, stark walls of limestone drop down to the silver gray of olive groves planted across the river valley to the shining Gulf of Corinth. The air is clear, the sky a beautiful blue, the wind blows through the pines. It feels like home in Arizona.

Twin crags, called the Shining Rocks, guard the Sanctuary of Apollo where the Delphic Oracle, Apollo's priestess, spoke prophecy to those who came. The oracle offered an interesting combination of contact with the spirit world and day-to-day advice. If you had a question about

Climbing toward Mr. Parnassus

foreign affairs to love affairs, you'd come here. "What is my destiny?" "Should we invade Athens this summer?" "Should I marry the daughter of Megacles or Pericles?" "Is my rich uncle going to die soon?" Your answer came through a prophetess, an old woman named Pythia, "inquiring one." Sitting on the sacred tripod and speaking in a drug-induced trance, her divinely inspired ravings would be cleverly translated by crafty men into elegant, ambiguous verse. As they had an excellent intelligence service, and the answers could always be interpreted many ways, the Oracle was rarely wrong.

For more than a thousand years, pilgrims trudged up Delphi's Sacred Way to consult the Oracle. Here to visit the Oracle came warriors, aristocrats, merchants and tyrants. Ruins of small "treasuries" erected by the city-states lined the way toward the sanctuary. Built to house offerings to Apollo, these little buildings held generations of riches from all over the Greek world, bronzes, sculptures, gold and silver. The Treasury of the Athenians has been rebuilt. It is easy to stand there and imagine the other ruins restored to beauty, the Sacred Way full of voices and footsteps as men out of legend paraded to Apollo's shrine. The leaders of Athens, the kings of Sparta brought gifts. Oedipus, King of Thebes came to learn of his dreadful crime. Jason for advice, Pythagoras (remember the Pythagorean Theorem?), the historian Herodotus, the biographer Plutarch. And a man called Alexander.

Of course, with thousands of years to draw from, there are many stories at Delphi. My favorite happened in 336 B.C. A blond, beardless young man walks quickly up the path toward the sanctuary. The priests are outraged, he doesn't have an appointment. He demands a meeting with the seeress. He is refused. He grabs the priestess and drags her into the temple. "My son," she cries, "thou are invincible!"

It was Alexander the Great.

It is possible to follow the exact path as the ancient pilgrims as they walked up the Sacred Way. And all the time you are climbing the mountain, you are aware of the panorama around you because the ancient Greeks' choices of location were close to genius. There is the Acropolis of Athens with its Parthenon gleaming above the city; there is the grand Temple of Artemis at Ephesus welcoming the pilgrims arriving from the sea, and there is the Temple of Poseidon, just north of Athens at Sounion, built on sheer cliffs above the water. Delphi was designed with the same brilliance. As the path winds up the hill, there is the great theater that overlooks the entire sanctuary and the valley. And farther up still, beyond the Sacred Way is an ancient stadium built in the 5th century B.C. and used for one of the Pan-Hellenic games. As the ancient Greeks stopped at each plateau, to pray at the Temple, to visit the Theater, to watch a game, the view would have been spectacular. The vista to the mountains, down to the valley floor and across to the Gulf of Corinth is glorious.

Once every four years athletes came to Delphi from all over the Greek world, from Asia Minor to Spain, to race chariots, wrestle, run, and throw the javelin and the discus. This is where the tradition of the victor's simple laurel wreath began as the glory of victory was considered reward enough. When the young men returned home, they were heroes for the rest of their lives.

When I was there, a group of Greek 4th graders had come to Delphi on a school field trip. They'd seen the sites, heard the stories, visited the museum. In a 2500-year old stadium that had seen the great Greek games and would seat 6500 spectators, they were yelling and running. I sat down and watched for a while. Blissfully oblivious to the history around them, they laughed and yelled and played sandlot soccer.

The Byzantine Chapel at Mistra

I Need to Go Back to Sparta

"An old man wandering around the Olympic Games looking for a seat was jeered at by the crowd until he reached the seats of the Spartans, whereupon every Spartan younger than him, and some that were older, stood up and offered him their seat. The crowd applauded and the old man turned to them with a sigh, saying "All Greeks know what is right, but only the Spartans do it."

Plutarch

Back when I had more time than money, more good luck than good sense, I spent a month or so in Greece. A friend and I bought an old, dented VW, and we went where mood and chance happened to take us.

Looking back now, we seemed to spend an inordinate amount of time in Sparta, in the tiny town of Mistra. Considering that the Spartans had "no walls but their soldiers," and that there is almost nothing there at all any more (it is now an ancient bump in the road), it seems silly to have been there so much. But you see, the roads were out. Every time we drove away, we were stymied by construction or boulders on the road or the road dwindling into nothing – so we would return to Sparta.

Over the course of several days we took alternate routes: On the first day we went north to Nafplion where they happened to be having "Independence from the Turks Day" with the bishop, a band and children dressed in national costumes. However, the onward road was blocked, so we returned to Sparta. The next day we drove through olive harvests south to Monemvasia on the coast which was freezing, so we headed back to Mistra. The third day we headed west to Kalamata, filling the trunk with oranges from the harvest, only to find there had been another landslide and we backtracked again to Sparta.

Every time we went back, we would stop at the bakery for macaroons. Did you know that the best macaroons in the entire world are made in Mistra, Sparta in Greece's Peloponnese? The last time through we took bread, cheese, cookies plus the free oranges and the olives for a picnic on a hilltop overlooking the Valley of Sparta. There was a little old church below, but we were tired and warm and lazy and didn't bother to explore.

I regret that indolence to this day. Let me tell you why

Byzantium, in the mid 1400's, was crumbling. Anyone with sense could see the handwriting on the wall (or in this case the marble). Many of the city's best and brightest left Constantinople and settled in a little town called Mistra beneath the mountaintops of southern Greece, close to the ruins of ancient Sparta. The emperor's brother went to live there, adopting a simple life and creating a small philosophical paradise. He was quite content until the family duties caught up with him and so the royal brother became emperor himself.

And on January 6, 1449, Constantine XI Palaeologos, knelt on the purple porphyry circle, the royal stone, set in the floor of the chapel I couldn't bother to go look at, and was crowned Emperor. He left Mistra and three years later, as the last ruler of an exquisite empire that had lasted a thousand years, joined his troops on the walls of Constantinople and died fighting with them as the Turks took the city. As the city was destroyed, Constantine is said to have cried, "The city is fallen, but I am alive." Realizing that the end had come, he discarded his purple cloak and led his remaining soldiers into a last deadly and suicidal charge.

And I didn't get off my duff to walk down the hill and poke my nose in that little chapel. I need to go back to Mistra, for more macaroons and to see the royal marble circle in the floor.

Olympic Heroes

I am an unabashed 'Olympicphile." Watching the Olympics is always a treasure; visiting Olympia is a gift. Ancient Greece was the birthplace of extraordinary legends and golden heroes. Two hundred miles south of Athens lie the remains of one of the great centers of ancient civilization. Today it is impossible to imagine the importance that this remote and ancient sanctuary of Olympia once held. It was not only the center of competition, but also of politics, culture and religion. The Olympics gave the world a dream of sacrifice, bravery and achievement.

Every 4th summer for a thousand years, multitudes made their way from every corner of the Greek world to compete in the greatest spectacle on earth. Visiting Olympia would have been a combination of going to the most incredible art gallery, the most fascinating museum, the Super Bowl and Mardi Gras – all at the same time. We're talking sweat, beer, sex, gambling, staying up too late at night and regretting it in the morning.

Columns in the Spring at Olympia

Held to mark a truce between warring cities, the Olympic tradition launched a millennium of games. Every four years, quarrelsome city states would lay down their arms in the name of peaceful competition. (Although one wonders how peaceful a chariot race was.) For a month beforehand, it was illegal for any Greek to fight. Anyone who did break the gods' truce was cursed in the eyes of Zeus.

This was a man's world where sports and war were obsessions. Those early games were some of the roughest, most exciting, most dangerous events every performed in the history of organized sports. It was a violent and brutal world where feared fighters and legendary heroes would come to battle for Olympic glory. The games would decide just one victor, whose reward would be honor and fame. Beneath the arch and onto an arena that would hold 40,000 spectators came the finest athletes of the Greek world. Naked before gods and man, the athletes would appear one by one from a tunnel built into the hillside. With the trumpet call from the sacred heralds, they would take their position at the starting line and at the mark would begin their race into story and legend.

The games we have now would seem a little bizarre to those ancient heroes. We allow both sexes (yeah!) and every nationality. But we have added competitions that would not seem viable to the ancient Greeks who saw the sports of the Olympics as mimicry of valued war skills. I strongly doubt that Achilles or Agamemnon would have seen much relevance in ribbon dancing or synchronized swimming.

The Olympic stories that I love aren't the flashy high-profile items, the swimming of Michael Phelps, the running of Maurice Greene; it's the little known events, the "small-guy" triumphs that I look for. It's watching the impassive 40-year-old, fat faced Chinese man with tears running down his face as he receives his gold medal for pistol prowess. It's the dashing, sideburned Italian boy (who obviously still lives in the 16th century) winning the gold for swordplay who does a double forward flip into the arms of his trainer. It's the determined faces of the rowers in the 8-man race. Put a Greek prow on that boat, surround it with Greek hills, watch the oars and muscles gleaming in the Mediterranean sun and it could be Jason and the Argonauts just starting out. It's the face of Otis Harris Sr., a large black preacher from Mississippi, who has come to watch his son run an Olympic race. It is the solemn face of a Kenyan lady runner standing on the winner's platform as an unexpected wreath is placed upon her head.

The world today holds a fragile peace. Held in Athens, the 2004 Olympics began with the phrases, "A thousand wars have flamed and burned. The world has been shattered and remade and the Olympic flame still beckons. Anchored by a romance of history, a new mythology is born in Athens with a new age of athletes which remind the world of what can be achieved in the marriage of body and soul….Return to an ancient dream of what we can become in a balance of power and grace and an uncompromising spirit."

Olympia lies in quiet ruins today. The columns have fallen into the grass, wildflowers marking where heroes once stood. But the arena is still there, and they say that the 210 yards of the clay running track in the center of the stadium was marked out by Hercules. When I was there in the cool and lonesome early morning, I curled my toes around the "balbis", the marble sill that still marks the starting line, and ran one lap for epic's sake. Go smell the olive branches, taste the wine, savor the victory.

India, Ancient and Enthralling

"So far as I am able to judge, nothing has been left undone, either by man or nature, to make India the most extraordinary country that the sun visits on his rounds. Nothing seems to have been forgotten, nothing overlooked."

Mark Twain

Facets of India

A study in contrasts:
The Victoria Memorial

And sitting in front, an Indian snake charmer. (Please note the cobra.)

India is the home of the Buddha and the British Raj, the riches of the Nizam of Hyderabad and the poverty of Mother Theresa, the Jewel in the Crown of the British Empire and the simplicity of Mahatma Gandhi, the sunrise perfection of the Taj Mahal, the slums of Calcutta. You can find Kipling or Rushdie, *Far Horizons* or Bollywood. It is an ancient country, full of contrasts and contradictions.

This is not a country for tourists. Traveling is cumbersome; cities can be overwhelming; poverty is apparent. But for a traveler, someone who loves different flavors, smells and sounds, India is a revelation. Like the god Vishnu who is both the creator and the destroyer, India has a multitude of faces. There is abject poverty of course, but there is also grandeur, learning, philosophy and a history of 9000 years.

I grew up on Kipling and the early exploits of Richard Burton, and I must confess the country had me from the first "salaam." I was staying high in the mountains at an old colonial hotel in the town of Darjeeling, a Himalayan "hill station" for the British Raj seeking relief from the hot summer plains. Everywhere you looked there were remnants of the Empire. The hotel was full of flowers, and I was guided to my room from the dining room by a young boy carrying a candle. Later a room steward dressed in a white jacket and wearing a turban, brought in an old silver tea service left over from the Empire, lit my coal fire and bowed, calling me "Memsahib." The next morning there were tea plantations below and the peak of 29,000-foot Kanchenjunga above. I was hooked.

The Kalighat Kali Temple in Kolkata (Calcutta) illustrates another example of India's countless faces. Kali, the dark mother, usually means "black" but can also mean "time" or "change." (You may remember the Golden Temple of Kali with its murderous thugs in the movie, *Gunga Din* and the "Temple of Doom" in an Indiana Jones' movie.) At opposite ends of the courtyard in the 400-year-old temple were two altars, both covered in red. One was red with flowers, offered by the vegetarians. The other was red with the blood of animal sacrifice. And everyone seemed perfectly happy worshipping at one or the other.

Also in Kolkata you'll find a little bit of England. In the middle of this huge, teeming city is a large and quiet island of green with an enormous, gleamingly majestic, white marble museum. This is the Victoria Memorial, built to honor the Empress of India. It is proper; it is British; it is surrounded by gardens and close to the Royal Calcutta Golf Course. Inside it was cool, quiet, uncrowded and full of European paintings and history of the British Raj as well as some obligatory Indian bits.

Ahead of us in the galleries walked two couples from the south of India (the clothes gave them away). The gentlemen were in traditional dhoti pants with silk kurta jackets, the ladies in traditional saris, fabulous fabrics shimmering and shifting colors as they walked. Because they were so traditional, the ladies weren't wearing "cholis," the cropped sari blouse. Instead, they wore only the silk sari fabric draped down from one shoulder. The silk covered them modestly, but it was not the American norm and I was a little uncomfortable.

However, I had Indian modesty (or lack thereof) shown to me the next day. We stayed at the Oberoi Grand, the elegant 125-year-old grande dame of Calcutta hotels. Getting back to my room the next afternoon, I planned on a very long, very hot shower. (Several days at a game preserve the week before with only cold outdoor showers had left me with an obsession for hot water.)

I called room service for several cold sodas, and they told me that it would be 45 minutes to an hour because they were so backed up. So I decided to go ahead and get in the shower, but just as I got under the water, there was a knock at the door. I grabbed a robe, a thick, tied, long sleeved, white terry robe which went down to mid-thigh. (I used to have dresses shorter than that.) I opened the door to a young attendant perfectly dressed in an immaculate white coat, with a horrified expression. With head averted, he put the tray on the table and with head still turned, held out his hand for the tip and got out of the room as quickly as he could. My uncovered legs had shocked him.

So, I shouldn't have been so puritanical about the ladies at the museum. With my bare legs, I had inadvertently been immodest too. Travel is wonderfully broadening.

Swimming With Care

When you go swimming in Hyderabad, little brown men wearing white conical caps come with you.

I was in the northeast of India as a guest of the Indian government and spent several days in Hyderabad on the Indian Ocean. Hyderabad may sound familiar as the home of the "Nizam of Hyderabad" whose many billions made him for a while the wealthiest man in the world.

We stayed in one of his many palaces that had been converted into a hotel. The palace was full of "Kiplingesque" features, broad verandas, beds hung with netting, salaaming staff and an overwhelming combination of Indian curry and British trifle in the dining room. Sitting on the veranda in the early evening, looking out to the sea, was a throwback to an earlier, gentler time.

Back to the swimming. It was off-season, nothing much for the hotel's staff to do. We had spent the day visiting temples and speaking to Northern Indian tourist officials. (There were a great many temples and very many officials.) And getting back to the hotel, a swim sounded like an excellent idea. I've always been very fond of the ancient belief that a day spent on the sea is a day that is not deducted from your life. It's like getting an extra one free.

I put on a swimsuit, grabbed a towel and headed for the water. During that short walk, a small brown man, also in a swimsuit, showed up, then a second, then a third. By the time I reached the water, I had an entourage of five. As we walked into the sea, they put on white caps with points on top, and I figured out what was going on. They were lifeguards, assigned to make sure the hotel guests had a safe swim. And if this foolish American lady was going swimming at dusk, they were going to keep an eye on her.

Far from home, swimming in the exotic Indian Ocean, I had a circle of babysitters. Every time I bobbed up in the water, there they were, little earnest brown faces with those silly hats, watching me anxiously. Surrounded by care, I just grinned and they smiled back.

Thanksgiving at the Top of the World

Next Thanksgiving as you lounge there recumbent and relaxed, replete from the holiday feast and considering just which of the leftovers to have for supper, take a moment to consider the plight of a poor traveler halfway around the world. Once I spent Thanksgiving in the high Himalayas.

Obviously turkey and dressing weren't on the menu. Instead, we had ginger-flavored pea soup, sautéed pumpkin and chicken curry, all accompanied by flaky paratha (the all purpose Indian fry bread), rice and emadatse, which is hot peppers stewed with cubes of cheese. (It is an acquired taste.) It was not the most culinarily satisfying Thanksgiving I have ever had (unless you are inordinately fond of curry or peppers), but it may have been the most memorable.

I was in the tiny state of Sikkim, a spot neither accidentally nor easily come to. Once independent, it is now a bulge on the map of India, between Nepal, Bhutan and Tibet. Whether by plane, train or car (and I used all three), the journey there is long and mostly at an upward slant.

Sikkim can give you a bad case of the Shangri-La's. There is only one main road twisting up through purple and pink rhododendron forests and across river gorges until reaching the capital. Gangtok looks out across the valley to the towering, snow-capped peaks of the legendary Kanchenjunga. We may not have had turkey and dressing, but you couldn't beat the view.

Sangachoeling Monastery in Sikkim, India

After lunch, our host took us across the valley to one of the hundreds of monasteries in the area. The sky was a hard, brilliant blue and the snow-bright peaks blazed in the sun. It was unbelievably beautiful. The mists from the mountain poured down toward the valley with its fragrances of azaleas and sandalwood. The laughter of little boys, already in maroon robes, balanced the low, deep tones of Buddhist monks chanting the cycle of death and rebirth. (It is one of those purely beautiful areas that drives you, albeit unwillingly, to lyrical descriptions.) Invited inside, there were ancient scriptures, small statues and everywhere the colors of red and gold. We set politely in straight-backed chairs, as shy little boys wrapped in stripped brocade and carrying small curved bows, sang and danced their way through a local legend about a mighty hunter.

91

Little boys raised at the monastery

Prayer flags in the wind

Outside in the courtyard, a great many people were just beginning an annual procession to carry holy books from the monastery down the mountain to another retreat. Complete with monks, cymbals and horns, there was a great to-do with much smiling, much bowing and much laughter. Go to the Himalayas at your peril. It is a place that can startle your heart with its uniqueness and beauty. I didn't get pumpkin pie that year and I missed the Macy's Parade, but it was a Thanksgiving I won't forget.

The Toy Train

Once I fell in love in India.

He was 130 years old and English, a small coal puffer left over from the British Raj, a tiny train remnant of the Empire's former glories. I admit to having an abiding love for trains and this one was just my type, exotic, old, experienced, with stories to tell. My new love was known as the "Darjeeling Himalayan Railway," or by its nickname, the "DHR."

The DHR is one of the most remarkable and unique railways in the world. Its engine was built in Edinburgh in 1867, and during its heyday it carried officers of Her Majesty's forces, planters, holiday travelers and British parents visiting their boarding school children. The train is quite small and is sometimes affectionately called the "Toy Train."

The train runs on a two-foot track from Siliguri to Darjeeling. Not surprisingly, I am not the first person to be overwhelmed with the trip. Mark Twain came before me in 1896, and his diary describes the "toy train journey" this way, "The railway journey up the mountain is forty miles, and it takes eight hours to make it. It is so wild and interesting and exciting and enchanting that it ought to take a week….The most enjoyable day I've spent on earth is of mixed ecstasy of deadly fright and unimaginable joy."

Puffing along its tiny track, the train begins to make its way through the dense jungle of Siliguri until it has climbed into the high peaks. The journey is only about 50 miles long, but the entire route is straight up, from an elevation of 300 ft on the plains to 7,200 ft in the mountains, and includes every curve, switchback and chasm available. It links the plains of Bengal with the grand Himalayas, takes eight hours to make the trek, and manages in its rapid climb to go through some of the most gorgeous country I have ever seen. At the start, the baby locomotive pulls three coaches along a track so hemmed in by jungle that you can't see the edges of the swath cut for the rails. Then with a series of complicated loops and switches, the landscape changes to tea plantations whose low green bushes are planted in a series of terraces which look like giant manicured steps going up the mountain. Then there begin to be massive teak trees, purple bougainvillea, lavender orchids and scarlet poinsettias. We passed spectacular waterfalls roaring over sharp cliffs, while below in the plains were ribbons of rivers.

All did not go completely smoothly. Because this was India, not Switzerland, we had to stop at watering stations to fill up the engine, and sometimes there was water and sometimes there wasn't. We had to spend some time going in reverse to get up another level. And we had to stop periodically to shoo children off the track. In the little town of Kurseong (which translates as "land of the white orchid"), the train was on street level. It went by shops and through the bazaar, and we were followed by an excited group of yelling children who apparently use this as a weekly excuse to run out of the schoolroom. They smiled and waved and giggled and jumped on and jumped off the train as it went through town.

And the train just keeps going up, and you keep thinking, "Well, we must be almost there." But you're not. At every bend there are children and wood carriers and saris and pine trees and vistas. Past loops named by some sadistic Victorian engineer, "Agony Point" and "Sensation Corner," the train climbs and climbs and climbs, through fog and tea gardens and mountains, until you are finally quite convinced that the next stop might be Heaven.

And then finally, nestled in a valley of the Himalayas with mighty Kanchenjunga and all the other peaks in perpetual snow presiding over it, is Darjeeling. The town is in the heart of the high mountains and was once the summer home of the British elite escaping the heat of the plains. They were joined by wealthy maharajas and landowners, the Zamindars. Precariously perched, the town is a marvelous blend of Victorian and Indian architecture which is always threatening to topple down the mountains.

During that long, breathtaking train ride, I met several people who lived in Darjeeling--a local banker, a Scottish minister and a lady who taught in a local convent. And while we traveled, they told me long, wonderful stories about the "DHR."

Once the toy train had to wait for hours on the narrow gauge track in the jungle because a tigress was lying on the tracks. The train was too little to take her on, and no one felt like getting out to ask the tiger to move along. So they politely waited, and she politely sat, and eventually everyone moved on again.

During its Victorian heyday, one of the guards was a Bengali gentleman, nicked named "Sugay" (parrot's beak) because of his nose, who worked for the line all his life. For a child growing up along the tracks, jumping on and off the train, playing hide and seek with "Sugay" waiting in ambush in some corner of a train car, was a treasured memory--at least for the children.

There were other stories about the incredible engineering skills that it took to build this line through the mountains among tumbling boulders and sudden, torrential waterfalls. The wife of the head construction engineer is credited with the idea of the "Z" reverse where the train is pushed backward through an up-gradient to reach the next level. However sometimes it tends to skid on the steep gradients, so a railway employee may be appointed the "sand man" and it is his job to stand on the front of the engine and sprinkle sand on the track to handle the problem.

The rail follows (more or less) the ancient Hill Cart Road which crisscrosses the line at 170 different spots. And while I listened to the stories, I was going through the forests and the jungles and the flowers and the tea gardens and the mountains. It was a magical day.

Danny Boy

"Oh Danny boy, the pipes, the pipes are calling
From glen to glen, and down the mountain side
The summer's gone, and all the flowers are dying
'Tis you, 'tis you must go and I must bide.
But come ye back when summer's in the meadow
Or when the valley's hushed and white with snow
'Tis I'll be here in sunshine or in shadow
Oh Danny boy, oh Danny boy, I love you so."
Traditional Ballad

Ross Castle reflected in
Lough Leane at Killarney

Ireland, Erin Go Bragh

Once I fell in love with an entire country.

"A Country we love, but a place we've not seen. My heart is in Ireland, it's calling to me." It is possible to be beguiled by a country even before you get there. I've always been a sucker for accents, and sitting on the tarmac at LAX getting ready for the takeoff of an Aer Lingus flight to Dublin, hearing something as mundane as, "Ladies and gentlemen, please fasten your seat belts," in a gentle Irish brogue made me beam. It is the delicate handling of the vowels, well mannered and quiet on the ears, that makes even common conversations musical. "We're cruising at an altitude of 30,000 feet," if said in an Irish accent, makes you grin and wiggle your toes. They don't mean the language to be so charming of course; it just can't be helped.

People smile when they talk about going to Ireland because they know they are giving themselves a gift. Of course the beauty of the country lies partially in its landscape, shimmering lakes, meandering rivers, soft green hills, unexpected rainbows and the nuanced and subtle "forty shades of green." But its other beauty is in the character of the people themselves who are full of lovely humor, wit and charm. We seem to view Ireland through a mist, not only through the rain that falls so often and turns the land such an incredible green, but also through the stories and myths of the Irish people.

Ireland is a place to explore slowly. It's such a small country that it is possible to drive the entire length in less than a day and to cross its width in a few hours. But instead of rushing, you should take your time and savor the trip, because the layers of history and legend run deep.

Standing stones and court graves, cairns and dolmens, holy wells and round towers, Celtic crosses and castles, the evidences of Ireland's long past are everywhere. But whether you're staying in a farmhouse or a castle, listening to the brogue in a pub or at a play, exploring a Neolithic cairn or a small fishing village, the magic of the country and the warmth of its people will be all around you.

A few years ago I traveled through County Mayo. The drive through the changeless, green country full of sheep, fields and hedges was lovely, of course. However, the most momentous event in Ireland that day was much more immediate. All eyes were focused on the televisions, not because of politics or terrorism or economic problems, but because it was the final qualifying round of the World Cup soccer matches. And Ireland was playing in the game.

Ireland played Iran, in Iran. They were only able to get 250 visas, so just a few supporters went to cheer-- against thousands of passionately screaming home team fans. And the whole of Ireland stopped for two hours to watch. We worked our sightseeing of castles and museums around the game so that we were in a proper Irish pub in the little town of Westport for the match. There was a peat fire, pints of Guinness and a crowd of Irishmen yelling for their team. The brogue got so thick that I'm not quite sure what was said half the time, but "kill the dirty so-and so's" and "off-sides" sound about the same in any language. It was the sort of special time that you don't forget. And Ireland won.

Not long after 9-11, I was walking down the street of a small village and passed some men working in a watery ditch, laying pipe. As I passed, one of them looked up and asked, "Are you American?" "Yes," said I. "Well, if it weren't for the muck from head to toe, I'd get out of this ditch and give youse a kiss, we're all so sorry."

Dublin, a Short Walking Tour

In Dublin's fair city, where the girls are so pretty,
I first set my eyes on sweet Molly Malone,
As she wheeled her wheel-barrow,
Through streets broad and narrow,
Crying, "Cockles and mussels, alive, alive, oh!"
Irish Ballad

Mythical and winsome,
"Sweet Molly Malone"

The Romans never got to Ireland; they didn't think it worth the bother. And so the streets of Dublin are laid out as nature and whim dictated; they meander by the river; they follow the game trails; they pass by the canals.

The parking situation may remind you of your own hometown on a summer Saturday when there is something going on in the city center. A story I overheard in a pub reminded me of home. "A man was lying in the street. 'Are you drunk?' says I. 'No,' says he. 'But I've found a parking space and I've sent the wife home to get the car.'" Luckily Dublin is such a delightful city to stroll around that a car and a parking spot are not really required for city sightseeing. Most of the main visitor attractions are within easy walking distance of each other, and the streets are picturesque and pleasant.

O'Connell Street is the city's broadest boulevard, planned as the central promenade. Start at the northern end, below the Gate Theatre, and look for the Gresham Hotel on the east side where you could have a marvelous Irish breakfast. Then on to Clery's department store which has been selling good Irish tweeds since 1853. Halfway down the west side of the street is the General Post Office, site of a key incident of the 1916 Easter Rising and the 1922 Civil War. Look closely and you will see the scars of shrapnel and bullets on the Ionic pillars. Listen, you might be able to hear those men and women of Ireland crying, *Éirí Amach na Cásca,* "Ireland unfree shall never be at peace," as they rebelled against British rule in the hope of creating an independent Irish republic of all 32 counties.

Cross the River Liffey over the bridge named for Daniel O'Connell, the famous Irish patriot, and then look back east for a good view of the majestic, domed 18th-century Custom House.

The colorful doors of Merrion Square – the 18th century's answer to an H.O.A.

If you go straight ahead on to Westmoreland Street and then right to Fleet Street, you'll be in the Temple Bar area. This is Dublin's bohemian district. (Of the city's 850 pubs, there are probably 600 located here.) If the walking has made you hungry, the Victorian pub, the Palace Bar, offers an excellent lunch of Irish pasties, smoked salmon and oysters.

Walking south on Westmoreland, you'll pass the entrance to Trinity College. Take some time and go exploring. "Trinity" is its nickname; it is formally known as the "College of the Holy and Undivided Trinity of Queen Elizabeth near Dublin." So there. The Old Library will offer you thousands of beautiful books in the "Long Room," which looks like something out of Harry

The irrepressible Mr. Wilde

Potter, as well as the extravagant and complex 9th century Book of Kells. There is a remarkable sense of history at Trinity College as you remember that on its cobbled stones have walked such alumni as Oscar Wilde, Jonathan Swift, Oliver Goldsmith and Samuel Beckett.

Straight ahead is the pedestrian Grafton Street, with a statue of Sweet Molly Malone to greet you. Although the shops here look like those anywhere in Europe, the street performers and the flower sellers with their carts are well worth the walk. As I threaded my way down the street, I came across a quartet of boys in their early teens singing Beatles' songs in perfect harmony, a musician playing an amazing steel guitar and a puppet so wonderfully handled that if you ignored the strings and the big feet next to it, could have been a living, breathing, small jester.

Walking east on Duke Street will take you past Davy Byrne's pub from Joyce's "Ulysses," and then south on Dawson will find you strolling past the Mansion House, the Lord Mayor's Palladian villa. Just across the way is St. Stephen's Green, a 19th century park which is an oasis of flower gardens, meandering paths and a quiet pond. At the end of Dawson, along Merrion Row, try to stop at the graceful old Shelbourne Hotel for tea and scones with jam and clotted cream. (You may note that I work in lots of stops for meals when I'm in Dublin.)

Turn left again at Merrion Street and a few steps down lies Merrion Square, the heart of the city's Georgian district. While a charming folk tale relates that the Georgian doors of Merrion Square were painted unique colors in order to help drunken neighbors find their way home, the real truth is that the 18th century developer required a dreary uniformity in style and architecture in the new Georgian townhouses. So to be unique, the residents added elegant fanlights, ornate knockers and painted their front doors whatever color struck their fancy.

The Square is still beautiful and elegant, and if you look in the northwest corner of Merrion Square Park you'll see a statue of Oscar Wilde lounging insolently on a rock. Carved in various marbles, the statue is appropriately colorful.

While you're out walking, be sure to listen for the stories, soak up the brogue, be charmed by the good humor and be glad you've had the chance to visit Dublin.

A Story of Inisfree

"Oh, Inisfree, my island, I'm returning
From wasted years across the wintry sea
And when I come back to my own dear Ireland,
I'll rest a while beside you, gradh mochroidhe."
Richard Farrelly

The little village of Cong, in western Ireland's County Mayo, is as pretty a place as you're ever likely to find. John Ford used it as the idyllic setting for the mythical village of "Inisfree" and made his iconic film, *The Quiet Man,* here in the early 50's. Never has this splendid country been more lavishly or lovingly displayed. The movie features John Wayne, Maureen O'Hara, Victor McLaglen and a company of extraordinary character actors. Full of wit, charm and blarney, it is perhaps the most marvelous film ever made about Irish rural life. I confess that I've seen it often enough to be able to quote bits of it, look ahead for my favorite scenes, and hum the theme from the epic donnybrook at the end of the film.

When I was in Cong, a little man with a thick brogue and an abiding fondness for the film gave us a walking tour of the town. We toured through the church and down the little main street, then along the crystal clear trout stream to the stone cross which serves as the central roundabout. We ambled past quaint cottages, stopped for a respectful moment at Pat Cohan's pub, crossed the bridge and meandered along the river, all featured in the film. As we strolled, he told stories of the making of the movie.

The movie reviews would tell it this way, "In one of the film's most fanciful, breathtaking, painterly scenes, Wayne walks to an emerald-green, grassy area and lights a cigarette. As he turns, he sees a transcendent, romanticized vision of a red-haired, blue-bloused, scarlet-skirted, bare-footed lass tending a flock of sheep in the meadow. He is so awed and dazzled by her beauty that he doesn't trust the fairy-tale he has seen." But my friend and guide, Paddy Rock, in a heavy Irish brogue, had a little more to tell about that opening scene.

"Now Mr. Ford planned quite an entrance for that lovely Irish lass, Maureen O'Hara. It would be the first time that the lucky hero sees her and Mr. Ford wanted it to be that colorful. For in a green meadow with black-faced sheep herded by a collie, would be a scarlet-skirted, barefoot girl with a blue blouse setting off her red Irish hair. And it would be the beginning of a faerie-tale.

"And so Mr. Ford borrowed a flock of black-faced sheep from a local farmer at lovely Hollywood prices and also brought in a special herding dog from the south to work the flock because he wanted Miss O'Hara to make her entrance in proper company. But that foreign dog they brought in special wouldn't be bothered. He didn't want to work the flock a bit and sat down on the job. And that's the top and the bottom of it all.

"Well, Mr. Ford was that angry. He threw his hat and stamped his foot and declared that he would have neither flock nor dog in his film at 'all. The farmer, for fear of losing all that

American money for the borrowing of his black-faced sheep, stepped up quickly with his hat in his hand and said, 'Good morning, sor. Now your honor, there's a thought that has come into my head for you. I've my own good dog at home who's the grandest worker in County Mayo. And sure if he'll not work for you, I'll not charge you a shilling for the sheep.'

"Well, Mr. Ford was that fond of his scene that he didn't want to lose it entirely, and so he gambled on the farmer's dog. And sure if that collie wasn't the grandest actor in the whole film? And didn't Mr. Ford have a fine shot of a lovely Irish lass with her sheep and her dog in the grand green of the country? And the

My new friend and I in County Mayo

farmer got a nice bit of money for the animals, too.

"And even better than that, the farmer got to drink free at Pat Cohan's pub for the rest of his days. For he'd tell the tale to all the American tourists who would come see the village where the film was made, and they would buy him a pint as a 'thank you' for telling them the story and meeting the dog. And sure, aren't movies a wonderful thing?"

The next day I met a fine Irish sheepdog myself. And when he stopped his work with the sheep for just a minute and jumped up atop a stone fence to say "hello" to me, sure and didn't I think that traveling was a fine thing too.

Legends of Lake Erne

The River Erne seems in no great rush to get to the sea and winds its way gently through watery, forested country until it runs into an enormous, island-studded lake of the same name. I was staying on Lake Erne, County Fermanagh in the north of Ireland. The northern part of Ireland has all the brogue and blarney of the more famous south (unless they're quarreling again), but there aren't as many tourists to clutter up the countryside.

Lake Erne is a huge stretch of fresh water, 50 miles long and split into two parts, with the ancient town of Enniskillen at the break. Its 300 square miles of fresh water is dotted with hundreds of little, green, wooded islands, many of them with medieval ruins and evidence of ancient cultures. There are ruined monasteries, pagan idols and stone crosses. The lake is a paradise for birds, flowers, fishermen and storytellers. So go get a cup of tea, sit back and if you can manage to hear an Irish brogue while you are reading this, all the better.

We were staying at a country manor house on the shore with sweeping views of the lake, beds as warm as the welcome, and a staff so kind that arriving felt like coming home. Apparently no one had told them we had left the 19th century and its level of service (and I wasn't going to spoil the stay by breaking it to them).

One afternoon after a lovely Irish tea, I ambled down to the lake. I had met a young gardener named Brian that morning and he was busy getting a very old rowboat ready to go out. Already sitting in the bow was an equally old man, Brian's grandfather. As I came up to say, "Good afternoon," my new acquaintance asked me if I would like to go along. He and his grandfather were going out for a bit of fishing and I was welcome to come. Invitations like that don't come often, so I grabbed my sweater and climbed aboard.

Brian handled the oars; I balanced in the middle and his grandfather, whose name turned out to be Daniel, sat in the front and soaked up the late afternoon sun which he said was good for his rheumatism. Coots, ducks, and mallards made their lake noises, and we trolled with copper baits past the jaws of big Erne pike. (Yes, I did have to ask what we were doing and what we were doing it to.) While drift fishing, Daniel told me stories of the lake, beginning with fairy stories, tales of the Good Folk. This isn't unusual. If you scratch most people, you'll find some sort of story. However, in Ireland you don't even have to scratch.

"You see those swans now, swimming by? Once there were three princesses and didn't their evil stepmother put a hex on them and turn them into beautiful white swans? They left their castle and had to go from lake to lake looking for heart's ease, and they came upon a prince of Erne who was fishing by the side of this lake. And they gave him a gold pin, and they gave him a gold ring, and one gave him her heart. So he followed them across the world and kilt the evil queen and married his own true darlin'. And she left off her swan dress and came to live with him here." I glanced at the swans for confirmation, but you know how smug swans are, they weren't talking.

"Have you been yet to see Devenish Island?" I confessed I hadn't. "Well it's best that you do, for it is a very holy place. They say Heaven is reflected in Lake Erne. Didn't St. Molaise first begin to build it, and after a while he was a wee bit tired, and he thought to take a rest under a great tree. And while he rested, he heard the songs of the Lord's birds singing him to sleep.

And when he woke up and looked around, sure and hadn't a hundred years gone by and wasn't the entire monastery all finished and built for him?" I promised to go visit such a miraculous spot.

Brian smiled and passed around a thermos of good hot tea and some cheese sandwiches he'd brought along. As he kept rowing, we went by one of the many little islands that dot the lake. "So you see that bit of wood over there?" I said that I did. "There's some that live there that we don't always see. For I've been out on the lake in the dark of the evening and seen little lights there, where no man lives. And sure it's the Daoine Maithe at their dancing." I glanced at Brian and he whispered, "The Good People." "Aye, for they have a great many secrets and if you're not respectful you can be pinched within an inch of your life. They can be a terrible bother. There was a man caught one night on that island, watching duck, and didn't they catch him and drag him through Hell and through Death and throw him back on that island the next morning?"

Brian smiled again and whispered, "I've always thought that a good excuse to his wife for not coming home at all that night," put his back into the oars and sent the small boat past the fairy islands and toward the shore. There were some old docks there, and Daniel asked, "Did you know we were famous here during the War? Did you know that great divil Hitler bombed Dublin and brought the Blitz to Belfast?" And then he leaned back on the boat's bench and settled in for another story. "The Yanks came and built a flying boat base here on the lake at Castle Archdale. And they brought sweeties and chewing gum with them as well. Have you no heard the story of the *Bismarck*?"

Brian shifted the oars and then handed me some hot tea from the Thermos. I can't do the story justice, but please listen in the brogue while I tell you what the old man told me. At Churchill's request, Catalina flying boats were given to the RAF by the United States. The big seaplanes were based on Lough Erne and were used on Atlantic coastal flights. Thousands of patrols were flown from the lake along the Donegal Corridor to the sea to protect the Atlantic shipping. "And sure," said Daniel, "didn't they call the Lough the most beautiful runway in the world." A desperate search was on for the "unsinkable" *Bismarck*, so the RAF divided the vast expanse of the North Atlantic into sections, and aircraft spotters were sent out from Iceland, England, and Argentina. It was the crew of a Catalina that took off from Lough Erne that spotted the great battleship. They stayed "on station" for five hours above the *Bismarck*. While the greatest ship in the German Navy took aim with barrages of deadly anti-aircraft fire, the sea plane from Lough Erne stayed at her post until the Royal Navy and the RAF arrived to sink the ship. It was a pivotal point in the war.

While Daniel spoke, the lake became full of brave and desperate men flying long and dangerous missions. His eyes looked across the water at the old docks and I think he was seeing heroes still there. The heroes are gone now, but the threads of remembrance remain of both the old legends and the new. I hope the old rowboat and the old stories will still be there when I go back again.

The Cliffs at the End of the World

When I saw the Cliffs of Moher on Ireland's west coast, my first thought was, "Land doesn't just end that abruptly, mist doesn't just roll in that quickly, and sea birds don't just appear on cue. This is too incredible to be real; Hollywood must have gotten here first."

But as extraordinary as the Cliffs are, the surrounding area is almost as remarkable. We were in County Clare, a little bit of a thing on the central west coast. Tucked in the northwest corner of County Clare is a vast limestone plateau, the Burren. The name is from the Irish "bhoireann" meaning a stony place and that's a terrific understatement. In the 1640's, Cromwell's surveyor (obviously not a big fan of Ireland) described it as, "a savage land, yielding neither water enough to drown a man nor tree to hang him, nor soil enough to bury."

He was right; it is a fierce and forbidding landscape. But looking closely, it is also a unique and matchless spot full of subtle miracles. Once the area lay beneath a warm tropical sea and then retreating ice-age glaciers left a limestone region of roughly 100 sq miles. For millions of years the rain and wind have worked there so that the Burren is now a dry and lunar landscape, composed of limestone pavements eroded in a unique pattern known as *karren* and crisscrossed by deep crevices known as *grykes*.

West Ireland's wild and rugged Cliffs of Moher

Underneath the plateau, the rain has gouged out an enormous cave system. This is a favorite area for spelunkers and others who have never read of Injun Joe's demise in *Tom Sawyer*. The biggest cave open to the public is Ailwee Cave which was found by an inquisitive sheep dog in the 1940's. There are large stalagmites, stalactites and remains of brown bears that have been extinct in Ireland for thousands of years. I did not go in; I have read what happened to Injun Joe.

The Burren also has vegetation rare to Ireland with Mediterranean, Alpine and Arctic plants all growing side by side. Although not normally even found in the same country, in the Burren you can see these plants sharing the same rock crevices. Walking there in the spring, you'll find a wild rock garden with gentian, orchids, and bloody cranesbill all growing together. And apparently all getting along, a lesson the rest of the country could take to heart.

For those of us who like really old stuff, the most marvelous sight on the way to the Cliffs is Poulnabrone Dolmen. (Poulnabrone translates as "hole of sorrows.") A recent excavation has dated the grave material to over 4,000 B.C. For archaeologists, getting to stand at a Neolithic tomb that is older than Egypt's pyramids is a goosebump moment. Some 22 burials spread over a period of 600 years have been identified, along with weapons and pottery, which indicate that this was probably a ceremonial cemetery for important individuals. The dramatic location, the extreme age, the idea that 6000 years ago men were buried there with such great care, makes this a marvelous visit.

And where the Burren runs into the sea, there are the Cliffs of Moher. Think of the verse, the drama, the music of Ireland. Think of the poetry and the pathos. All these qualities are embodied in this landscape. But trying to describe them is a little like talking about the Grand Canyon; you may be able to convey an idea of the overwhelming power and intensity, but it still won't be enough. The five miles of cliffs rise 700 feet above the sea in a vertical wall from Nag's Head to just beyond O'Brien's Tower. The sandstone and shale, looking axed through, form a sheer drop to the crashing waves below and are a slice through geologic time. On a clear day the view is spectacular; the Aran Islands are visible in Galway Bay as are the hills of Connemara. The wind blows; there is the smell of kelp; the sea birds keen as they hover and soar; the clouds drop down to shroud part of the Cliffs and the ocean pounds on the high cliff.

That day was mist-shrouded; there was a light drizzle with clouds rolling in and an unlikely rainbow in the distance. I walked along the edge of the abyss with the booming of the waves below and only the company of the seabirds. I was at the end, or the beginning, of the world. I was in the spot where the legends of Ireland are born.

The Scattering, Leaving Home Forever

"You're picking up a pebble?" asked Donald, my Irish friend. "And sure you should, for these cliffs are some of the very last bit of home that many saw for the rest of their days. And many the tear that was shed and many the prayer that was said as they sailed away from Ireland forever." (I'm not really sure that this bit of land would be the last thing the emigrants saw, but Donald was a poet and never let the truth get in the way of a good story.) These cliffs would certainly be a proper spot for a "good-bye." The Cliffs of Moher stand at the edge of the world with nothing but the cold North Atlantic between the soft green grass of home and the harsh realities of beginning again in the New World. They fall straight and hard to the sea, and when you stand there with the waves crashing below and the lonesome cry of the gulls wheeling above, it does seem like the end of everything.

"Diaspora" is Greek for a "scattering of seeds" and is used to refer to any people who are forced to leave their homes, dispersed throughout the world. While there have been many such tragic events, the tale of the Irish is particularly poignant. In the middle of the 19th century, as the potatoes died in the fields and the folk died in their cottages, the Irish were scattered to the ends of the earth.

It's a sad story we are all familiar with and was brought home to me a few years ago at the Ulster American Folk Park in Northern Island. The Park is an enormous open-air museum in County Tyrone that tells the story of the Irish emigration to America in the 18th and 19th centuries and gives the visitor a "living history" experience with authentic Irish homes of the period and costumed reenactors. It includes 30 buildings (and a ship), 300 acres and 2 extra centuries.

An 18th century Irish cottage

The Irish peasant experience has been romanticized in story and song, but stooping to go into a little, dark one-room cabin is dreadfully grim. A late 18th century hovel, which was moved from the foothills of the nearby Sperrin Mountains, had a dirt floor, a small peat fire, with a bed frame, a table and a few stools as the only furniture. It would have been home to as many as 12 whose life there was dark and dirty, cold and fragile. Most peasants were poor tenant farmers whose principal source of food was the potato. And when the potato blight struck in 1845, the food rotted in the earth.

The more prosperous families practiced a craft, weaving or smithing for example, with space laid aside in their homes for a loom or a forge. So the Park has a working forge, a dyer and a spinner. There is also a Presbyterian Meeting House, a good-sized thatched building with a proper minister. But a majority of the Irish folk were at a hand-to-mouth, subsistence level. And so when the only major source of food was destroyed by disease, they died or moved. Two million people left their homes, heading by sea into the unknown, leaving friends, family and country behind, enduring the torment of the passage to escape the *an Gorta Mor,* "the Great Hunger."

In a large exhibit hall, the Museum offers an amazing series of life-size dioramas telling the story of a ship's voyage. There are songs of lament that will break your heart with their strains of longing, anger and despair as you listen to narrations of the crossings against a backdrop of sounds of the gulls, the roar of storms and cries of children. The stories speak of loneliness and disease, hunger and hopelessness, about the long walk across Ireland to the strange and busy ports, and about the "Living Wake," the final farewell given to a loved one by the family who stayed behind.

Walking down a recreation of an Ulster main street, you can board a full-size reconstruction of an early 19th century sailing vessel. Crammed with small berths, the *Brig Union* is the sort of sailing ship that would have carried thousands across in their holds. The North Atlantic is not a benign sea, and a rough crossing, plus illness, plus babies must have been wretched. If the captain was skilled and the ship was well built, the crossing could be relatively swift; the average length was 40 days. But there could be storms and icebergs, doldrums and disease, and it could have been miserable. (I will think of that next time I am complaining about being squished on a flight to Europe.)

The path through the *Brig Union* takes you from the Old World to the New, from famine-stricken Ireland to the energy and optimism of the United States. I know that this was just my imagination, but while the "Irish" side was dark and cold and rainy, on the "American" side the sun was out. As I walked down the gangplank, I started whistling *God Bless America* (much to Donald's confusion). There were American hand-hewn log cabins and farmhouses, along with herb gardens and smoke houses, brought to Ireland all the way from Pennsylvania. Obviously there was a lot of hard work involved in starting over in the New World, but there was also great strength and promise.

I was happy, even symbolically, to be home. And proud of what it took to get there and what it means to be an American. Go out and see the wide world, then come back and love ours all the more.

Conversations in an Irish Pub

 Now the first thing you must realize is that I'm not a drinking woman. Anything that smells that bad, tastes that bitter, and costs that much isn't something I'm going to encourage. Besides I've found that a sip of whiskey will cause me to lose my "edit button," which is a fearful thing to contemplate. So when I tell you that I nursed a glass of Irish single malt for an entire evening in a Dublin pub just so I could listen to these stories, you will appreciate the effort it took. Eavesdropping is not polite, but sometimes the results are worth the bad manners.

   Also, please understand that a pub in Dublin is not like a bar in the U.S. It's a spot where friends meet, families gather, lovers embrace and enemies duel. A pub is the pulse of the city and its heart as well. It's a place to enjoy a nice brew, a good meal and the warmth of the people themselves, who are full of charm, humor and stories (and lies). These stories may be a little lengthy because the Irish are culturally incapable of getting directly to the heart of the story, but must circle around it for a while. I promise, eventually we will get to the point.

   There are all sorts of pubs in Dublin, and if you're not careful you may end up in one of the trendy ones in the Temple Bar area with mirrors, tourists and potted palms. Instead, go a little farther away, down one of the colorful, winding lanes until you run across the genuine article, perhaps with sawdust on the floor, dark wood on the bar and a warm welcome for you.

   This particular evening, I stopped at the Stag's Head on Dame Street. (To find it, walk down the left side of Dame Street from Trinity College until you see the mosaic of the stag on the pavement. Down the cobblestone alley, you'll find the three-story, brick Victorian building tucked away on the left.) The Stag's Head is an atmospheric place with an interior of dark mahogany, mirrors and tiles all dating from 1895. During the day, it's a quiet sanctuary. During the evening, the activity builds around the head of an unfortunate stag mounted over the bar. If you're new to the pub, the barman will tell you that a 14-point bull stag was captured in Dublin. And when the poor rebellious creature broke loose, it crashed headlong right through the wall of the Stag's Head. So they left it there. With an introduction to blarney like that, how could you not sit and listen to the conversations around you? So we grabbed a bench seat under the stained glass windows, put our whiskeys down on a small marble table and got ready to listen. (As most of the stories I heard had a broad dialect to them, while I'm remembering them to you, you'll need to use your imagination a little to hear the Irish lilt. Because part of the magic is in the brogue.)

   To the left of me were two men in suits, one of whom had just gotten back from a car trip north to visit his wife's family. "Now her parents have moved to a smaller spot and we were having a bit of trouble finding it. There was a fella by the side of the road with a car no better than he was and the wife insisted I ask him. Well I knew the moment I got out that it was a hopeless thing, for the cigarette ash was spilling down his shirt, and the reek of the drink had me stop upwind. But I pulled out my map and showed him the place we were going. He squinted down and said he knew right where the place was, the problem being, he didn't know where we were just now. The best advice he could give me was, 'If I was going there, sor, I wouldn't start from here.' "

The other suit said he had a bit of bother in the same county but for an entirely different reason. "Sure we were driving as straight as a string, making good time when all of a sudden we went down into a valley, and the road took a terrible bend around a bit of a tree before it straightened out again. I asked my brother-in-law riding next to me what was the reason for the hiccup in the road. He said there were wee folk living under the tree and the highway department had given up trying to argue with them. So they'd moved the road."

Sitting to my right on the red leather bench were two working-class men having a quiet time with a brew before going home to face the wives and kids. "Sure it's not always easy to find a pint in the North, for all they're that civil. We stopped the car to have a sip of something at a pub in one of the Glens of Antrim. Have you been there? You'll want to have a care, then. The pub was a long, low building with a long, low sign and a lot of doors going in. My friend and I went in one, and as there was nobody about we sat quietly until the landlady came and so we ordered two pints. She looked a little sad and said she was that sorry, she only had bottles to give. But perhaps we could try the pub next door? We stepped into her front parlor by mistake."

Later in the evening, three old men deep in conversation, moved over to the bench commiserating with each other about their marriages. "Ach," said one, "It's been a fine 50 years. Mind you, she wasn't always the wonderful wife she is now. We had a bit of trouble or two when we were first wed, but we got over the rough spots. Except I do remember the terrible problem with the button.

"Well, back then we used to wear union suits, the great, long underwear. And I had an old set where the buttonhole in the back had torn so that the button would keep slipping out. So I asked my young bride if she would mind fixing the problem? 'No,' she said, 'she'd be happy to help.' So I gave her my suit without another thought. And she set mending in front of the stove and wasn't it a fine sight for my newly-wedded heart?

"The next day, I put my underwear on and went off to work. All was well until I went to sit down and then such a pain I had in the rear part that it was almost intolerable. So I went off for a bit of privacy to see what the problem was. And there, hadn't she gone and fixed it though. She hadn't sewed up the torn button hole at all. Instead she had sewed on a bigger button and that was what I was sitting on! We've had many a laugh about it since. But 50 years ago, I wasn't that sure I would live through the first year of wedded bliss."

There are supposedly 450 pubs in Dublin, each with stories to tell and all will greet you with "Cead Mile Failte" or "One Hundred Thousand Welcomes." You may not sit down at the Stag's Head, but in the pubs, in the lanes, in the neighborhoods, you will meet a hundred kindred spirits.

Italy, the Fortunate Country

"The Creator made Italy from designs by Michelangelo."   Mark Twain
"You may have the universe if I may have Italy." Giuseppe Verdi

The Faces of Venice

Venice is a city of illusion. A combination of light and air and water so full of movement and shadow that is impossible to be sure what is real and what is daydream. Half the city isn't really there at all, but instead a reflection in the legendary canals and lagoons. Even its most famous profile, the beautiful mask of Carnival, is a masquerade, disguising what lies beneath.

I took this photo a few years ago because this incredibly exquisite collection of masks seemed to symbolize the entire city as precisely as any shot of its grand buildings or picturesque gondoliers. The city is lovely, unique, deceptive and oh so fragile.

"To sail in a golden gondola in a city where the streets were not paved with noisy cobblestones but in silent and silver water and where the sun was so hot that it could melt the ice out of your heart and the pain out of your mind. No one ever grew old in that city and love never died." I suspect I'm not the only one to love this city.

Centuries before the Renaissance and the European age of exploration, Venetians began a series of journeys to the Orient and transformed their little mud bank settlement on the island of Torcello

The masks of Venice

into the greatest city of the Mediterranean. Forced into the lagoon by warlike neighbors, it was the water that gave the city its wealth. With their legendary fleet, the Venetians dominated the sea routes of the Mediterranean and traded salt harvested on the flats of the lagoon for spices and then spices for gold.

"La Serenissma" was the greatest marketplace in Europe where goods from Persia, India and Africa, silks and spices, dyes and porcelain, were piled beside the ores and cloths of northern Europe. Venetian merchants maintained outposts in the Orient, Africa and Arabia, and the wealth of Byzantium, Alexandria, Baghdad and Damascus flowed down the Grand Canal. The great galleys would enter the city with their flags flying and trumpets ringing out. Their officers, dressed in silk, would be received by the Doge and his powerful Council of Ten. The glimmer of water would be matched by the gleaming of jewels.

Venice was built to awe and impress her rivals and her people. The city's reflection in the canals which doubles the impact was not created accidentally. Her ornate palaces, her public festivals, her extravagant water processions were all designed to astonish and amaze the visitor and assure her citizens that their city was the "Queen of the Seas." Ruskin wrote, "While the burghers and barons of the North were building their dark streets and grisly castles of oak and sandstone, the merchants of Venice were covering their palaces with porphyry and gold."

Go to the Plaza San Marco either very early in the morning or very late at night, when the mobs of backpackers and busloads of tourists have vanished for the day. Known as the "the most beautiful drawing room in Europe," it really hasn't changed much since the late 16th century (except for Napoleon ripping down a church at the far end to put in a ballroom). Surrounded by the city's most important historical buildings, sit for a while in the centuries-old center of Venetian and have an incredibly expensive but worthwhile espresso at an outdoor cafe while watching the pigeons flap indignantly at your lack of popcorn.

Facing the waterfront and directly in front of the Basilica are three columns. These are ships' masts from the glory days of trading, and since 1480 have flown the colors of St Mark during feast days. Take a good look at the Horses of St. Mark on the top of the Basilica. They were stolen from the Hippodrome of Christian Constantinople as part of the loot sacked by the Christian armies of Venice during the Fourth Crusade. (The enemies of trade obviously being more dangerous than the enemies of religion.)

Cross over the Grand Canal on the Rialto Bridge, once the city's commercial center. "What news on the Rialto?" asks Shakespeare's Merchant. Looking down to the water, you can get an idea of the commotion of daily life taking place here for the last 900 years. Very near the Rialto is the Campo delle Peccaries where produce and seafood have been sold for almost 600 years. In the early morning, in open-air stalls under stone columns decorated with monkfish, the mists rise off the lagoon and piles of fresh-caught fish glisten in the sunlight. Stocky lady shoppers haggle with the fishmongers as burly men in rubber boots and plastic aprons unload fish, verci clams, mussels, cuttlefish and silvery sardines for Venetian dinners.

Wander down the maze-like warren of small side streets and watch a carnival mask be made at Emilio Massaro in the San Marco District, have a bitter chocolate ice cream at the Hotel Cipriani, enjoy a gelato cone almost anywhere. Any everywhere you go, look for marvelous, museum-quality art hanging in the corner church, the corner palace and the corner hospital, and all of it placed where it was meant to be, not in a frozen museum but in the center of vibrant city life.

As the sun goes down, locate a neighborhood "bacari," or wine bar. This is where most Venetians go after work, before dinner to have an "ombra" or shadow, a glass tumbler of wine to ease away the day's dilemmas. Then saunter out to see Venice at dusk, when the light and the water and the air turn everything shadowy and pink.

Getting Lost in the Vatican

Once I got lost in the Vatican.

I have a knack for turning the wrong direction. Leaving a football game, a concert, a store, if I turn to the right, people with me know that the car is parked to the left. It's a skill I have. I'm fine in the woods, it's just civilization that confuses me. And the more civilized a city, the more muddled I get. So it's no wonder that I was bewildered in Rome. Rome is an ancient city of small wandering lanes and alleys, a confusing warren built up over the centuries. The roadways that were once the center of the world are narrow, curving and sneaky. This is even truer in Vatican City.

Work on the original St. Peter's Basilica was begun in 324 A.D. by the Emperor Constantine (who must have been dissatisfied since he picked up and moved to Constantinople six years later), and through popes and kings, cardinals and bishops, has been enlarged, renovated, demolished and rebuilt. Through the millennia, it has possessed an incalculable amount of influence, power and wealth, so it is also full of the labyrinthine dealings that accompany those

Saint Peter's Piazza and Basilica

pursuits. It is full of intrigues, glory and honor. It is also brimming with magnificent treasures, Michelangelo's Pieta, Bernini's canopy, Raphael's tapestries, the wonders of the Sistine Chapel.

Stepping inside the Basilica is a little surreal. You are already aware of how imposing, magnificent and vast it is supposed to be, but nothing quite prepares you for your first look. The nave, the central approach to the high altar, is more than a city block long; the main ceiling is 140 feet high, and the dome soars up to 440 feet. Conceived by Michelangelo and built during the high Renaissance, there is not one subtle plank in its entire construction. Replete with marble, gilt, mosaics, legendary paintings and sculptures, it represents massive wealth, privilege and the finest work of some of the greatest artists of Italy.

It is easy to meander, awestruck for hours. Just looking at the incredible mosaics and paintings on the soaring ceilings hundreds of feet above will give you a serious crick in your neck. But inside all the brilliant splendor of St. Peter's, there are also smaller treasures for you to be aware of. And I think it was looking for all these lesser pieces that was the beginning of my "directional difficulties."

Once inside the Basilica, ignore the glory spreading out in front of you, turn around, and go back for the moment to the entrance directly inside the Great Doors. (You can't go straight in through the front doors because they are reserved for "Holy Year" which only happens every quarter century.) On the floor, right in the beginning of the nave, is a disc made of purple porphyry marble. Porphyry was used by the ancient Romans to designate their Caesars. On

Christmas Day, 800A.D. Charlemagne knelt there to be crowned Emperor of the West. Charlemagne's knees were on that spot. Somehow I am always overwhelmed by that detail.

Turn around then and look toward Bernini's enormous (and very ornate) bronze canopy over the Papal Altar. At the center of the crossing and directly under the dome which marks, in a monumental fashion, the place of Saint Peter's tomb, you will see the results of a "my church is bigger than your church" contest. The measurements of the "largest" in the world are recorded in brass letters on the center of the marble floor. (Guess who wins.)

Another often overlooked place is the poignant memorial to the last of the Stuarts. As you enter the church, take a left along to the corner and then a quick right, and in front of you is the Stuart monument. After his aborted attempt to regain the English crown, the romantic and foolish Bonnie Prince Charlie was exiled to Rome and is buried in St. Peter's along with his father and brother. (One would wonder why the carvings show Prince Charlie's father facing away from him, but I'm probably being needlessly melodramatic.) Every true Scot should stop to make a respectful genuflection and leave a blessing.

Near the High Altar is a 13th century bronze statue of St. Peter. In a pleasant but unsubstantiated myth, it is said that the statue was made from the bronze statue of Jupiter on the Capitol. Notice the right foot of the saint. It is worn thin from the kisses of thousands of pilgrims throughout the centuries asking for mercy or forgiveness. Whether you are a believer or not, that level of faith through the millennia is tremendously moving.

It was looking for these little things that got me into trouble. I turned left when I should have turned right, went up a corridor instead of down a gallery, up a long flight of steps instead of down a ramp. I was off the maps, away from the groups, past the guides. I finally pushed open a heavy door at the top of a particularly long series of steps, and unexpectedly I was outside. There was an old man there in a uniform. My Italian is limited to "please," "thank you" and "may I have more pizza?" but he smiled at me, so I didn't think I was in too much trouble.

He motioned me around the door to the side and finally I knew where I was. I was on the roof of St. Peter's. I was at the foot of Michelangelo's dome with a grand view of the Piazza San Pietro and the city of Rome. There are enormous statues there of Christ and his Apostles looking out over the city, and standing very small, I was looking out over the city too.

Sometimes getting lost can be a wonderful talent.

One of Capri's gorgeous views

Villa Michele in Ana Capri

Jasmine on the Isle of Capri

I bought my favorite perfume at the edge of a cliff on the island of Capri, in a tiny, family-owned perfumeria. And when I put it on and close my eyes, I can smell jasmine, feel the warmth of the Italian sun, the satin softness of the breeze and still hear the sound of the sea. Capri is the stuff of legends, one of those places you don't believe will be quite as breathtaking as described, just because it is so famous. After all, it has been a vacation mecca, a paradise for lovers of beauty for the last 3000 years.

In the Bay of Naples, six miles from the mainland, are three islands, Ischia and Procida which are volcanic (remember Vesuvius is ominously close) and Capri, which is limestone. The island's limestone composition is the reason the cliffs plummet to the sea, that there are dramatic, creamy rock towers, that the grottos are blue. There are hydrangea, oleander and bougainvillea that cling and climb up the stone walls. The light plays with the blues and greens and golds of the mountains and the water. And everywhere are the scents of jasmine and the call of the waves. (I apologize if this is a little lyrical, but Capri does that to you.)

It is not easy to get to paradise. First a long, numbing flight to Rome, then another flight to Naples, an histrionic taxi ride to the pier, a hydrofoil to the island, a funicular ride up the mountain, and then a stumbling walk to the hotel. The small villa where we stayed was built into the hillside with gardens surrounding the rooms. We were met by the owner/manager who offered us a glass of compari and a quiet seat on a balcony filled with orange, red and yellow blossoms overlooking a turquoise sea. Perhaps because it was such a difficult and lengthy journey to get there, but I've never felt so welcomed and surrounded by beauty. (And another confession, I fell asleep on the balcony, my wine in my hand.)

Capri has been a lure for artists and refugees, poets and lovers, pirates and playwrights since the Greeks and Phoenicians first landed. Odysseus sailed by, tied to his ship's mast to escape the call of the Sirens from the island's sea caves. The Romans followed the Greeks, and then

Saracen pirates, Norman princes, Renaissance courtiers came after. The well-heeled and the well-oiled have always loved Capri.

The Emperor Tiberius, retiring from the dangers and intrigues of Rome and never one for simplicity, built twelve sumptuous villas on the island. Now only three remain and you can still walk in the ruins of the Villa Jovis. It's a heck of a hike up the mountain to the remains of the villa, but the climb and the views are worth it as you follow stone staircases along twisting lanes, fragrant with lacy swaths of wisteria and jasmine. The villa itself is built into the mountain with grand rooms and balconies in the front and small servants' quarters in the back (of course). The engineers among you will be interested in the system of canals and cisterns for water usage. The historians will note the lurid details of Tiberius's scandalous hobbies and the artists will delight in the beauty of the place. With the riches of the entire civilized world to draw on, it must have been an incredibly spectacular palace.

Hiking in Capri can be rewarding. The tourists tend to stay in just a few areas, the Piazza, the Gardens of Augustus, and the Blue Grotto, so once you are away from those you will hardly meet anyone. Further from those tourist haunts, Capri has a wild beauty that can be explored as you climb up and down the cliffs. There are well-marked trails with spectacular views. One path, modestly called the "Walk of the Gods," takes you through fields of wildflowers, groves of cypress and past staggering sea-views. Abandoned 16th century towers perch on the edge of vertical cliffs, and at every turn is the incredible azure blue of the Mediterranean.

While the Blue Grotto is usually full of tourists and the rough sea waves make it tricky to swim, there are other grottos on the island to explore. In a little boat called a "gozzi," you can visit the White Grotto, the Coral Grotto and the Emerald Grotto. Seeing Capri from the sea will give you a whole new perspective on beauty. And if you would like to swim, the Emerald Grotto is a perfect place to stop. Make sure your boatman speaks English (if your Italian isn't up to it), and he will tell you marvelous stories of nymphs and sirens, pirates and kings. Just believe everything he says and tip him generously. And in the evening, after the day-trippers are gone, sit in the Piazza, have a coffee, and you will be reminded of the warning, "Don't stay in Capri too long, you may never leave."

There really isn't a lot to do on Capri. There are paradises of flowers, long alleys of ancient Cyprus trees, the smell of flowers, the blue of the water. You can eat and sleep and walk, smell the juniper, wild sage and orange blossoms, listen to the sounds of the sea and perhaps find out that this may be quite enough. All it needs to take me back there is the scent of jasmine

On the Virtues of Hot Water

Have you ever had a horrific day with appointments and meetings, clients and kids, no time for a break or a breather, not a minute for a meal or a short walk outside? When the only remedy is going home, standing in the shower and letting the warm water wash away the day's dilemmas? When only an empty stomach or running out of hot water will make you leave the tub and dry off?

Of course, that happens to everyone sometimes. And standing in the shower with the water pouring down, the muscles in my neck and back unkinking one by one, I've thought about the blessings of hot water. I spent a college summer on a dig on Arizona's Mogollon Rim with only the cold water of a nearby stream for absolutely everything (which was not as picturesque as it sounds), and it left me with an abiding appreciation for indoor plumbing. Hot water cleanses, relaxes, rejuvenates. The desire for it, and the engineering skills necessary to produce it, help to define a culture. Barbarians use cold water only when compelled; civilization views hot water as a necessity.

The Baths of Caracalla

Go to Rome and visit the Baths of Caracalla.

The city of Rome dates from the 8th century B.C. when the wolf-suckled twins beat up the Etruscans and put the city on the map. From primitive huts on the Palatine Hill, it grew to become the grandiose centerpiece of a vast empire. Augustus bragged that he had found Rome a city of bricks and left it a city of marble. Later emperors added to it with temples, theaters, public baths and arenas to please the gods, the people and mostly themselves. Nero exclaimed, "Finally, I can live like a human being," when he moved into his Golden House with its own private lake.

If you can bear with my history obsession for just a minute, in 64 A.D. great fires decimated the center of Rome so the emperor took advantage of the empty property and began building. The Golden House with its hundreds of rooms, gardens and artificial lakes may have covered as much as 300 acres in the heart of the city. After Nero's suicide, (that would be after the infamous violin recital), the pleasure palace was destroyed and the materials used to build both the Baths of Caracalla and the Coliseum, occupying the same prime location in Rome. Until the end of the 15th century the palace was covered with tons of dirt and debris, forgotten until a boy fell through a cleft in the rocks. Michelangelo, Raphael and other artists crawled under-ground and found the mosaics, frescoes and architecture of Nero's palace, and these discoveries nurtured the early Renaissance. Not too bad for a mad emperor's extravagance.

The Baths are just a little southeast of ancient Rome's center and it's not a bad walk if you like exploring. That so much skill and so much money could be invested in such an undertaking is awe-inspiring; and of course, I find the combination of history and engineering absolutely irresistible.

115

The Baths of Caracalla are a vast 33-acre complex built in 212-17 A.D. of red brick faced in white stucco, with bathing facilities for more than 1600 people. (Imagine St. Peter's as an enormous spa.) The interiors were richly decorated with marble seats and mosaic-covered walls and floors. There were enormous frescoed vaults, marble fountains and statues. Gray granite and purple porphyry from Egypt, yellow marble from Numidia, green marble from Greece, the complex wore all the riches of the Mediterranean empire. The whole area was actually a multifunctional leisure center with gymnasiums, libraries, gardens, art galleries, restaurants, hair salons and shops. And in underground levels, slaves kept the baths at just the right temperature by burning ten tons of wood every day.

The hours were divided into segments, men in the mornings, women in the afternoons and slaves between 4 and 6 p.m. Bathing and socializing seem to have been relatively egalitarian. Different classes (although not sexes) mixed comfortably, lounging on the steamy seats and indulging in the need for cleanliness, relaxation and beauty beneath the soaring arches.

And bathing was just not hopping in and out of a shower. There was a hot bath in the caldarium, then a lukewarm dip in the tepidarium and finally a quick splash in the cold frigidarium. All this came with conversations with your friends, oiled massages from bath attendants, music, gambling and wine. One ancient Roman lamented that he had time to go the baths only once a day.

The engineering involved was also fascinating. Robert Harris in his novel *Pompeii* writes about their aqueduct, "Oh, but she was a might piece of work, the Augusta – one of the greatest feats of engineering ever accomplished…Somewhere far out there, the aqueduct captured the springs and bore the water westward – channeled it along sinuous underground passages, carried it over ravines on top of tiered arcades, forced it across valleys through massive siphons…a distance of some sixty miles, with a mean drop along her entire length of just two inches every one hundred yards…And the roar of the water was the music of civilization."

In 537 A.D. the Goths finally cut the great aqueducts that fed the city. But the proof of creativity and brilliance are still there to see. While walking through the ruins, I met a Roman cat perched on a crumbled brick wall energetically giving herself a bath. Cats being the way they are, I'm not sure she was as struck by the coincidence as I was. But it was reassuring to know that someone was still getting clean at the Baths of Caracalla.

The Amalfi Coast from the sea

The Amalfi Coast, with Flair and Élan

"This is where all the lovely myths go when they die, and we no longer believe in them."
Anonymous

Positano, Ravello, Sorrento, say those names aloud. Don't they roll off your tongue like smooth wine? Driving to visit them on the Amalfi Coast should be done with flair, élan and utter disregard for personal safety. (It also helps to have red hair, a quick smile and be able to say, "I'm sorry" in Italian.)

South of Naples, the narrow, twisting, coastal road stretches from Sorrento to the Gulf of Salerno, past the beautiful villages of Positano and Ravello and then to the village of Amalfi. The roadway has only occasional railings to keep your car from plunging into the craggy rocks and the sea far below. The faint of heart take the northbound route, hugging the cliffs. The foolish and foolhardy take the southbound direction that hugs the sea cliff edge and gives the most spectacular views. (It was early in the tourist season, or we would not have tried it.)

Driving the Amalfi Coast is a little like navigating our Pacific Coast Highway. There are crashing waves, sheer rocky cliffs and rolling sunlight instead of fog. This achingly beautiful area is justly considered the most lovely stretch of scenery in the Mediterranean as steep cliffs plunge into water the color of sapphire, opal and jade; picturesque villages cling to the rocky sides and at every curve there are breathtaking views. Looking down from the road, you will see

117

private coves and terraced gardens, with purple, pink and red bougainvilleas tumbling down into the water.

The driving part, however, is a little bit tricky. The beauty of the bright, lush flowers growing wild, plus all the views of the deep blue sea, make it difficult to concentrate. But the proximity to the cliffs does tend to keep you wonderfully focused. John Steinbeck, who used to come here in the '50s, claimed the Amalfi Drive was "carefully designed to be a little narrower than two cars side by side." There must have been a thousand turns in the road between Sorrento and Salerno as we drove along the edge of the mountains, navigating twists and hairpin turns, tunnels and bridges, as the cliffs plunged vertically into a shining sea. Driving through an ordinary tunnel, suddenly an infinite expanse of sea and sky would burst into view. Looking down there were terraces, towers, gardens and verandas all the way down to the Bay of Salerno with the islands of Capri and Ischia beckoning in the distance.

The sun is bright, the sea is that lovely turquoise and you realize you are following in the wake of Odysseus. Along the coast, there are gleaming villas clinging with no visible foothold to the sheer cliffs. (One of them belongs to a current Italian goddess, the divine Sophia Loren.) Odysseus' alluring sirens and much later the charismatic Rudolph Nureyev lived on the island of Li Galli in the Bay. It's reassuring to know that beautiful people can't resist this coast either.

The towns along the way are all worth stopping for a day, a week, a month. Sorrento is an ancient Etruscan clifftop town beautifully located on the white cliffs and enclosed by the mountains. Its breathtaking sunsets and the fragrance of the orange and lemon groves have been luring the traveler for millennia. Positano is a "vertical village" with pastel-colored houses and terraced gardens clinging to impossibly steep cliffs straight out of a postcard. Steinbeck wrote, "Positano bites deep. It is a dream place that isn't quite real when you are there and becomes beckoningly real after you've gone."

We meandered up through winding paths past art galleries and expensive shops, cafes and beds of bright flowers. There was a cobbler putting together a pair of brown sandals from butter-soft leather and around the corner a shop that sold creamy, peach gelata. There were intricate and colorful handmade dresses, Amalfi ceramics in the famous blue and yellow patterns and everything in the world that can be made with lemons. (The lemon soufflé is excellent.) Beautiful baskets filled with the large yellow fruit and its glossy green leaves are in every shop. There were lemon biscuits and perfume, candles and excellent homemade Limóncello. I have a yellow and blue Sorrento olive oil carafe sitting next to my stove, but the Limóncello liqueur is long gone. The guard towers to protect against Saracen pirates are still there, but now the beach is a peaceful place for fisherman to bait their hooks or mend their menaiche, the traditional hand-woven nets.

At Positano, you can walk to a relatively uncrowded beach off to the right or clomp straight down steeply circling stairs to the noisy, crowded beach in front of the cafes. Swimming in the Mediterranean is better than any other place. (I'm sorry, it just is.) You're swimming in cool, clear water of almost mystic azure blue with Odysseus and Poseidon and the rest of the nymphs, and if the gods won't help you to stay afloat, the extraordinary salinity of the water will do the trick.

Founded in the 9th century, the town of Amalfi lies about halfway between Sorrento and Salerno and was the maritime rival of Genoa and Venice. Its name is derived from the nymph, Amalfi, beloved by Hercules. Legend has it that after she died, he buried her in the world's most beautiful spot. (See, even then it was lovely.) In 337 A.D., Roman nobles on their way to Constantinople were shipwrecked along the beautiful coast; they decided to keep away from the dangerous morass of Byzantine politics and stay put. Centuries later the 19th century Italian writer, Renato Fucini, wrote, "When the inhabitants of Amalfi get to heaven on Judgment Day, it will be just like any other day for them."

Its grand cathedral of striped marble and stone was built in the 9th century and is a mongrel of Byzantine, Gothic, Baroque and Arab-Norman architecture. The ancient power of the city is evident in the grand steep stairs which approach it and in its tall bronze doors which were cast in Constantinople around 1066 (This makes the U.S. look just a little juvenile.) Through the main doors is the "Cloister of Paradise" with its intertwining arches surrounding an enclosed garden. Inside the basilica it is cool and fragrant with incense. There are rich and elaborate frescoes on the walls and ceilings and lavish marble and gold on the altars and shrines. The relics of Saint Andrew the Apostle are housed in the crypt of the cathedral and St. Francis of Assisi visited them in the 13th century. (Yup, still feeling a little young.) Please note that the relics were "purloined" from Constantinople along with the rest of the loot during the Fourth Crusade.

We stopped at a café, had a cup of espresso and watched the world go by, a perfect thing to do on the Amalfi coast. There was a ferocious game of kayak water polo going on in the harbor with two teams of ten men ferociously paddling and passing the ball toward a net. On shore, little boys and little dogs ran about in excitement with much yelling and barking, much splashing and a lot of laughter. Obviously they were rather more blasé about the 11th century Cathedral doors than I was.

We moved on from the espresso in Amalfi to the village of Ravello for a late lunch. That choice for a stop was made partially because we were told that the best views of the coast could be seen there and also because it was a chance to unpry driving hands from the steering wheel. This small and elegant village is perched on a ridge above Amalfi and has breathtaking panoramic views of sea and sky and two beautiful English/Italian gardens. In a small café, we sat outside in a shady grape arbor overlooking the sea. With the sun shining green and gold through the leaves and the azure Mediterranean below us, we ordered lemon soufflé. It was an absolutely perfect day.

The entire country of Italy is filled with splendor. But especially on the Amalfi coast there is beauty in the sea, beauty on land, the Isle of Capri, the enchantress Circe, the fascinating Sophia. It's so magnificent that Odysseus may have been sorry he left, deciding he should have stayed and listened to the sirens' song. I've seen the island of Ithaca, and now I've been to Positano. Faced with an aging Penelope on a barren island and remembering lovely Circe on the "Divina Costa," I suspect he had regrets.

119

The "Speaking Statues" of Rome

I confess, I'm a meanderer by nature, a slow stroller, a stopper and reader of any and all historical markers. Put me down alone in the middle of an old city with a good guide book and I'm as happy as a clam. So I was pretty chipper when I had a free afternoon in Rome. I had been in the city before for much longer stays and already had the chance to see the "big" sights, the Vatican, Coliseum, Pantheon, Forum and so forth. So dressed in jeans and tennies and clutching my trusty *Michelin* guide, I took myself on a "small" tour to the Piazza Navona. I had "Millefoglie con Crema alla Grappa e Rabarbaro," (which is both a verbal and a gustatory mouthful) and tea at an outdoor café and watched the pigeons, balloon sellers, tourists and such mill around Bernini's world-famous "Fountain of the Four Rivers" with its heroic figures of the river gods.

The guide book also took me to some not-so-famous statues. The "talking statues" or the *arguli* (the witty ones) are not as lovely and polished as their more famous cousins, actually they are kind of crummy, but they have a famous history and a practical use. Until the 19th century, the citizens of Rome were able to criticize and complain while safely retaining their anonymity by hanging signs from these marble figures. One wouldn't want to put his real name to "Since Nicholas became pope and murderer, blood is abundant in Rome while there is lack of wine," unless one had a death wish.

For example, near the Piazza Navona is "Pasquino," an armless statue who "spoke" about the papacy. (A dangerous discussion in the best of times.) Although the "official" reports state that Romans were "overwhelmed and enraptured" with the "Four Rivers Fountain," "Pasquino" didn't like it and complained, "We do not want obelisks and fountains, it is bread that we want, bread, bread, bread!" The pope authorized disguised spy patrols to watch the statue. Imagine sneaking around a piazza in the middle of the night to protect an ugly, battered statue.

"Pasquino" also traded insults with another statue, "Marforio" in the courtyard of the Palazzo Nuovo. The statue of the water porter in the Facchino Fountain on the Via Lata spoke for everyday people, while the women used the impressive figure of Madame Lucrezia near the Palallo Venezia to gossip and complain. The "Babuino" (baboon) statue above a fountain near the Spanish Steps tells crude jokes, and the elegant "Luigi Abata" statue near the Sant'Andrea della Valle uses satire to get his point across. "Quod non fecerunt Barbari fecerunt Barberini." "What the Barbarians did not do the Barberini did." This "statuesque" correspondence has possibilities; think of the statue of Abraham Lincoln at the Capitol writing mash notes to the Statue of Liberty, or the Borglum bronze of the legendary Buckey O'Neill, captain of the Arizona Rough Riders in my home town, writing a list of suggestions to the city council, or all of the presidents carved on Mt. Rushmore sending suggestions to the White House. The mind boggles.

The "witty ones" are only one tiny bit of a huge, ancient and complex city. But if there is only a short amount of time to sightsee, it is much better to explore just a small area and do it well. The statues give personality and character to the city, and it is a fun way to spend an afternoon.

Modern History, Montecassino

I was on the road from Naples, heading north towards Rome. I had been to Pompeii and Herculaneum, to Tiberius's villa on Capri and the ruins near Sorrento. There is enough ancient history in Italy to satisfy the most ardent scholar, and I was a happy camper. On the mountaintop ahead, however, there was much more recent history to study. The history of Europe is not usually determined by calm decisions and wise agreements. Instead petty disputes and regional jealousies, rivalry, pride and greed lead to blood and brutality. What is most remarkable is that from this evil may come a heightened sense of goodness, from this destruction may come a stronger knowledge of beauty.

About 50 miles south of Rome is the city of Cassino. On the top of the dominant hill overlooking the city, the Abbey of Montecassino stands in the warm Italian sun and the spotlight

of history. Originally there was a Roman fortification built on the mountain along with a temple to Apollo in a nearby holy grove. Then in 529 A.D. Benedict and his monks moved to Montecassino and began the work of founding a monastery which became the Abbey. Great and imposing, it was one of the most influential religious and cultural institutions of the Middle Ages and was famous for its learned collections of manuscripts, frescoes and mosaics. Its monks went out all over Christendom to spread the gospel.

The Courtyard of the
Abbey of Montecassino

Standing on the top of the mountain, the first thing you notice is the excellent view of the surrounding valley. It's quite obvious that whoever controls that hill controls the Liri Valley and the road to Rome. Now, if I would notice that, you've got to be sure everyone else would too. It's another "popularity via location" issue. In 577 A.D. the monastery was destroyed by the Lombards. It was rebuilt in the 8th century. In 883 A.D. the Saracens invaded and attacked the Abbey. It was rebuilt in the 10th century. And in 1349 A.D. Mother Nature took a turn and an earthquake destroyed it. It was rebuilt again. Through all the centuries, it was looked upon as a glorious place of holiness and culture until the Germans took the high ground in the last days of World War II.

The area around the Abbey was used as an artillery observation post, a key German defensive hub in the Nazi effort to block the Allied advance on Rome. The Allied generals, believing that the hilltop housed German positions, decided that their men's lives were worth a great deal more than ancient buildings, and on February 15, 1944, Allied aircraft bombed the Abbey. In three hours, the 1,400-year-old monastery was reduced to rubble. When I was there, our guide was an elderly local man, Antonio Scolari, who had been a teenager during the war. "There was nothing standing," he said, "not even a statue. There was so much damage the

Americans needed bulldozers just to get up there. I thought it was all gone forever." He had told the story so many times that the shock was dulled by time, but even 50 years later knowing that something so ancient, solid and sacred to God had been destroyed was painful.

The monastery became an abbey, the Abbey a palace, the palace a fortress. It has known honors and burdens and been put to the sword. More than 1000 Polish soldiers who lost their lives storming the burnt-out Abbey are buried there in the War Cemetery. A white marble obelisk stands in their memory with an inscription. "We Polish soldiers, have given our bodies to Italy, our hearts to Poland and our souls to God for our own freedom and for the freedom of others."

After the war, the Italian government began the seemingly impossible task of rebuilding Montecassino as it had been in the 16th century. A guidebook tells about the bronze doors first cast in 1066 that were recovered, restored and put back into place. The archives and library were rescued, and the abbey's decorative detail was replaced. Antonio told us, "It took a few hours to destroy, but it will take many years and many lives to rebuild it." Some of the walls are still only debris and rubble. Mr. Scolari says, "They are waiting for the right painter to be born."

Montenegro, Simply Breathtaking

Kotor, the Fisherman's Story

Let me tell you the story as it was told to me.

Now fishing's not an easy job. First, you've got the sea and the waves and the wet. There's the boat that's too old and too leaky, and then there's the fish, starving when there's none and smelly when the catch is good. And once you're ashore, there's the old wife to deal with and the kids always underfoot.

So when such a fisherman found a painting of the Virgin and Child washed up on a sea rock in the middle of Kotor Fjord, of course he took it for all the luck he could.

Now whether he noticed when he was fishing or not, but the Gulf of Kotor is one of the most spectacular landscapes of the Adriatic Sea, where rugged mountains meet calm waters in the long, deepwater fjords. The land has known Greeks, Romans, Byzantines, Normans, Venetians, Turks, Serbs and Slavs. But beyond the picturesque coves and azure waters and into the black mountains, lies a land of fierce tribal warfare. There are bandits in the mountains and pirates in

Chapel of Our Lady of the Rocks

the seas. A man needs faith and a little bit of luck to guard himself and his family. So it's no wonder that if a fellow finds a painting of the Madonna and Child on his way home, that he just might take this as a very fortunate event.

Already there was a bit of an island there called Sveti Djordje or the "Island of St. George." It is also called "the island of the dead captains," because according to legend, a French soldier, shooting a cannon towards the mainland, hit the house of his sweetheart and killed her. (One would think "the island of dead girlfriends" would have been more appropriate.) On this island, there is a Benedictine monastery from the 12th century and an ancient graveyard for sailors.

But a special spot was needed to give a home to this sacred icon, so when our fisherman found it in the 15th century, local people began to build their own man-made island. Whenever a sailor or a fisherman came home safely, he dropped a stone in the spot. And over the centuries, the rocks dropped by these seamen formed an island. They used the hulls of scuttled ships and then boatload after boatload of stones. By 1630 there was enough of a rocky perch in the Bay to hold a small votive chapel, and 100 years later the islet was large enough to build a small baroque church, *Gospa od Skrpjela* or "Our Lady of the Rocks."

On the mainland there are a myriad of lovely and elaborate churches built by wealthy men, while this little spot with its small chapel was created by ordinary people. There are stone benches in front of the church, a "place of reconciliation" where a man could work out arguments with his neighbors in the shade of the sanctuary and avoid the Venetian courts. To maintain the island, every year at sunset on July 22, the *fašinada* or "scattering stones" still takes place, when locals take their brightly decorated boats out to throw rocks into the sea to add to the tiny island, and with music and folk-singing keep the fisherman's promise.

I sailed around these islands once. I want to go back again. Kotor is a delightful, walled medieval city with winding streets, squares and markets just perfect for exploring. Although not as famous or large or polished as neighboring Dubrovnik, it is an easy spot to linger. Built of the local granite, there are labyrinths of winding streets with sudden flights of steps and arches covered in vines with bright red flowers. There is the ancient cathedral, St. Tryphon's to explore, sidewalk cafes for sipping coffee and innumerable cats to meet. With the rugged, jagged mountain peaks behind it, the churches and cathedrals, palaces, and museums, and the multitude of narrow streets, squares, elegant boutiques and local markets, Kotor is a marvelous place to meander.

I want to go back and climb the thousand stairs up the stony mountain to where the 600-year-old city wall rings its way around the city. I want to smile and nod to shepherds on the mountainside, its slopes filled with yellow, white, blue and purple wildflowers. I want to watch fishermen pole skiffs down narrow channels to the gleaming waters framed by mountains, blue and violet.

As we sailed away past the little town of Perast, (Peter the Great sent young nobles to attend their Naval School and learn the tactics of the Adriatic pirates – such are the rewards of fame), people waved from shore, and some stood in their open windows waving white sheets in farewell. I want to go back, wave "hello" and stay for a while.

Norway, Land of more than the Midnight Sun

Treasures of the Vikings

Can you imagine being a poor, illiterate peasant farmer, living in a hut in a small village on the northern coast of England, never having been more than ten miles from home your entire life - and all of a sudden, several of these ships show up one foggy morning? What could you have done but drop down on your knees and pray, "From the fury of the Northmen deliver us, O Lord."

Isn't this a fabulous ship? As you can see, the romance of the sea is not a recent development. This photo was taken at the Viking Ship Museum in Bygdøy, Oslo, and the story of this ship is a tale of romance and plunder, hidden treasure, determination, and of course, adventure on the high seas.

The Viking Museum is one of two buildings that make up the Museum of Cultural History. (In the same area of Bygdøy are also the *Kon-Tiki* Museum, the Norwegian Maritime Museum, and Roald Amundsen's ship, the *Fram*. So if you are a maritime buff, this is the place to head.) In the museum are grave goods from Tune, Gokstad, Oseberg, and Borre. This photo is of the Oseberg

The Oseberg Longship, a Viking ship built in the 9th century

Ship, which was excavated from a Viking burial mound on the Oslo Fjord in 1904. Found with the prow pointing toward the sea, the ship was reassembled and gently moved to a museum built especially for it. Piece by piece, rivet by rivet, for 21 years conservators put the puzzle back together. Now she is as elegant and full of grace as she was 1,200 years ago when the Vikings sailed the seas.

This longship was built around 815-20 A.D. and became the burial ship for an older woman of the high aristocracy who died in the middle of the 9th century. Next to her were placed the remains of a younger woman as well as valuable possessions. Laid in blue clay on a turf-built mound, the ship and its contents are beautifully preserved. Wood, leather, silk and wool all survive to tell us a little of what life was like so long ago.

While the barrow was plundered in ancient times and thieves stole the jewelry, gold and silver that would have been buried there, the tremendously rich grave goods that remain are actually a greater treasure. There are three intricately carved sleds, an ornately carved four-wheel wooden cart, a leather saddle, battle axes, the skeletons of ten horses and two oxen, tents, bed frames, beautiful weavings and wood carvings The full set of 30 oars is there, as well as a mast and rudder, all ready to go sailing again.

Who were they? Romantics like to believe that the older woman may be Queen Åsa Haraldsdtr, mother to King Halfdan the Black and grandmother to King Haraldr Fairhair. She was abducted by Gudrod the Magnificent (love the names, wish we still did that) and forced to marry him. According to legend, she had him murdered as he lay in a drunken stupor and assumed the throne until her death.

Remains of the two women were first exhumed during the original ship excavation and later reburied waiting for better scientific techniques. Fearing that the remains might be disintegrating, the graves were reopened in 2007 and the bones taken back to the Museum for more study. While a genetic profile could not be recovered from the older woman, a DNA sample of the younger indicates that her family may have come from the Black Sea. Okay, that is very fun. A young Persian slave buried with an old Viking queen. That is the stuff that bad movies are made of.

I know that some folks aren't too fond of museums; they think they are boring and full of old stuff. But if you go to Oslo, visit the Viking Ship Museum and remember that a queen was buried on that beautiful ship. She was interred with magic, ritual and sorcery and surrounded by the goods that would accompany her to Valhalla, or wherever good Viking ladies went. Circled by riches of silk and jewels, she may have been accompanied by an unwilling Persian slave girl. That notion should spice up your visit.   And then there are the curious points: Was the ship buried with stones in order to keep the lady in her grave? Why was a small leather pouch of hemp seeds buried with her? Do we have this the wrong way 'round and was it a young exotic princess buried with an older attendant?

A final confession. Although I know that these "traveling farmers" were marauders, destroyers of peaceful towns and churches, despoilers of innocent maidens, when I see a ship like this I remember the musical score from the movie, *The Vikings,* starring a marvelous, scarred Kirk Douglas and a too-pretty Tony Curtis. Do you remember the movie? The opening theme goes, "Ta DAAA da, Ta DAAA da, Tum te tum te tum te tum te TUM!" The music is strong and heroic and makes you want to boldly go where no man has gone before, to strike out through unknown and dangerous waters on a great journey. There is "poetry of sailing as old as the world." This ship embodies that longing.

A monk from a French monastery tried to describe these "towered ships." "When at length they were all gathered, they went on board the towered ships...On one side lions molded in gold were to be seen on the ships, on the other birds on the tops of the masts indicated by their movements the winds as they blew, or dragons of various kinds poured fire from their nostrils...But why should I now dwell upon the sides of the ships, which were not only painted with ornate colors but were covered with gold and silver figures?...The blue water, smitten by many oars, might be seen foaming far and wide, and the sunlight, cast back in the gleam of metal, spread a double radiance in the air."

The Vikings' bravery, their skill, their adventuresome spirit "to strive, to seek, to find, and not to yield," should be admired and cherished. These qualities are all splendid, as long as you weren't one of those frightened peasants watching them sail toward your little village.

And the path just kept going on and on

Portugal, Land of Discoveries

"Getting lost is just another way of saying 'going exploring'."
Justina Chen Headley

Getting Lost in Bucaco Forest and Not Minding a Bit

I'm going to call it the "Hansel & Gretel Syndrome." I am walking alone in a foreign wood. I'm not worried because it's a perfectly nice forest and I know where the lodge is; I can see the sun and I know which direction is north. Besides, I'm tough; I'm from Arizona; I'm used to hiking in the woods. But not these woods (major, arrogant error). This is not an Arizona forest where God, the rainfall and the elevation dictate the growth. Instead, imagine trees that are older than time, a primordial forest with trees as tall as cathedrals that has been growing and developing for a thousand years, a forest that has been nurtured and cultivated for centuries, a forest that has its own dark soul, a Portuguese Fanghorn Forest.

Bucaco Forest was already old in the 6th century when Benedictine monks built a hermitage there among the immense oaks, cypress and cork trees. Located north of Lisbon, Portugal, it was guarded, gardened and preserved by the priests of nearby Coimbra Cathedral for 600 years, and by the Discalced Carmelites, a hermetic order of barefoot monks, for 200 years more. Obviously not willing to share the woods, the monks built a monastery and surrounded the entire 250-acre forest with a wall. Over the centuries, the monks and the government foresters who succeeded them, have planted nearly 400 Portuguese varieties of trees, shrubs and flowers while importing hundreds more from all over the world.

I stayed at the king's 19th century hunting lodge, which was built for the Portuguese royal family by an Italian operatic scene painter and architect, and looks it. Fortunately it is now accepting more common guests. I only had one night there, so I got up early the next morning before the sun rose, threw my clothes on, grabbed an apple and was outside at first light. I knew we were leaving early and I wanted a little time to explore this marvel.

I have no words to describe the forest well enough to you. I cannot do it justice. Imagine for yourself having 800 uninterrupted years to cultivate 250 acres of dense woods and hills with a labor force of men devoted only to God and the trees. (It was protected by a 17th century Papal decree that threatened to ex-communicate anyone who damaged it, as well as another Papal edict during the same era, which declared that women entering the forest would be cursed.)

Do you remember the stories your grandfather read to you when you were small? About the little boy and girl who walked through a gate at the bottom of the garden and found a magic land? That's what this walk was like; it was enchanted. With the mist still on the ground, surrounded by towering trees, there were paths down the slopes and little bridges across the creeks. There were open meadows where the sunlight caught silver in the dewdrops of the grass. There were mossy stone benches placed just where a meanderer might sit to eat her apple. And in this vast and quiet place, everywhere there was the loving hand of man.

There was a spring that came out of a hillside into a large, old stone catch basin; from there it spilled down in a waterfall to a pool and then cascaded between massive stone steps down the hill. At the bottom of the water steps, the waterfall became a small, quiet lake surrounded by blue hydrangeas and pink magnolias. In the lake, black swans swam toward me, assuming I would leave a little bit of my apple for their breakfast.

It was a whole new world and I got blissfully lost. My watch went unnoticed and my schedule ignored, as I wandered up and down hill, past chapel and path, lake and stream and the giant, beloved trees. It was so lovely that I almost forgave the monks for not originally planning to let me in. And yes, my friends held the car for me, but I bought everyone wine that evening as an apology for making them wait.

In his elegant and erudite little book, *The Art of Travel,* Alain de Botton writes that the reason we love to travel is to see ourselves more clearly. "It is not necessarily at home that we best encounter our true selves." De Botton reminds us. "The domestic setting keeps us tethered to the person we are in ordinary life, who may not be who we essentially are."

In other words, getting lost may be the best way to find yourself. Push yourself out of the comfort zone and go traveling. I promise, it will be the best gift you could ever give yourself.

Meandering in Lisbon

The cobblestones under my feet were rough, uneven and old. The closed walls on either side of the narrow, winding street reached up to block any view. The shadowed maze of lanes twisted off in several directions. The doors were closed, the windows shut, and I was alone in the man-made canyons of the Alfama.

This is the oldest part of the city of Lisbon, a warren of narrow winding streets that date back nearly a millennium to when the Moors ruled the Iberian Peninsula. This area was the old souk, and its tell-tale maze of streets is filled with colorful tiles, flower-covered balconies, wonderfully historic shops and marvelous restaurants. I was exploring the old quarter with friends and a guide, and as the group turned left onto a lane, a rooster flew directly in front of me and turned right. The rooster is the symbol of Portugal, and a possible photo of the bird, the tiles and the flowers in the Alfama was too much to pass up. So I turned right too.

That elusive Portuguese rooster

I followed that silly bird for a block or two, waiting for it to be picturesque, and it finally settled long enough for me to get a camera on it. I wasn't crazy about the car it chose to perch on, but I couldn't afford to get picky. And then I realized I had done it again, I had misplaced myself. I wasn't too worried though; it was sunny weather; I had my credit cards and I can say, "Please" and "Thank-you" in Portuguese.

So I turned back the way I had come, sort of. Then I veered in the direction the group had gone, sort of, and began to walk downhill through the web of twisting, cobblestone streets. The city of Lisbon is built beside the Tagus River, and I knew that along the river there would be taxis. But I didn't need to go that far. As I passed an open window above me, an old lady dressed in black looked out and smiled. Obviously a lost tourist was nothing new. She waived her hand to keep going down the lane and then turn left. I followed her hand signals and arrived at the large fountain which stands at the entrance to the Alfama. There were my friends beginning lunch at an outdoor café, and accompanied by teasing, I sat down and had fresh sardines grilled at the table with olive oil-drizzled, crusty bread and bought the wine again. The rooster didn't join us.

Singapore, the Lion City

Hunting for Mr. Greenstreet

Once I think I just might have seen, perhaps, the last little bit of Sydney Greenstreet's huge, dirty white blazer as he disappeared behind a potted palm. Now the skeptics among you might think this is a little difficult, as Mr. Greenstreet died a good many years ago. But Raffles Hotel in Singapore is that kind of place.

It was a balmy spring evening and I was sitting in a peacock chair with an after-dinner aperitif on the veranda of one of the world's most historic and treasured hotels. Dinner was salmon and lemon soufflé served by white-coated waiters who didn't realize that the British Empire had left. Twilight had come and gone as we lingered over dinner, and I was in one of those beatific moods that only an excellent meal, good company and superb service can provide.

Raffles Hotel is full of legends. The original hotel was built in 1887 by four Armenian brothers, the Sarkies, who named the property for Sir Stamford Raffles, the founder of modern Singapore. The classical buildings are set in extensive tropical gardens and feature high molded ceilings, polished teak, gleaming marble floors, exotic oriental carpets, circling ceiling fans and offer all the ambience you could wish for in a grand hotel.

All the great and the grand visiting the Orient stayed there - Joseph Conrad, Rudyard Kipling, Somerset Maugham, Noel Coward, Ernest Hemingway. History has it that guests had at their disposal luxuries as varied as a post office, a theater, and for one particular gentleman, a dark room. The restaurants alone are worth the jet lag - the Raffles Grill, the Tiffin Room, the Raffles Courtyard, and especially the Long Bar where the Singapore Sling was created, and more cigars smoked and more lies told than anywhere else in the world. Imagine sitting at the Long Bar between the World Wars. What stories you would have heard! (There is an unsubstantiated tale that when the Japanese invaded in 1942, they found the guests of the Raffles Hotel dancing one last waltz.)

When you can tear yourself away from the hotel, the city of Singapore will be waiting for you. Singapore is a unique spot, where the flavor of the East is blended with the comfort and efficiency of the West. While it is no longer the legendary city of rickshaws and opium dens, pearl smugglers and pirates, you can still have a gin sling at the Mountbatten Club or dinner at a renovated quay along the Singapore River where merchant ships once docked. And amazingly, in the center of the mysterious Orient, the British Club still has a full green cricket lawn.

There is another thing you can look for in Singapore, the Lion City, but will never see. There are no lions. Never have been any lions, probably won't be any showing up any time soon. But there is a Malay legend to hold on to. A visiting Sumatran prince in the 11th century saw a fearsome creature and called it a lion. Deciding it was a good omen, he founded the city as a minor trading post for his empire, naming the settlement *Singa* the Sanskrit word for "lion" and *Pura,* the word for "city" and used the new name as heroic advertising for his new city. Oh those sneaky Sumatrans.

There's shopping...

And more shopping...

And pedicab rides to Raffles Hotel

As with many great cities, it was location and trade that built the town. Ambitious entrepreneurs between India and China stopped by, as well as the Sumatrans, the Malaccans, the Portuguese, the Dutch and the British. Trade is definitely a wonderful encouragement for growth.

The city exploded in 1819, when Sir Stamford Raffles and the British East Indian Company came hunting for a deep-water port in a good location to use as the British base in the area. Raffles "reestablished" a local sultan who in return awarded Britain the right to set up a trading port. The free port became the hub of the busy trade route from China to India, and within three years, the obscure Malayan jungle village of 1,000 became a boomtown of 10,000. Starting from scratch, a modern city was built. Roads, schools, hospitals, a military and naval base with British law were all established. And immigrants and fortune seekers from Europe, China, India and Arabia, all attracted by the tariff-free port, poured in.

Trying to minimize racial tension, Raffles allotted sections of the city to different immigrant groups. Therefore it is possible to spend several days in the city and see a smorgasbord of Asia. All of the great Asian cultures are represented, so that in just one city you can sample little bits of the entire continent.

In the crowded streets of Chinatown, you can find fortune-tellers, calligraphers and little gray-haired men gingerly taking their birds out for a walk. Ignoring the lessons learned in Busaco Forest, I went out for a meander in the early morning hours. Stores selling incense, interesting Chinese medicines and bamboo gifts for the funeral pyres (also interesting), little ladies on their way to worship at the Thian Hock Keng Temple or bartering for ginger root and Chinese herbs, letter writers, open air markets (pressed duck anyone?), and take-away restaurants, all crowded together in the streets.

In little India, there are silks and spices in the shops and a temple to Kali the Courageous. You can smell curry powder and perfume and hear the shrill notes of Indian music. Shops sell gold and garlands of flowers, an interesting mingling of the enduring and the ephemeral.

On Arab Street, there are antiques for sale and the call of the imam can be heard from the Sultan Mosque. People gossip in doorways and small closet-size shops are crammed with silks, batiks and rattan.

A cab ride to the top of Fortuna Peak will give you the chance to ride a funicular (aerial tram) across the water to Sentosa Island. The Island contains hotels, an amusement park, restaurants, an excellent aquarium, a very strange "Boulder Museum," and an especially memorable museum dedicated to the history of the city. Life-sized dioramas and wax figures tell the entire story of Singapore, but it is the area devoted to World War II that is the most heart-rending. Surprised by a Japanese land invasion, the city surrendered quickly and many of the Europeans were herded first to the open fields of the Padang Cricket Ground and then on to Changi Prison, the most notorious prison camp in Asia. With photographs and in recorded messages on wall-phones, the survivors tell their own grim stories of those horrible years.

Spend a few days in Singapore and feel the warm breeze waft over the quay as you take a water taxi. Visit the Merlion, the city's symbol that guards the entrance to the Singapore River. Bend an elbow at Harry's Bar, a haunt of rogue trader, Nick Leeson. There's a jazz club upstairs, still crowded with bankers and brokers with ties undone and a gleam in their eye. The ancient opium traders and pearl smugglers may be gone, but there are still pirates in the city. Did I see Mr. Greenstreet? Probably not. But there was a glimpse of large, fat man expansively mopping his brow and just a whiff of cheap cigar smoke lingering in the corner of the lobby. Singapore is that kind of city.

Frenzied fans at a soccer game

Spain, Fierce and Beautiful

"De sangre y oro es nuestra bandera. No hay oro para comprarla, ni sangre para vencerla."

("Of blood and gold is our flag. There is no gold that can buy it, no blood that can conquer it.")

Viva Bilbao!

I have the same problem with soccer that I do with football. Although I have sat courteously through innumerable games, trying not to ask questions in the middle of a play, to cheer politely at appropriate times and to speak only when there is a time-out or a commercial, I really don't have a clue what is going on. But one evening in Madrid I had one of the most marvelous nights of my whole life and it was because of a soccer game.

Spain is one of those "onion" countries where you just keep peeling back one extraordinary layer after another. After spending two weeks in the country stopping in small towns and chatting with courteous, gregarious people, I thought Madrid was formal and pretentious. We made the requisite pilgrimage to the Prado, strolled the shopping boulevards looking for black pearls, bought antique prints and Sherry wine. It was all predictable and scripted. The only spontaneous thing that happened was when I stopped the cab and ran across three lanes of traffic to a soda stand near the Ritz. They were selling Tab Diet Cola, and I hadn't seen any since I had left home.

Madrid was very grand but very stolid and urban. Then we went to a soccer match. The concierge at the hotel had a brother who had a friend who knew the assistant manager of the visiting soccer team, and somehow they got us tickets. Football (soccer) holds a special place in the hearts of the Spanish people and fanaticism reaches a frenzied height during the champion-ship games. We were lucky enough to see the game between Madrid and Bilbao (a smaller city in northern Spain). Apparently all the residents of Bilbao had closed their stores and their houses and piled on trains to Madrid so that they could live and die with their team. I really don't know exactly what happened during the game; just watching the stands was entertain-ment enough.

It was an explosion of noise, smoke bombs and flag-waving with thousands of people on their feet yelling, crying, cursing and cheering. The soccer match was more about energy than the game itself. It felt like being in the middle of the French Revolution or at the Coliseum in Rome when a lion ate a gladiator. We were in a section near the fans from Bilbao who had to be the rowdiest folks I have ever seen, and I learned some choice Spanish phrases, none of which I can ever repeat. It was fabulous.

Bilbao, the underdog, won. And there was much jubilation.

Later that evening we went to dinner at the Restaurante Botin, just off the Plaza Mayor, which claims to be the oldest restaurant in the world. The restaurant was dark and glowing; paintings decorated the walls; the open kitchen had hanging copper pots and 18th century tiles lined the counter. It was a favorite haunt of Ernest Hemingway who raved about their suckling pig. Even by Madrid's standards we were there late and just as we were getting up to leave, the Bilbao fans we had met came into the restaurant.

They were none the worse for the evening's celebration, and when we saw them, someone at my table yelled, "Viva Bilbao!" That made us dear friends and drinking companions for the rest of the evening. We left the restaurant wearing gifts of scarves with the Bilbao colors and pledges of eternal friendship.

I love museums and archaeological sites and rubble, but absorbing a place through your senses, the way it tastes and smells and feels, is what truly makes a country come alive. People often make a checklist of things they have to see while touring and in doing so often miss the real identity of the area. When you travel, be sure to look for the soul of the country, for the passion that drives her people.

Viva Bilbao!

Thailand, the Land of Smiles

Treasure of the Golden Buddha

Being raised in Nebraska, that sane and stable center of the country, gave me a hankering for the exotic, a craving for the unusual, a yearning to see what was on the other side of the corn-fields. Thailand was one of those spots where I had no doubt that I was a long way from the barn. During one visit, I rode an elephant, was encircled by an affectionate python, tiptoed through gilded temples, ate a sultry dinner by candlelight while sailing along a Bangkok khlong, had a two-hour massage and sauntered through local markets where the offerings included silks, silver and live frogs.

Visit Thailand and you will begin to understand the word "exotic." Go north to Chiang Mai and you will see strange and unfamiliar country, as dragon stairways on misty mountains lead to curious temples and saffron-clad monks. Everywhere people greet you with a shy smile and the delicate, graceful hand-clasped bow called a *wai*. (There's a whole branch of wai-ing etiquette, three different types of bows, who to wai, who to be waied by.)

Visit Bangkok and you'll be overwhelmed by the gleaming sky-scrapers, the noisy but speedy tuk-tuks (rickshaws with motors), the crowds of city-dwellers and the many tourists. Surprisingly Bangkok is not all that old. While one of the world's first Bronze Age cultures began in Issan in the northeast part of the country about 4,000 years ago, Bangkok, the "Village of Wild Plums," doesn't have much of a history behind it. It was only established in 1782 by the first king of the current ruling house. Never conquered by imperialistic Europe, Bangkok has an unfamiliar structure. There is no central square, no Roman grid; the city just meanders, following the rivers and the canals in a sort of Asian time warp.

The Golden Buddha of Wat Traimit

There are saffron-robed monks with cell phones, traffic noisily rushing by serene golden-leafed Buddhas, teakwood houses with elaborately carved spirit houses standing near 21st century office buildings.

Bangkok is also a city of temples; more than 400 Buddhist temples are sprinkled all over the city. Peaceful sanctuaries in the middle of the city's rush, they are full of calm, incense and legend. Let me tell you one story as it was told to me.

Many centuries ago, a wealthy king of Siam wished to demonstrate both his riches and his piety. And so he gave the monks of a great monastery an immense statue of the Buddha, ten feet tall, weighing five tons and carved of solid gold. The statue gleamed with such richness and purity that even unbelievers were inspired by its strength and power. The monks treasured the gift, and for many years it was the center of the temple and the object of deep devotion.

But great riches bring great peril, and when enemies invaded the country, the high priest feared for the safety of the precious statue. Choosing only a few discreet monks to aid him, they hid the image in an old cellar in an unused part of the temple complex. Not only did they

136

hide the golden idol, they also covered it with plaster so that it looked old, unused and unwanted. When the invading armies came, the temple was destroyed; the priests fled or were killed and the secret of the treasure was lost.

Centuries later, a poor Buddhist sect in Bangkok needed a statue of the Buddha for their small temple, but could not afford to buy one. One of their monks came from a small jungle village in the north and remembered playing as a child in an abandoned temple complex where a huge, rough plaster statue stood. So the monks took a large cart and oxen and traveled the long way north. Finding the ruins in the jungle and the abandoned image, they loaded it onto the cart and began the trek home.

Just outside of Bangkok, a fearful storm began. The pilgrims took shelter, leaving the statue in the cart on the road. Suddenly there was a terrific clap of thunder and an enormous bolt of lightning struck the image. The thunderbolt sheared off a large piece of the plaster covering, revealing the solid gold underneath. Awed and terrified, the monks crept out of their shelter to realize that they were bringing home to their little temple, not a shabby, dusty statue, but one of pure gold.

Is this story true? Perhaps. My host, a well-dressed old Thai gentleman, who leaned across the dining table at the Oriental Hotel and whispered it to me, certainly believed it was. Does it matter? Not really. Treasure lost in the jungle, golden idols, virtues rewarded are the stuff of legends and myths. And all an excellent reason to go traveling.

The Temple of the Emerald Buddha

The name change from Siam to Thailand occurred in 1939 when Field Marshal Phibun Songkram and the Thai military government decided that the switch was logical since the correction now represented the country's majority and was popular with the people. I'm not sure the people were actually consulted.

I represent a one-woman movement to change the name back to the original "Siam." The restoration would be logical on many levels. It would be historical significant as Siam has been the name of the kingdom for almost 800 years. It would be culturally appropriate as there are many more ethic groups living in the Kingdom than just the Thais. And most importantly, it would sound prettier.

And in my quest for all things far away, romantic and unobtainable, I spent a whole day in the Grand Palace Complex and the Temple of the Emerald Buddha searching for Yul Brynner. I am sure I just didn't look behind the right stupa.

I hunted and hunted, but no luck at all.

Still, it was a great excuse to be there.

The fabled Blue Mosque of Istanbul

Turkey, Exotic and Fascinating

Anatolia, Asia Minor, Lycia, Pontus, the land we now call Turkey, is a little like the Grand Canyon – and seems almost as old. Each level has a different history; every stratum represents a different epoch. Starting from the beginning, or nearly so, was the world's first known settlement, a Neolithic city which dates back to 6,500 B.C. This was followed by Assyrians, Akkadians, Hittites, Assyrians, Urartians, Lydians, Persians, Greeks, Pontusians (are you keeping track?), Romans, Goths, Byzantines, Arabs, Ottomans and finally in 1923, the Republic of Turkey.

Turkey is the land bridge (if you can call such an enormous country a bridge) between East and West. It is the route through which all the goods of the Orient and of Europe passed, the silks, spices, porcelain, jewels and slaves. Then the knowledge, the art, the religion and all the other non-material items that were carried along with the merchants were shared as well. Look for an interesting mythological or historical figure and he might have been there. Achilles, Herodotus, Alexander, Cleopatra and her Antony, St. Paul and St. John were all drawn to this crossroads between East and West.

And for each culture there are different languages, art, architecture, history, etc. Combine that with courteous people, terrific weather, marvelous food, a fabulous coast line, darling children and 3,000 year-old ruins, and Turkey is practically perfect. (Except for the eggplant.)

Now a confession. I don't know about you, but when I was introduced to world history the basic flow was Greece, Rome, Barbarian hordes, Dark Ages, Crusades, Renaissance, Reformation, Enlightenment and so on. Au contraire, Rome did not fall, it just moved. Somehow my Euro-centered, Anglophile history and literature lessons glossed over Constantinople, if they mentioned it at all. Basically the short form is that Constantine, the emperor of Rome, moved the capital there in 330 A.D. And until it fell to the Ottomans in 1453, it was the grandest city in the Western World. So, you've got the Byzantine Empire and its capital city of Constantinople, with its labyrinth of power and luxury, that metamorphosed into Istanbul with the Ottomans in control. And no matter the name, some things did not change at all. The exploration and creativity, the wealth and power, the skullduggery and tricky dealings were all still there.

And somehow we think it was the Dark Ages.

A short word about Byzantium, Constantinople, Istanbul. This city comes up a great deal when talking about Turkey, and it should, as it has stood at the crossroads of Europe and Asia for the last 1350 years. In the center of the city, near the magnificent Hagia Sophia, is a monument called "The Milion." The "Golden Milestone" was the beginning of distance measurements to all the major cities of the Byzantine Empire.

I suspect, however, that the residents took it for granted. They were already sure that they lived in the center of the civilized world and didn't really need to see how far away any other cities were.

Incredibly old and incredibly beautiful, Hagia Sophia

A golden mosaic of Christ Pantocrator, the Ruler of All

The Last Mass at Hagia Sophia

The heart of Constantinople is Hagia Sophia, the Church of the Divine Wisdom. The Basilica is too old, too complex and too vast to photograph or attempt to describe. So I'm going to tell you just one small story from its 1,500-year history.

Walking into Hagia Sophia in Istanbul is like entering St. Peter's in Rome, Chartres in the north of France or Seti's tomb in the Valley of the Kings. One is struck by immense silence, huge cold space and over-whelming age. Vast and mysterious, these places demand humility and a sense of wonder. The legend of the last church service at Hagia Sophia is a story of despair and hopelessness that was conquered by courage and faith, reminding us of the strength and nobility of the human spirit.

During its 1,000 years as a Christian house of worship, only the Emperor was allowed to use the Imperial Gate, the great bronze doors at the main entrance of the Cathedral. God's "Regent on Earth" prostrated himself before crossing the marble threshold, while in a mighty mosaic over the Imperial Door, Christ Pantocrator, the Ruler of All, looked down at his chosen repre-sentative. Using tiny bits of glass, some ancient artistic genius portrayed the strength, pity and love of Holy Wisdom as his worshippers entered Hagia Sophia.

A pilgrim would enter the Church through one of four side doors. Stepping down on the marble threshold's single, shallow step, worn in the center by a millennium of devout footsteps, what he would see is light. The great dome curves upward and daylight comes in through hundreds of windows as immense piers support the Basilica. The walls are left open for the sunlight which reflects from marble and jewels, gold and silver so that the entire interior of the Church is glowing. I'm sure that during its construction, someone said, "Let there be Light." And there was.

The walls are of veined marble, and the vaulted ceiling is covered with mosaics. Far ahead and far above are semi-domes, one with a golden mosaic of the Madonna and Child and floating far above that is the great dome of the Basilica. A 6th century historian wrote that it "does not appear to rest upon a solid foundation, but to cover the place beneath as though it were suspended from heaven by the fabled golden chain."

Because I am of a practical turn of mind, I am always interested in the logistics. This building which was designed by two Greeks, one a physicist and the other a mathematician, is incredibly complex and complicated. This ultimate symbol of power and faith, which combines both science and art, stands in one of the most deadly earthquake zones on earth. The church sits on top of a massive fault but while everything else has gone to rubble, Hagia Sophia is still there. The engineering innovations which allowed the construction of the largest dome in the world are a marvel of creative genius.

Then there is the question of what sort of society would support the amount of time, energy and money that such a massive undertaking would require. I am always amazed at the quantity and quality of faith that holy places represent, the prayers that have gone up during their construction. Faith really does move mountains.

The history of Hagia Sophia is both rich and violent. The Byzantine Empire that created her stood at the geographical and culture center of the European and Middle-Eastern world for more than 1000 years. Constantinople was the "Queen of Cities," overawing visitors from other lands with her wealth and culture. The City's focal point, the great church of Hagia Sophia, was built between 532 and 537 A.D. The Emperor Justinian enlisted 10,000 workers, and from the four corners of the empire he brought gold and silver treasures, icons and ornaments. Forty thousand pounds of silver encrusted the sanctuary. Ancient temples in Egypt, Syria, Rome and Ephesus sent their finest possessions. It surpassed all other churches in size, beauty and riches and became the light of Christianity in the East.

Although the center of the Greek Orthodox Church, the city was also a hotbed of religious controversy and dissension, discord and conflict. Quarrels erupted over coffee in the morning, over ayran at lunch in the cafes, over wine in the evening. Violence flared and hate filled the air over inconsequential doctrinal matters and differences in ritual or phrase. Was the trinity 3 in 1, or 1 in 3? Christ's humanity or Christ's divinity? Just how many angels could dance on the head of a pin? For centuries disruptions, disagreements and disputations were the norm.

The awe-inspiring interior of the Church of Divine Wisdom

A small, overwhelmed tourist

Then in 1453 Mehmet the Conqueror, who wished to capture the "Pearl of his Dreams," attacked the grand and glorious city. Through the centuries, Constantinople with its massive walls had withstood every assault, but this time its people faced starvation and exhaustion and knew the end was coming. Shortly before dawn on May 29, Ottoman cannons made huge holes in the triple walls, and the Janissaries poured through to destroy the city.

During the last days of the attack, realizing that they were doomed, the contentious men who had argued so violently over religious trifles came together for one last Christian service in the sacred heart of the city, Hagia Sophia. Forgotten in the greater peril were the unimportant doctrinal differences. On the night before the city's fall, the sophist and the cynic, the deeply religious and the vaguely agnostic, were all drawn into the magnificent depths of the mighty cathedral to pray. United in danger where they had been divided in peace, there were a few moments of true charity.

Imagine the immense church lit by candlelight and the incense rising to the dome, the light playing on the gold and silver and the air filled with prayer, while outside the armies of the conqueror howled. Knowing that death was coming, with one last service they finally came together. When the world they knew was crumbling around them and the barbarian was at the gate, the people of Constantinople forgot their differences and celebrated Christ's story together.

There is a wonderful legend that while lighting candles during the service, the priests took the sacred dishes and escaped through a secret door behind the Grand Altar. They will return to finish the Mass in Hagia Sophia when the church becomes Christian again. Eternally optimistic, I always look for that door when I am there.

Captivated by Topkapi

I've always been a sucker for dashing adventures filled with swords, capes and captured maidens. I try to demand some quality of writing and some historical accuracy, but I'm honestly not all that picky, and when it comes to feats of derring-do, periodically a good schmaltzy book is just the thing.

Topkapi Palace in the city of Istanbul is the sort of spot where this stuff really did happen. Ancient and magical Istanbul, divided by the Bosphorus, straddles two continents and is a sophisticated combination of many cultures, offering Greek statues, Roman roads, Byzantine churches and Ottoman mosques and palaces. In the middle of it all, among the magnificent domes and minarets of Hagia Sophia and the Blue Mosque, stands Topkapi Palace.

Built with the stones of ancient Byzantium, scented by jasmine and roses with a lovely view down to the sea of Marmara, this enclosed city with its harem, eunuchs, palace plots and betrayals is the stuff of old movies and junk books. Built in the mid 1640's, of marble probably pilfered from ancient Byzantine monuments and soon after the Ottomans had made the city of Istanbul their capital, the sultan's palace stands on the finest location in the city. Parks and gardens, adorned with pavilions and fountains, are laid out on slopes falling away to the sea. The palace is not a single building but a complex of buildings grouped around a series of courtyards, the second largest royal compound in the world

Walking through the grounds of Topkapi Palace

Someday you will visit Topkapi. Next to it, Versailles looks nouveau riche and glitzy, Windsor, cold and clunky. Dryansky writes, "Power expressed in sensuality and sensuousness... the awesome proclamation of itself that power can achieve. Nearly everything in Topkapi is voluptuous." Like a series of fitted Chinese boxes, the courtyards fall back to reveal one treasure after another. The barracks of the elite Janissaries and their armory surround the first and most public courtyard. Children chosen from poor Christian families, the Janissaries were forbidden to marry and dedicated to war. They died with the certain expectation of paradise which made for a very effective fighting force.

Through the Gate of Salutation (where badly behaved officials were publicly beheaded) is the busy world of the second court where the imperial council and ministers labored. In the mysterious and perfumed third court are the sultan's private apartments where the sultan's mother, sisters, wives and 300 concubines lived in seclusion, guarded by a corps of 200 eunuchs.

The logistics alone are overwhelming. The members of the palace were divided into the Outer and Inner services. The former included Janissaries, household cavalry, gatekeepers, standard–bearers, musicians, artisans, physicians, astrologers and gardeners. The latter category contained the sultan's eunuchs, personal attendants, pages, valets and the 20,000 slaves necessary to serve them all, each wearing a costume whose design and color proclaimed his position in the hierarchy.

The harem was just as rigidly organized. At the bottom were the novices, and above them a series of grades, called the privileged, the favored, the fortunate and finally the princesses, those who were lucky enough to give the sultan a child. The supreme ruler was the sultan's mother, the Valide Sultan. It takes only a little imagination to visualize the effect that the combination of wealth, indolence, seclusion, beauty and power would have had on several hundred young women cloistered together. Along with the fragrances of flowers and perfumes, intrigue filled the air.

For 400 years, Topkapi was the heart of one of the world's most powerful and long-lasting empires. The Ottoman Empire controlled Europe and the Middle East from Greece to Austria and from Russia to Arabia. Those lucky enough to reach the throne could call themselves, "Sultan of the Sultans of East and West, Fortunate Lord of the domains of the Romans, Persians and Arabs...Sultan of the Mediterranean and the Black Sea, of the throne of Egypt, of the lands of the Tartars, of Kurdistan and Luristan, etc. etc." Ottoman royal politics being what they were, it was a fortunate man who stayed on the throne long enough to hear the entire recitation of his title

The Sultan's Throne Room

During the 16th & 17th centuries, the sultans were the most powerful potentates on earth. Tribute and gifts came from everywhere. The English sent gilt plate and elegant clocks, the French, parcels of Lyon silk, from Russia came bales of rich furs, and there was porcelain from China. In the treasury rooms were enormous emeralds and diamonds, gold and pearls, rich weapons and armor, maps and paintings. Gazelles, deer and peacocks roamed at will over the green lawns, songbirds lived in the willows and cypress, roses bloomed and perfumed the air.

Walk with me down the paths, smile as a lovely odalisque glides by, sit under the trees and listen to the bird song and the fountains, smell the lush flowers. Look at the treasures on display, marvel at the jewel-box richness of the vividly tiled rooms, each more elegant than the one before. Now one can only imagine the splendor of the Seraglio in its heyday. The brightly colored tiles remain, but most of the painted paneling and silk hangings are gone. The gold paving of the royal reception chamber disappeared long ago, but if you try, you can people the rooms with stately processions of soldiers and dignitaries in robes of satin, velvet and cloth of gold. Listen, and you can still hear the tinkling of the fountains and the laughter of the harem.

In my dashing romance novels, the beautiful heroine either grabs a scimitar, skewers the sultan and escapes back to her own true love. Or she enchants the ruler of the world, marries him and converts the entire country to the virtues of hard work and clean living. Both endings work quite well.

Remnants of the Great Hippodrome

The Great Hippodrome
of Constantinople

It's early morning at the Great Hippodrome in Istanbul. "Shush, what do you hear?" "Nothing," I answer, "Only silence."

Far on the other side of the park, there is the sound of an early morning tour bus and the hushed conversations of a few sleepy tourists. Closer, there is the murmur of mourning doves and the splashing of a fountain. The rest is quiet. Today the Hippodrome is a square named Sultanahmet Meydani, a park for the beautiful Blue Mosque. But stand quite still and your imagination may let you see the shape of a giant oval and hear the roar of the crowd and the thundering hoofbeats of the great horses.

If you had been there 1,500 years ago, the Great Hippodrome would have been entirely different. The cheers and screams of the crowd, the magnificent horses thundering around the track, the purple and gold, brocade and jewels, dust and chaos would have overwhelmed you. Then Constantinople was the Queen of the Ages, the proud center of the world. While Rome fell and the western Empire crumbled, she endured, a shining city. Layer upon layer of buildings climbed the steep cliffs overlooking the Bosphorus, and at the top, the white marble of the palaces and the golden domes of the churches glittered in the sunlight.

At the center of it all was the Hippodrome of Constantine, the social heart of the city. It was an enormous oval, 1,500 feet long and 426 feet wide with seats that would hold 100,000 spectators. The Great Palace of the Emperor was connected directly to the Imperial Boxes by private passage. (No treading on mortal ground for these folks.) Four splendid horses, made of gilded copper shining in the sun, stood on the roof of the Hippodrome Boxes at the northern end. The track was a long oval of golden sand split down the center by a low, narrow wall of brick, holding trophies from faraway lands. There was a bronze column from ancient Delphi and a pink granite obelisk from Thebes on the center island, and lining the track were bronze statues of famous horses and chariot drivers, statues of gods, emperors and heroes. One could get huffy that the Venetians stole their famous Four Horses and put them up on the front of St. Mark's Basilica, but then one would have to explain the bronze column from Greece and the obelisk from Egypt standing in Constantinople.

Had you gone there to watch the races, you wouldn't have paid much attention to the impressive monuments that bordered the race track or the grandeur of the Imperial Loge, there would have been many more immediate distractions. When you left your home, the great Mese, the main thoroughfare, would have been already crowded with people jostling each other. Families carrying small children, noisy gangs of boys, merchants and their wives, slaves, beggars, hawkers, a vast noisy crowd all going to the Hippodrome. Reaching the colossal entranceway, there would already be a line of people with their cushions, picnic baskets, jugs of wine, all arguing about the drivers and placing wagers on the teams. They gamble and swear, swagger and sing slogans while looking for an excuse to start a fight with anyone who is not of their team, the Blue, the Green, the Red or the White.

Finding your spot on the benches and waiting for the races to begin, there would be entertainment, clowns, acrobats, trick riders, jugglers. Finally to a flourish of trumpets, the Emperor enters the Imperial Box. Sitting godlike, he is very small all the way up in his private balcony, but you can see the shine of gold and purple, the gleam of jewels and the fluttering of silks, and you shout, "Hail, Basileus!" along with everyone else.

The golden Emperor stands, drops a white cloth, the starting gates open, and eight chariots each drawn by four horses charge down the track. The crowd leaps to its feet and screams as the greatest drivers and the finest horses in the Empire thunder by in a swirl of gleaming muscles, flashing wheels, whips and dust. Down the track they go, hurtling through the straightaway, careening around the corners, forcing each other out at the turns. Seven times they make the circuit as the crowd yells, swears, cries and roars. Finally, the Greens pull ahead and cross the finish line, and you collapse on to your seat, exhausted but with seven more races to watch.

Late in the afternoon, everything gets packed up, the cushions, the empty wine jugs, the empty picnic baskets, the tired and dirty children. With your neighbors, you wearily trudge home, knowing that you have been to the greatest spectacle in the greatest city of the world, the Hippodrome in Constantinople.

Now there is only an empty green park and silence.

The Basilica Cistern, What Lies Beneath

When we walk down a city street we see the pavement, we notice the gutters, there might be a hill to climb up or a slope to slide down, but we pay little attention or think at all about what may lie below. And the older the city, the greater the treasures that may be down there. This is especially true in Istanbul, a city so rich in history and so full of cultural layers that it is only to be expected that the physical strata would be just as enticing. This is an elaborate way of saying that with 10,000 years of history and 12 dominant empires, there is a lot of neat stuff in Turkey, and some of it is underground.

Let me set the stage. Overlooking the Sea of Marmara and the Golden Horn is one of the most matchless and unique peninsulas in the world. Lying at the edge of Europe with Asia being literally a stone's throw away, this is where you'll find some of the finest churches, the greatest mosques and the loveliest palaces anywhere. I was so overwhelmed by Hagia Sophia, the Blue Mosque and Topkapi Palace all in one area that it's no wonder the first time I was in Istanbul I didn't even notice the little sign that said *Yerebatan Sarnici* (Sunken Palace) and the small door leading down.

The next time I was in the city, I knew better. Through a nondescript entrance, I walked into a small lobby, bought my ticket and then went gingerly down narrow, wet, marble steps into darkness and the sound of water. Just below the tram lines and busy city streets is the subterranean world of the Basilica Cistern. I was in a palace of marble with row upon row of soaring pillars that towered up in the darkness to support the arches and vaults of the ceiling. The columns were enormous, perhaps six feet thick, all different, all unique. There were hundreds of them, a forest of white marble vanishing into the dark. The floor was rippling water

The Basilica Cistern of Istanbul

148

spreading in all directions, cold and clear and green. I could hear the echoes of water dripping, and there were fish in the water, silver flitting shapes.

This was a palace built more than a thousand years ago by Justinian as part of his grand plan to bring fresh water by aqueduct to Constantinople for its gardens, fountains and baths. One of many used to supply water, the Basilica Cistern was designed specifically for the Great Palace, but the memory of it was lost after the city was conquered by the Turks. Sunk under the city, it remained hidden and secure while the buildings overhead were destroyed and rebuilt and destroyed again. As the centuries passed, the pipes clogged, the Cistern fell out of use, and for many hundreds of years it was completely forgotten. No one knew that under their feet was a massive underwater chamber.

It was rediscovered by a Dutch traveler who was told that people in the area were getting fresh water and even catching fish by dropping buckets through holes in their basements. He scrambled down a dark well and holding a lantern aloft, rowed about in a boat taking accurate, Dutch measurements. What he found was an underground chamber of 470 by 215 feet, capable of holding 100,000 tons of water. The large room was broken up by a forest of hundreds of marble columns of many styles, each 30 feet high, arranged in 12 rows, each consisting of 28 columns.

What he couldn't see until the water was drained was the mystery on the northwest side. In the very far corner of the Cistern, wedged under the weight of two columns are two giant heads of Medusa. One is placed upside down, the other on its side. No one is quite sure why they were put there so long ago, to stare out blindly under the deep, cold water. Although of course, there are many theories. The least exciting notion is that they were used to prop up shorter columns. Another is that they were placed there to guard against the palace's water supply being poisoned. My own favorite is that they are there for the same reason you can find the Medusa on many important Roman buildings, a female dragon of the underground to turn enemies to stone. But mystery is appropriate in a magical sinking palace under the traffic of a modern city.

When you go, save a few minutes for a Turkish coffee by candlelight in the underground café. And keep your eye out for Sean Connery, who filmed a scene in *From Russia With Love* in the Cistern. Obviously he knew a romantic and exotic spot when he saw one.

The narrow, blood-soaked beaches of Gallipoli

and the rows upon rows of memorials

Gallipoli, the Forging of a Nation

"Here's rosemary, that's for remembrance," said my Australian friend as he broke a small twig from the long, low hedge and handed it to me. I recognized the quote from Hamlet but here on the Aegean coast of Turkey was an odd place to hear Shakespeare. I shouldn't have been surprised; the plant grows wild on the Gallipoli Peninsula and is an ancient symbol of remembrance and fidelity.

Driving along the Dardanelles, it is difficult to believe that this quiet and peaceful place was the site of one of the greatest British disasters of World War I, and for almost a full year a scene of unimaginable carnage. While we headed up along the coast, the sun was warm, there was the scent of lavender and oleander in the air, and the color of the crystal blue Aegean was exquisite. Because I know more about ancient history than modern, I was already familiar with the classical associations of the region. This is where the ancient Greeks sailed on their way to Troy, where the Persian king, Xerxes built his bridge of boats, where Leander swam the fierce currents to his lady love and where the romantic Lord Byron attempted the same thing. But I was not prepared for Gallipoli.

It was just past dawn when we got there, and the sky was still streaked with gold and red. Apart from a call to prayer echoing from a nearby village, there was only the quiet sound of the waves. Overhung by steep cliffs there is a sheltered rocky beach, and near the beach are the graves and the graves and the graves. Tens of thousands are buried there; in row after row the soldiers lay. Privates, lance corporals, gunners and seaman, all with lives barely started; the British, the French, the Irish, the Australians, the New Zealanders and the Turks are all buried where they fell.

If you don't know the history, let me give you a brief and imperfect background. During World War I, the British Royal Navy planned to blast its way through the Dardanelles and the Sea of Marmara and by the sheer magnificence of its presence, cow the Turkish government in Istanbul into submission. Then the sea lanes to the Black Sea would be opened, Germany and Austria-Hungary would be exposed, and the newly supplied Russia would steamroller into Berlin. It didn't work. The battle raged, the Turks were not overawed, and the fleet withdrew.

The next day the land campaign began. It was supposed to take three days. Just land the soldiers, get rid of the Turks, clear off the seaward defenses and get on with the conquering of

Istanbul. It didn't happen that way. For 259 days, from April 1915 to January 1916, the Allied Forces held onto their toeholds on the narrow beaches at Gallipoli. Approximately 500,000 men were landed there over the course of the campaign, and almost half of them became casualties. Historians say that the Turks alone may have lost half a million men, but no one is quite sure. No one counted the Turkish dead.

The bloody beaches of Gallipoli destroyed the myth of British imperial might. But it also provided Australia with the blood-sacrifice that united their new nation. I was fortunate enough to be at Gallipoli with six Australians. As we stood there silent except for tears, one said to me, "This is where we showed the world; on Anzac Day we wear rosemary to remember." And then this big, gruff Australian got a little misty.

Gallipoli was also a crucible for the Turkish nation. Although poorly equipped, they stood up against the greatest empire in the world, and their courage and determination won the admiration of their enemies. Their leader at Gallipoli was Mustafa Kemal, one of the greatest soldiers his country has ever produced. He would go on to become Kemal Ataturk, the Father of his nation.

Christian and Moslem, the men at Gallipoli fought bravely, and on the silent battlefield they rest in peace together in the democracy of death. There is a truly touching memorial there written by Ataturk in 1934. "Those heroes that shed their blood and lost their lives...you are now lying in the soil of a friendly country. Therefore rest in peace. There is no difference between the Johnnies and the Mehmets to us where they lie side by side here in this country of ours. You, the mothers who sent their sons from far away countries wipe away your tears. Your sons are now lying in our bosom and are in peace. After having lost their lives on this land they have become our sons as well."

It's no wonder my friend got teary-eyed. Sometimes there is nothing quite as heartrending as travel.

Magic Carpets

I watched a girl named Sedrah sitting in front of a large loom that held a half-finished carpet, its surface glowing with designs in rich red, green and azurite blue. She turned and showed her weaving to me, taking a strand of woolen yarn and weaving it into the pattern and slowly explaining that each square inch held 50 small, tight knots and that it took about five months for her to complete a carpet. Then she invited me to try. I managed two knots in five minutes and would still be working on that one warp line if she hadn't taken pity on me.

I was back in Turkey, "The Land of the Heart's Desires," with its enthralling mixture of Greek and Turkish cultures. As the spot where East has met West for millennia, Turkey is also the marketplace of the world, and its most famous creations are its world famous rugs. It is unusual for so much of a people's history and tradition to be represented in a single handicraft, and it is rarer still to receive instruction in its creation. Turkish carpets are not the over-civilized remnants of ancient Greco-Roman history but instead represent the nomadic and aggressive Turkish tribes who invaded Asia Minor in the 15th century and made the land their own. Come traveling with me while I have my own "carpet lesson."

Even wih an excellent lecture...

this slow and earnest weaver doesn't have much chance.

Turkish carpets were brought to Anatolia by the nomadic tribes of Central Asia. Woven for centuries in patterns and colors passed down from generation to generation, the rugs were used by the herdsmen on their tents' floors and walls for warmth. The looms were horizontal, quickly dismantled, and the rugs were easy to pack and simple to unload as the tribes moved with the herds. The tradition has continued in Anatolia since the late 11th century, and the carpets have been treasured in Europe since Marco Polo first wrote about them. Their brilliant colors, their distinctive patterns and motifs have made them valued worldwide.

We traveled in the central plateaus of Anatolia toward gorgeously eroded Cappadocia whose tufa villages and fairy chimneys have been famous for centuries. There were small villages in the countryside where lengths of spun, dyed yarn hung outside to dry in the sun. On some houses, the wool was drying on the rooftops, joined by layers of golden apricots. The women of the household were drying the fruit for the winter and preparing their dyed wool to be woven into treasured carpets - all in the open air.

We stopped at a carpet weaving center where local women could bring their wool to be colored with native plants, mader for red, boiled woad (gathered at the edges of fields) for blue, ox-eye chamomile for yellow and the fruit and leaves of the walnut tree for brown. Can't you imagine nomadic women keeping an eye out for plants as they traveled to use in their dying and weaving? I had a fascinating lecture from its director who explained that carpets are either flat-weave (kilims) or pile carpets where short strands are knotted and cut. The density, the number of knots per square inch, indicates the quality and durability of the rug. A superb rug of woven silk may have more than 500 to 1,000 knots per square inch. Some carpets may take a few months to complete while others may take years.

The next day we drove south to the sea port of Antalya where I was introduced to the owner of a carpet center whose family has been collecting and selling village carpets since the 1920's. While we sat in his office and sipped apple tea, he described the richly designed Anatolian rugs that are woven in hundreds of small villages. Each has its own distinctive pattern, design or symbol, passed from mother to daughter for centuries and all unique for their family. And the older the rugs are, the more cherished they become.

Created in a nonliterate society, it is possible to read the feelings and sentiments of the woman who wove the carpet and used these symbols to tell her story. A certain flower can represent an emotion and even the color may have a meaning. A pink hyacinth is love, a purple one sadness, a white one loyalty. Poppies mean spring, tulips show love and carnations are peace. Many carpets guard against evil, perhaps with a sacred number pattern to protect the user; for example the numbers 3, 5 and 7 all have a special meaning. A woman who has lost a child may weave her grief, while a woman who is happy with her husband may weave her joy, all in the designs and colors of their carpets.

Different regions also create their own patterns. The priceless Hereke carpets interweave vines and flowers as a sign of infinity and their tulips are a symbol of the Ottoman Empire. The Yuruks use different pointed stars to represent the universe, wisdom or virtue. The carpets of Bergama have triangles in their corners to protect against the evil eye, a sheaf of wheat for fertility and the eagle for holiness. In Cappadocia, a pattern of diamonds and triangles means a girl is looking for a husband. A white rose means love, a red one passion and dots stand for fertility and abundance. So, if you were a young bachelor and the girl you liked was weaving a carpet with diamonds, triangles, red and white roses and lots of dots, you had better look out.

When we went into his showroom, my new friend and his staff laid carpets before me, one after another after another, an Ali Baba's cave of treasures. The carpets, hundreds of them, were the finest in the world; each filled with color and rich patterns and gathered from "the pages of fairy tales and forgotten songs." First I was watching primly from a bench and then I was on the floor, touching and learning about all these glorious rugs. It was like first understanding the alphabet so that you could read fabulous books. I'm still at the kindergarten level.

Mark Anthony and St. Paul both walked these streets.

Ancient Ephesus, Center of Faith and Power

"If you were a Roman lady, 2,000 years ago," said my Turkish friend as we walked down the main street of Ephesus, "here you would stop to buy silks from China, there you would look for a perfume from Araby and across the way you could taste spices from India. All the wealth of the world came across the Silk Road to this city. The port was full of trading ships while the streets were crowded with pilgrims to the great temple of Artemis. You might have passed Alexander the Great or perhaps Anthony walking with his Cleopatra or heard St. Paul preach. This was one of the great centers of the ancient world." The city of Ephesus on the western coast of Turkey is an irresistible combination of history, engineering, power, money and faith, all my favorite things.

Before we get to the sexy stuff, the power and the money, let me give you a little history. This being Turkey, every Mediterranean and Middle Eastern culture dropped by. Neolithic man came first, followed Bronze Age Hittites; the Mycenaeans came over and the Trojans came through, escaping from their conquered city. Later came Androcles of Athens, Croesus, Xerxes, Hannibal escaping Carthage, Julius Caesar, and Antony who spent a winter's carnival before the Battle of Actium. Ephesus served as a political pawn among the Persians, the Greeks, the Romans, the Byzantines and the Ottomans. Although American, British, European and Turkish archeologists have been exploring her various sites for over 100 years, only about 25 percent of the ruins has been uncovered. (Realizing that the large hill to the north is the unexcavated acropolis will make you crazy.)

And if all that marvelous history weren't enough, there are the brilliant feats of engineering to investigate. The pipes are still there from one of the most advanced aqueduct systems in the ancient world. Copious supplies of hot and cold water were piped into public fountains, private homes and luxurious baths with their mosaic floors, salons and central heating. There were miles of underground pipe as well as beautiful arched aqueducts that brought in roughly 100 gallons of water per person to a population of half a million. Another engineering marvel is the impressive Roman roads that brought St. Paul to Ephesus. Laboriously constructed with five separate layers, the roads are still there and walkable. I wonder if they'll be able to say that about our highways in 2,000 years?

And then was the mighty temple. Greater than the Parthenon in size, status and fame, the Temple of Artemis attracted more pilgrims than any other shrine in the ancient world. Destroyed several times by fire and flood, it was rebuilt each time with an unmatched genius in engineering and design techniques. The enormous marble blocks were cut by hand at a quarry, put into wheeled wooden cradles and rolled the eight miles to the building site. Using scaffolding, the builders assembled the columns with stacked marble drums, each weighing more than eight tons. Each of the 127 columns contained 30 drums, and then the giant unmortared lintels were placed precisely on top. It took 120 arduous years to complete.

Now the money angle - location, location, location. The harbor was a perfect crescent on the eastern Mediterranean facing directly toward Athens and attracted trading ships from all over the world. The nearby mountain passes brought the Asian caravans along the famous Silk Route. Caravans leaving China carried silk, ceramics, spices, ivory and bronze while the China-bound caravans heading east were loaded with woven goods, tapestries and carpets, furs, honey and slaves. At the extreme ends, the Silk Road connected Xian with Rome. And Ephesus lay in between.

And finally, faith. First there was the Temple of Artemis. One of the Seven Wonders of the Ancient World, it was the preeminent shrine in the Grecian world. ("The sacred house of Artemis, reaching the clouds.") Open and airy and standing on the shores of a beautiful bay, it was the size of a football field with mighty pillars six stories tall and could be seen glimmering in the sunlight from eight miles out to sea. While a cynical observer might note that the thousands of pilgrims who came annually brought gold to the city coffers, the faith that attracted them should not be discounted.

Christianity brought its own pilgrims. St. Paul stayed in Ephesus for three years, establishing it as a center of early Christianity. The Virgin Mary is said to have spent her last days there in the company of St. John. In the 6th century, a magnificent brick and marble church was built over St. John's tomb by the Emperor Justinian (of Hagia Sophia fame). One of the great churches of Christendom, the exterior of the basilica was built in the shape of a cross with six massive domes, and the interior gleamed with marble courtyards, frescoed walls and mosaic floors.

At its height, Ephesus was a glittering, opulent city. But eventually the harbor silted up, the Ephesians abandoned their goddess, earthquakes and erosion ruined the fertile valleys and the world forgot. Silk is now delivered by freighter, and the site of the enormous Temple of Artemis is marked by a single, forlorn column built from bits and pieces. One hundred years of archaeological excavation has uncovered some of the city with much more still to be found. But if you try hard enough as you walk down those streets today, you can see the sailors as they saunter up from the harbor, hear the fountains, feel the silks, smell the perfumes and know what it is like to be in one of the world's great ancient cities.

Troy, Beware of Greeks Bearing Gifts and Vice-Versa

A giant reproduction of
Troy's mythical horse

Schliemann's levels of
"many-towered" Troy

A tiny tourist replica of the Trojan horse sits on my desk. It's pretty corny, but if you've been waiting all your life to visit a legendary site, it is the sort of thing you can't help buying. I love it because no matter the size or authenticity of my little souvenir, it is from that city of myth and legend. That little horse embodies a story of treasure and treachery, passion and war, the stuff of a Hollywood hit or an ancient fable.

The site of ancient Troy is located in the northwest section of present day Turkey, only a few miles from the entrance to the Dardanelles. We all know the story of the kidnapping of the lovely Helen by Paris the prince of Troy, and the ten-year campaign waged by the Greeks to rescue her. The giant horse, seemingly left as a tribute to the gods which carried Greek warriors hidden in its belly, finally brought the war to a bloody end.

That is the fable that everyone knows and for centuries that was what Troy was believed to be, a city of fable, a myth. But in 1865 an Englishman named Frank Calvert excavated trial trenches in a field in north-west Anatolia. Then, unfortunately for his future as a well-known archaeologist, he met and convinced a wealthy German entrepreneur, Heinrich Schliemann that this area was the site of ancient Troy. Poor Mr. Calvert faded into obscurity.

Clutching Homer's *Iliad* and accompanied by great fortune and good publicity, Schliemann set out to prove the truth of the story. Six years later, underneath the hills and sand dunes of western Turkey, he began to uncover one of world's most famous lost cities, the ancient city of Troy.

Since then excavations have found at least 13 cities built one on top of another dating from 3000 to 100 B.C.; Troy VII is considered the most likely city for the legend. To be honest, Schliemann misjudged the depth of Homer's Troy, burrowed a little farther down than he should and pitched a bit of the legend on top of the dirt pile.

Troy was ancient when Cleopatra visited, when Alexander the Great made a pilgrimage and even when Homer wrote his epic. The layers of the city are sliced through in the gullies like a giant wedding cake, exposing 4,000 years of life. But when the wind gusts and the dust swirls, I did wonder just which century was blowing by.

Ancient and fabled Troy
and its indifferent cat

 The story of the Trojan gold is not quite as hazy. During the dig, Schliemann uncovered "Priam's Treasure," a great golden hoard of ornaments and artifacts. Mrs. Schliemann posed for a photo while bedecked in the ancient earrings, a golden diadem and other gleaming jewels of the booty. This was probably the last time the fabulous jewelry graced a pretty throat and brow before it was stuck away in a dusty old museum. Schliemann and Co. smuggled it out of Anatolia, and most of it was "protected" and removed (read stolen and smuggled) to a museum in Berlin. During World War II, the Russians Red Army "liberated" the treasure from Germany and took it home with them. The gold is still in Moscow. "Finders keepers, losers weepers." I suspect it will be a cold day in Turkey before it is ever returned.

Rather than the myth, the less romantic truth is probably that Troy was a rich and prosperous Greek city state with the normal warlike trading rivalries with its neighbors that periodically flared up into actual conflict. But the legend of the love of Paris, the vengeance of Agamemnon, the death of Achilles, the destruction of the city, have had a much more famous and enduring existence. Those stories have become a catalyst for immortal painting and poetry, sculpture and architecture. The myth became reality and transcended its origins.

And I got to be there.

I watched a cat perched on a Bronze Age wall, close to the spot where millions of dollars of golden treasure had been found and where the most famous war of all time was fought. There were riches and legends, blood and conflict, death and glory. The cat didn't care; it just washed its face.

Cappadocia, an Indiana Jones Moment

"Be careful and watch your head," said my Turkish friend as we entered the dark tunnel. "Some of these ceilings are very low and the rock is very hard. We are going to explore a hidden underground city."

Would you like to channel your inner Indiana Jones? Would you like to explore secret cities, face ancient demons, search for hidden treasure and see sites so foreign and exotic that you will never forget them? Go to Cappadocia.

A few hours' drive south of Turkey's capital city of Ankara, Cappadocia is located in central Anatolia, the region between the Black Sea and the Taurus Mountains. The towering peaks that surround the region were not always so quiet. For millions of years, these volcanoes spewed out tons of lava and volcanic ash that in time formed deep layers which blanketed the area and deposited porous tufa. Wind, water and time have eroded the soft stone to create peaks, crags, stalagmites and giant cones, cheerfully called "fairy chimneys."

Geologic spires, or "hoodoos".

This is the cradle of civilization. Archaeologists excavating the nearby Neolithic settlement of Catalhoyuk date it from 7,500 B.C. The area was part of the ancient Bronze Age Hittite Empire and has been crisscrossed by the Assyrians, Persians, Greeks, Romans, Byzantines, Ottomans and now by modern tourists.

Above ground there are marvelous treasures. First there is the landscape which is beautiful in a bizarre sort of way. Stone towers and turrets, caves and caverns are everywhere. There are literally thousands of strange rock formations that rise stories high, the most spectacular of which are the enormous, improbably boulder-capped pillars with the lovely euphemistic name of "fairy chimneys." The terrain is black and white, pastel pink, yellow and green with deep, stream-carved gorges enclosed by sinuous, curving walls streaked with swirls of color.

And as if that weren't enough, many of these strange formations are pitted with small doors and windows. During the last few thousand years, humans have helped the erosion along by carving homes, churches, chapels and monasteries into the soft rock. Early man used primitive tools to gouge caves out of the volcanic rock, and ten thousand years later there are still homes hollowed out in the stone with children who climb as easily between the caves as we would walk from room to room.

Other aboveground treasures are the chapels and monasteries that have also been carved into the rock. Hidden throughout the region are hundreds of frescoed churches. In the Goreme Open Air Museum alone, there are more than 30 rock-carved churches and chapels dating from the 9th to the 11th century.

In the cool early morning we walked down a stony path, clambered up a stairway, through a small door cut in the rock and into a jewel box. Standing in a large, dark room lit only by light from the doorway, the walls were covered with wonderful primitive frescoes, their colors of red, green, gold and azurite blue still rich and bright. Carved out of the stone was a church with its vault, columns, arches and transepts all covered with scenes from the Bible. There was the Last Supper, Christ on the cross, Christ as King, St. George attacking a dragon, Judas' betrayal and the Emperor Constantine and his mother, all in the company of smaller creatures - rabbits, roosters, fish, and all drawn in vibrant colors.

There are hundreds of these chapels, some small and others quite large, and all enticingly named after the frescoes you will find there. The Snake Church, the Sandal Church, the Dark Church, the Apple Church are all a thousand years old, all with incredible paintings, all stuck out in the middle of the back of beyond. Don't you just love traveling!

Underground, there are more marvels. When invaders arrived, the locals went below ground to escape the marauding hoards, carving elaborate, multileveled cities out of the soft stone. Dating from as far back as the Hittites, most were built between the 6th and 8th century A.D., first to escape Roman persecution and then to avoid other tribes of invaders. There are at least 40 of these underground cities discovered so far, some with as many 16 levels. (One was found in 1972 by a local farmer who was concerned about disappearing crop water. Investigating, he found an underground room which, when later excavated, revealed an entire city which would hold an astonishing 60,000 people for up to three months.)

Who knew what wonders lay beneath? Ignoring my "Injun Joe" issue, I walked down the small, sloped tunnel entrance. Stooping over, it was obvious that the size of the door would force invaders to attack while bent over and in single file. As the small entrance went down, there was level upon level of rooms, each serving a special purpose, store rooms, kitchens, livestock pens, churches. Through a labyrinth of long tunnels and down steep stairs, the rooms were clustered around ventilation shafts. The entrance of each level was closed from the inside by "millstone doors," massive round stones which were rolled across the doors, impossible to open from the outside. (This was an Indiana Jones moment.) The city I was exploring could hold 20,000 people and their animals and keep them safe for months.

Tourist standing in front
of rock-cut shrines.

There were storage areas for food and for wine, a kitchen located beside a well with niches for oil lamps. One room had two troughs carved into the stone floor. They made wine there. Another held storage bins carved into the walls. They fed their animals there. There were vertical communication shafts making it possible to speak to another person on any level. (Kind of a geological party line.) Soot on the ceilings, mortar and pestle grinding stones still in the kitchens, all left silent evidence of the thousands of people who lived in these hidden cities.

There are more levels that have not been excavated, more cities that have not been found. Our guide was a little old man who gave us a full tour of the city using smiles, gestures and inventive body language. We were the last of the group to climb back into the sunlight. As saying "thank you" in Turkish is a 16-syllable word, I did what I usually do at such times. I nodded "thank you," smiled and put my hand over my heart.

Reflections on Travel

I've been traveling now for over 40 years and one of the more rewarding discoveries I've made is the amazing number of everyday similarities we share. In the middle of all the exotic sites, the familiar and normal suddenly pop up. Everyone must eat and sleep; everyone has perplexing problems; sometimes everyone needs help and advice; everyone laughs, gets tired or becomes angry; everyone likes children and music. We may answer these problems in different ways, but solve them we must. The following are small pieces about travel and some of the common bonds that unite us.

Kitchens I Have Loved

I love kitchens; I'm even very fond of my own. Kitchens are one of those common threads of humanity. No matter the country, no matter the era, everybody has them. They're the heart of the palace or the house or the hovel. And what makes them particularly intriguing is what they explain about the people who use them. They can be Spartan or exotic, simple or high-tech, comfy or barren.

Especially when I travel, I look for those things we all have in common and kitchens are a perfect example. It's fun to see how

One of the enormous kitchens at Hampton Court
(The black above the fireplace is soot.)

everyone else handles the same problems because no matter the country or the century, everyone needs essentially the same features. They should find some way to heat liquids, someplace to bake, somewhere to store grain, spices, game, etc. (And, of course, some way to make coffee.) If you look closely, the room will reveal a tremendous amount about the people who live there, a window into other lives.

When I was in Bangkok, I stayed at the Oriental Hotel which is reputed to be the best hotel in the world, and I am not going to argue. (It's the sort of place that when you send out laundry it comes back gift wrapped - with an orchid.) When I met the hotel manager, he asked if there was anything special I would like to see. What did I ask for? The kitchens. It was an excellent choice because their kitchens are elaborate and fascinating. Besides the standard prep areas for such a large facility, there was a separate room for the beef, one for the chicken, one for the pastry making and a whole "cool room" to prepare their candy. Normally I am shown the meeting rooms and the suites, but this was a much more distinctive and interesting part of the hotel.

I visited a similarly complex kitchen in France's Loire Valley, albeit centuries older. The Chateau at Blois has all the prerequisite number of grand ball rooms, elaborate chambers with sumptuous tapestries. In the several buildings which make it up, there are 564 rooms and 75 staircases. You know, one of those cozy, lived-in places. The most remarkable rooms in the chateau? The 600-year-old kitchens with their monumental fireplaces, massive spits, gleaming copper pots and scrubbed oak tables all waiting for the cooks to prepare the vegetables, the game and poultry, the sweets, the cheeses, the wines to serve the king and his guests.

At about the same time across the Channel, the kitchens at Hampton Court were cooking for Henry VIII. He was the golden prince, the Renaissance marvel, and the logistics of feeding and entertaining his vast staff and guests were overwhelming. If you visit Hampton Court today, you'll see the kitchen area faithfully recreated, a great open room flagged with stone to defend against fires. The knives are sharpened and the fires blazing, just waiting for the cooks to begin the banquets.

The visitor's guide will give you some idea of the size and scope of the enterprise. "The king's kitchen employed nearly 300 people to cover all the facets of the meals. It consisted of 52 rooms which covered 36,000 square feet and the staff was responsible for serving up to 1,000 guests for important events. The kitchen complex had 15 offices and a separate gatehouse through which all the supplies for the court were brought. The spicery was responsible for exotic spices from the Orient as well as huge quantities of fruit produced in the palace gardens. The pastry house had 10 ovens, the largest measured 9 feet. There was a confectionery, a meat larder, a fish larder and a dry larder. The kitchen complex itself had six great fireplaces which could each roast a spitted cow. The master cook directed 12 other cooks and another two dozen assistants." This makes fixing Thanksgiving dinner at home look a little anticlimactic, doesn't it?

Halfway across the world, the Ottoman Sultan in Istanbul kept an equally elaborate kitchen. By the 17th century, the huge kitchens at Topkapi Palace were housed in a complex of immense rooms topped by chimney-shaped domes. These kitchens were the largest in the world with 1,000 servants working around the clock to feed the 5,000 who lived in the palace. And that number could grow to 15,000 during special holidays. The enormous cauldrons are still there hanging over the fire pits, but the sultan is gone, the ovens are cold. If you listen, you can hear hungry ghosts crying in the harem.

In contrast to the grandeur of Blois, the splendor of Hampton Court, the magnificence of Istanbul, I have also visited the other end of the spectrum. In Ireland's Ulster Province, there is an outdoor museum with a collection of homes that were used by the Irish in the early 18th century. Beside the comfortable homes of the wealthy and middle classes, there is an example of one of the "picturesque" peasant cottages, the home for most of the rural poor. It is only picturesque from the outside with its thatched roof and twining roses; inside it is a dirt-floored hovel. As many as twelve could live there, with straw mats for bedding and a kitchen consisting of only an open hearth and pivoting hooks to hold the pots. With babies crying in that little dirty space and not much food, imagine trying to cook for a family. For me, that kitchen put a face and heart on the potato famine and the Irish immigration to the U.S.

We are not unique in our time. We are not different or better than our great-great grand-parents. We all face the same problems--the need for shelter and community and the same quandary of feeding a hungry family. When I travel, the differences are readily apparent. It is the similarities that are fascinating to find.

Why the Ancient World Crumbled

Delphi rests on the slope of Mt. Parnassus, sacred to Apollo and the Corycian Nymphs and the home of the Muses. It is built on a series of high plateaus and terraces that cling to the mountain, giving the visitor a marvelous panorama of the ravines and gorges below, the rich and fertile Amfissa Valley off to the right and lower still, the Bay of Itea. I was standing looking at the view, musing, (pun intended), and it occurred to me that I hadn't seen one single golf course in the whole country. Now granted, the sort of ancient rubbley places I like don't encourage parkland, let alone a links course, but I should have run into at least one. Then I had an epiphany.

I believe that I may have finally found the answer to a puzzle I've been mulling over for years, the reason for the deterioration of Greece, the decay of ancient Egypt, the decline and fall of the Roman Empire. How could civilizations so advanced, cultures so deeply rooted, societies so widespread have crumbled and dissolved? The answer has finally become apparent to me. They didn't play golf.

All the pretentious ego, the vaunted and destructive superiority of the Romans, would have been humbled with a single muffed chip shot. The arrogant precision of the Praetorian Guard, the insane pride of the corrupt emperors would have been laid low by a bad slice. Never having played golf, their self-image was badly inflated. They would never have felt that growing feeling of inadequacy caused by a duffed drive or a pitch shot that flies the green. No matter how much of the known world they conquered, if they had played golf they would have known they were merely human.

Julius Caesar wouldn't have thought he was such hot stuff if he had played to a 16 handicap on his home course.

Carrying this a little farther, the mind boggles at the implications. Alexander might have stayed home instead of conquering the world. How could getting to India compare with the satisfaction of improving your golf game? If Ramses had paid more attention to his bunker shots (and there certainly is enough sand in Egypt to take care of that), he wouldn't have had to lie about his "victory" in Kadesh. Attila the Hun wouldn't have bothered to go pillaging across the steppes if he'd had a nice 18-hole links course to work out his frustrations. And Ivan the Terrible might have turned out to be a regular sort of fellow if he had Sunday afternoon rounds with the boyars.

Isn't travel broadening?

Lord Byron left his mark

And so did the some of the "working girls" of Pompeii

Graffiti's Silver Lining

"The words of the prophets are written on the subway walls and tenement halls."
Paul Simon

I have a confession to make. I realize that graffiti is horrid. It is evil, wicked, mean and nasty. The traditional definition is "pictures or writing placed on surfaces, usually outside walls, without the permission of the owner." It is tacky, low-rent and people caught doing it should be forced to scrub everything within a two block radius. That acknowledged, there are some circumstances where it can be fun. Marks left on walls can say, "I was here. I existed. A man stood here and left a record of his passing." Let me share with you some of my favorites. Most I've seen, one has yet to be visited. I think every one of them hold that special feeling of immediacy, of reality.

In 1995, a bushwalker discovered a cave in a remote part of the Wollemi National Park northwest of Sydney. Eagle's Reach Cave contains some 203 paintings, some of them 4,000 years old. There are 11 layers of work, the oldest dating to an age when the Egyptians ruled the Nile, Knossos was being built and the monoliths of Stonehenge were being lugged across Salisbury Plain. The rock shelter is 12 meters long, 6 meters wide and holds delicately drawn paintings and stencils of animals and humans created over a 4,000-year span. The one that touches me most is a simple handprint, saying in the dim dawn of time, "A Man stood here."

In the pyramids of ancient Egypt, in places never meant to be seen, the tomb builders left their calling card. In the weight-relieving rooms above the King's chamber in the Great Pyramid of Khufu, the working gangs made their mark. Usually it is the pharaohs who are remembered while the men who sweated and strained over the great blocks of stone are forgotten. But because of their scribbles, we know that the "Drunks of Menkaura" gang was there and they competed against the "Friends of Khufu" crew. And we know that those stupendous, gigantic, polished, white limestone marvels, blazing in the sun, were made by real people.

Giovanni Belzoni left a more modern example of graffiti in a pyramid. He shouldn't have, of course, but I'm glad he did. Belzoni stood six foot seven inches tall and was an Italian circus strongman who performed in London in the late 18th century. An adventurer and self-taught archaeologist, he ended up working for the British Consul, bulldozing through monuments in Abu Simbel and Luxor. Returning to Giza, he spent three weeks at the pyramid of Khafre, discovered the hidden entrance and was the first modern man to see the sarcophagus. By then, the treasure and the mummy were gone, but Belzoni left his name in 1818 on the south wall of the burial chamber, evidence of a fascinating if unsubtle man.

The Roman city of Pompeii is covered with graffiti, a great deal of it boasting about unlikely bawdy accomplishments. But on the wall of one workshop I found evidence of real women. The names of women workers and their wool allocations are scribbled. "Amaryllis, Baptis, Damalis, Doris, Lalage and Maria" worked there. Were they happy? Did they see Vesuvius erupt? Did they get away in time?

Desecrating, but still delightful, I ran across Viking graffiti at Hagia Sophia. On top of the marble balustrade in the South Gallery of the great cathedral, among the gold and gems, the incense and sanctity, the mosaics and marble, a Viking wrote in runic letters 1000 years ago, "Halvdan was here."

My favorite graffiti? I think I have three. Robert Dudley, Earl of Leicester, loved Elizabeth I until he died. Imprisoned in the Tower of London as a young man, his future was dim. His ambitious father had the bad sense to marry a son to Lady Jane Grey, make a try for the throne, and be executed for his trouble. Robert, brother and son to two convicted traitors, was held in the Beauchamp Tower only a walkway away from the Bell Tower where the young and vulnerable Elizabeth was kept prisoner by her sister. Legend has it that they met there and remained in love their whole life long. Beauchamp Tower is cold and dank, a dreary place to be imprisoned. And "Sweet Robin" bored and afraid, carved his name on the stone. You can practically touch him.

And just as cold, gray and wet was Cape Sounion, an hour's drive along the winding coast road from Athens. With its marble columns and panoramic view, the Temple of Poseidon is one of the most famous and picturesque places on the peninsula. Set back from the sheer cliffs, poised on the edge of the Aegean Sea, in ancient times mariners would see the marble columns and know they were close to home. Once full of worshipers, now it is home to the ghosts of ancient Greece and one foolish and idealistic English poet. Lord Byron went to Greece to indulge his fondness for life and somehow to aid in the fight for independence. He swam the Hellespont, wrote poetry, carved his name on one of the columns and died in Greece. You can practically touch him.

My favorite graffiti is in our home. If you open my hall closet door, there are the "birthday marks." Every year we stood my daughter up against the wood and drew a line at the top of her head. The first few marks are small and discreet. I was keeping track and I didn't want to mess up the wood. But by age 10 or so, when she was making the marks herself, they become large and black and proud. "I have grown 3 inches this year. I am growing up. I am here."

There were cats on Santorini,

A sheepdog in Ireland

a python in Bangkok

Animals I have Met
"Lots of people talk to animals.... Not very many listen ,though .... That's the problem..." Benjamin Hoff, *The Tao of Pooh*

I have been spat upon by an obdurate Egyptian camel at Giza, patted on the shoulder by a curious Sikkimise elephant at Gangtok, stoically ignored by a Balinese water buffalo and beamed at by a cheerful Hawaiian dolphin in Kona. And along the way I've also been peeped at by a French swan, glared at by a one-horned rhino in India's Kaziranga Preserve, munched on by an Irish donkey in County Kerry and then "kissed" by an exuberant working sheepdog the same day, "hugged" by a Thai python in Bangkok and charmed by a Greek kitten on the island of Santorini. They do form as interesting an assemblage of acquaintances and as remarkable a set of memories as anyone might hope for. (That camel and I never did become fast friends.)

Spinner dolphins in Kona,

a camel in Egypt,

and a very sweet donkey in County Kerry

All the treasures of the world can be found in Istanbul's Grand Bazaar.

There Were the Markets

I have a confession to make. I am not a shopper. Not for me the slow meandering through malls, the studied numbness of investigating innumerable departments, the rummaging through sales racks of unnecessary paraphernalia.

I make a list. I'm in the store. I look for the stuff (growling if it isn't there), I spend money, and I get out. And I better get it right because I hate to return things. Please note that I am still on my first husband, my first kid, my first house and drive a 1970 MGB. Do it right the first time and you can go on to other more interesting activities. There are books to read, gardens to tend, walks to take, golf to practice, food to cook and most especially trips to plan, all of which are much more appealing.

That said, I must admit that my distaste only holds true at home. I love shopping overseas. I love markets. I love watching people. I am fascinated by what is considered essential versus a luxury in other cultures. I love the memories I bring home as well the cool stuff I've bought. So let me tell you some shopping stories.

I was in Egypt, in the city of Luxor on the Nile. We had spent the last two days in the Valley of the Kings. I had been down in tombs, up on mountaintops and through deserts. It was incredible but hot and dusty, and I wanted a galabeya. Those are the long flowing cotton over-gowns that are worn by everyone there. They are cool and comfy, perfect for the climate and for sitting on an Egyptian boat in the evening watching the Nile go by.

Early in the morning, the sky over Luxor changes color from enamel blue to clear, brilliant turquoise. The air was clear and warm as I left the hotel to explore the morning market in Luxor. I could hear a dozen different languages, none of which I understood, but the odors were familiar, tar, fish, spices, dust, coffee and perfumes. Everything was a soft sand color shifting into darker terracotta; wide avenues lead into small dark alleys; shoppers wore pale robes, men with turbans and women with flowing scarves. The air was full of laughter and Egyptian conversation and now and then a call from the minarets.

Optimistically I knew that shoppers had been coming here for 3000 years, so there was a definite precedent for spending money, and I plunged in. The market was full of small shops, open stalls with the proprietor smiling in front. I found one with a nice chubby lady standing outside with lots of galabeyehs hanging in front and went in to pick one out. The first gown I tried on was fine - big, long, white, flowey, and I was good to go. Then she offered me a scarf for my head, and I put it on just to be polite. A friend of hers peeked in the shop and suggested another scarf to hide my face, so I put it on too. By that time, we had quite a group of Muslim ladies giving me a fashion critique. The general consensus was that I looked much better in the traditional Arabic dress than in tourist khakis. I only bought the galabeyeh, but I'll always remember the kindly advice.

Once in Dijon, I found a bakery by following the smell of fresh bread around two corners, and there was the window, piled high with bowls of candied cherries, plates of thinly layered Opera Gateau, shell-shaped Madeleines smelling of lemon and butter and golden flaked pastry. Inside there were stacks of long, hot crunchy loaves. I bought enough to gain ten pounds, but it was worth it.

There was bread in Dijon,

In India, I drove east from the city of Puri to the Temple of Konark, the Black Pagoda. The temple itself is 13th century and was built in the shape of a massive chariot, carrying the Sun God across the heavens. Because of its tremendous size, it was used by Portuguese explorers as a landfall on the Bay of Bengal. Every inch of the enormous structure is covered with sculptures. There are thousands of gods, warriors, dancers and lovers; there are scenes of courtly life, hunting and battles; there are warhorses trampling a fallen foe; nearby a delicate parrot sits on a lovely lady's shoulder while 2,000 elephants march past, oblivious to the horses or the lady.

But it's not the age, nor the carvings, nor the history that I remember most. In the courtyard, there sat an old monk, a holy man who had given up the things of this world for contemplation of the next. With him was his "chela," a young boy who would help and learn from him "to prepare tea for him and to fold a blanket for his head." It looked exactly like something out of Kipling's *Kim*. Next to them was an old lady sitting on a blanket, selling hand-hammered brass bowls. I gave the boy a respectable donation and bought the bowl from the old lady to remember the day. The bowl sits in all its battered glory on my dining room table. It is priceless.

You find the market in one little Spanish town by following the noise. Rickety stalls are put up for the day in the town square between classic columns, and between the columns are round smiling women loading up their booths. In our antiseptic grocery stores, the fruits and vegetables are scrubbed, graded, grown into polite uniformity and then artistically arranged. In this market, however, the fruits and vegetables were big and boisterous. Rowdy tomatoes looked like pumpkins, heavy and dark red; radishes big as plums, unruly heaps of bursting sugar peas piled on large trays and instead of the tidy bunch of bananas we're used to, there were thick clusters, hanging upside down. There were baskets of enormous lemons, crates of sunny peaches and huge golden onions hung in red nets. It was overwhelming; I bought a bunch of lily-of-the-valley and charged right in.

In the floating markets of Bangkok, there are flower-filled dugouts poled through the canals, bright scarlet and lustrous purples, sunny yellow and brilliant blues reflecting on the water just begging for a painting. Children dive off the sides of the boats, and little brown men smile and nod and offer their wares. It is a water world with houseboats, spirit houses and vendors floating together. The klong is not only transportation; it is home, livelihood and laundry. The babies, the clothes, the dishes, your teeth, your hair are all scrubbed in the canal. You could buy anything there, silks and orchids, incense and spices, lemons, kaffir lime and fragrant cilantro. Bargaining can get you clothes or lunch or a monkey.

Leaning out from our boat, I waved at a young boy who paddled over with a dugout full of embroidered cloth. I picked out a bright, red belt covered in flowers and gave him twice what

Silk in Bangkok,

he asked, thus ruining the game for the next bargaining tourist. But I wasn't buying the belt, I was buying a memory. And that was priceless.

The fish market in Istanbul has trays on the concrete with buckets of coral prawns. Fishermen in faded trousers bring in trolleys loaded with boxes as you watch, octopus from Bodrum, calamari from Antalya, shrimp from Canakkale, grouper from the Saroz Bay. Fat, silver fish lay artistically fanned on one counter, on another, eels are tangled beside a heap of blue mussel shells. There are nameless fish, purple-blue and bright pink, silver pinstriped in yellow. And all over, people smiling, chatting and bargaining.

Turkey's Goreme Valley is a land of underground cities and cave churches. By the side of a path there was a small stand run by an enterprising Turkish family. The wife sold wonderful, hand-woven woolen shawls, her husband offered tourist rides on a camel, and a little boy and girl sold apple tea from a homemade stand. I picked out a shawl as the camel peered down to help me choose and drank the children's apple tea. That was the day I learned to say, "Thank you very much, you have a beautiful family," in Turkish. I still have the shawl.

Finally and most especially, there is the Grand Bazaar of Istanbul. Built in 1455 by Mehmed the Conqueror to restore trade to the conquered city, it stretches over 75 acres and contains 4 main gates, 61 "streets" and 3,000 shops. Although the stone entrance looked like a well-guarded door to a massive fortress, once through the pointed archway and into the maze of covered streets, I was overwhelmed by the labyrinth. The number of shops was astonishing, and the passageways through them were sometimes wide, sometimes narrow and seemingly infinite. I felt I just might need Theseus' string or I'd never get out again.

Stepping inside I entered a tale from *One Thousand and One Nights*. I was in Scheherazade's boudoir seeing gold, everywhere gold. The ceilings were high painted vaults, the streets were paved with marble and the glittering shops were full of gold and silver, with silks and jewels spilling from their windows. It was Ali Baba's cave. "Gleaming with lanterns, piled with carpets and heaped with spices, it is a fantasy of Eastern opulence."

Although it may look like a maze when you first enter, there actually is a semi-organized system. The Bazaar is grouped into areas or "hans" where different items or crafts are clustered together. Helpfully, the streets may reflect the specialty as well. Through the Nuruosmaniye Gate, the main street is "Hatmakers Street," although the jewelry stores have pushed those craftsman out. You will probably stroll down "Jewelers Street" and "Pearl Merchants Street." Many of the guilds are remembered only through these names. There is the "Street of the Handkerchief Sellers," the "Street of the Turban Makers," "Slipper-makers," "Mirror-Makers," 'Fez-Makers," "Quilt-Makers," "Fur-Makers" and "Silk-Thread Makers." (The trades were very, very specialized.) In this city within a city, there are mosques, banks, police stations, restau-

Lemons in Positano

rants, coffee houses and workshops. Bathrooms, however, are a little tricky to find.

On the southeast corner of the market, and through a main gate, the Nuruosmaniye Kapisi ("Light of the Ottomans"), you will find the endlessly tempting shops of the Kalpakçýlarbaþý Caddesi ("Gold Jewelers' Road") that pay the highest rent, have the most enticing salesmen and are as close to a main street as the Bazaar has. And down about three blocks, on a right hand corner is #24, the shop of Mehmet Ceylan, the "Scarf Guy." There will be several years between my visits, but he always pretends that he remembers me, invites me in to the back of his shop to sit down and have tea, asks me about my family and tells me about his. There is no selling involved, just innate courtesy. I love it.

In the older and more traditional hans, you will find two stories of craftsmen and their shops surrounding a central courtyard. Some of these areas have been operating in this same setting since the 15th century, and many of the families involved have been there for several generations. If you can find it, visit the Sandal Bedesten off Kalpakçýlarbaþý Caddesi. It is called "The New Warehouse" because it wasn't built until the 17th century. Its rectangular hall with a domed roof supported by 12 large pillars is a good example of the structure of the original hans. Here in centuries past were found the most valuable items and that is still true today. You may find old coins, antique weapons, beautiful Turkish carpets, glazed tiles, glass and crystal, leather, copper, ceramics, gold and silver jewelry.

Farther from the center of the Bazaar, you can visit shops that are not as fancy as those in the central areas, but they're not as aggressive either. There it is still possible to watch a goldsmith or silversmith at his work. Take a good map, some comfy shoes, good humor and some patience, it is possible to wander there forever and not see everything.

Classically, of course, travel is meant to broaden our perspective and introduce us to a new world and a new sense of self. Unfortunately, my new self just might think that spending $200.00 on a silk robe in Hong Kong is brilliant only to get it home and have my real self think it was an incredibly stupid buy. Those fabulous suede boots purchased in Lisbon hurt like the dickens. The silk sari I bought in Calcutta won't

and flowers in Hong Kong.

stay up, and the keffiyeh I bought in the Upper Nile Valley looks just like Yasser Arafat's. On the other hand, I am still kicking myself for not buying the patina replica of a Bronze Age antelope in a shop near the fabulous Anthropological Museum in Athens. But I'll get back to Athens-eventually.

I've bought grapes in Capri, sausages in Salzburg, oranges in Nauphilon, noodles in Singapore, bread in Paris and spices in Istanbul. When I'm out in the wide world, going into a market will give me more of a window into that world than anything else I can do. It shows the personality, the richness or poverty, the soul and sensibility of a country more accurately than anything else I know. The fact that I do not understand the language, am unfamiliar with the food, the money and the customs is unimportant. I can learn enough to plunge right in.

There Were the Trains

"My heart is warm with the friends I make,
And better friends I'll not be knowing,
Yet there isn't a train I wouldn't take
No matter where it's going."
Edna St. Vincent Millay

I never saw a train I didn't want to board. I never saw a track I didn't want to follow, not for the arriving, but just for the going itself.

Everything is possible on a train, a good meal, a good night's sleep, an intrigue, a unique conversation, a cutthroat card game. With a comfortable seat, a good book and the possibility of a stranger's story, the journey itself is enough. Framed like small paintings the world goes by, the sari-clad women bending over immaculate green tea bushes, the lithe brown girl with a baby on her hip standing knee-deep in a lavender hyacinth-filled pool, the small Italian town painted in muted tones of washed-out pink, chalky yellow, surrounded by azaleas in bloom.

Arriving has its pleasures too. Entering a city is like the beginning of a symphony; the first few buildings are the soft opening woodwinds; a little more traffic brings in the entering strings; then clusters of shops add the brass, and finally more buildings and people and traffic until you are hurled headlong into the thunderous crescendo of the city itself. And you know you have arrived.

Trains have such bewitching names, the Royal Scotsman, South Africa's Blue Train, the eternally entrancing Orient Express. Just getting to ride the Orient Express itself would be an excellent excuse to travel; Lady Chatterley took it, and so did Hercule Poirot, James Bond and that canine nemesis, Cruella De Vil. The storied trains will give you a history of kings and courtesans, celebrities and spies. You might take trains purely for the efficiency of travel, but

The trains and the stories go on and on.

174

on the journey you will meet strangers with stories to tell, and this is what you will remember. The stories Chaucer's pilgrims told are the heart of that tale, not the arrival at the shrine.

From Rome to Brindisi on the coast, we were in an uncomfortable compartment with two Italian college students and their grandfather. They spoke no English and we spoke no Italian, but they spoke French and I sort of spoke Spanish and we had a French-Spanish dictionary. Figuring out how to communicate and exchanging personal bits and pieces made the long, rattley trip speed by. Incredibly they were related to every famous Italian I could think of. "My brother, my uncle, my cousin," they exclaimed in mock surprise as they tapped their chests. (One could wonder how one single family could be related to Sophia Loren, Robert Baggio and Luciano Pavarotti, but I wasn't going to doubt them. Besides, I told them that I was related to Tom Brady and Sandra Bullock.) Even the reserved old man unbent after a while and told us about growing up in his little northern village.

On the aged but elegant night train to Assam in Northern India, I spent most of the trip in the club car with a Darjeeling attorney and his wife. He was going for business while she was going for shopping. (It's hard to buy clothes when you live at the tip-top of the Himalayas.) We talked about children and politics and books. They thought I seemed a little Indian (the ultimate compliment), I thought they seemed marvelous.

On a train out of London, I met an entire college soccer team who were going to Cambridge for a match. Puppy-like, they spilled out of the seats and into the aisles, big-footed and eager. I got a very earnest and in-depth education on English professional soccer and the god-like virtues of Manchester United.

On a TGV high-speed train from Paris to Bordeaux, I sat near a well-suited gentleman who was using a lovely laptop. We went from computers, to the need for reading glasses, to golf, to restaurants in Bangkok, to his son's marriage. As his chauffeur met him at the station in Bordeaux, he thanked me for the conversation and said he was happy he had broken his own rule about talking to strangers.

On a train to Athens and at the other end of the social ladder, I met a graying, heavyset lady from the Greek countryside going into the capital. She was so thrilled at the trip that she didn't need any coaxing to talk. Her son was a member of the Presidential Guard, the Evzones, who with their kilts and embroidered jackets are such a distinctive guard of honor in Athens. That month he was assigned to the Tomb of the Unknown Soldier, and she was going into the city to see him. Her English was sketchy and my Greek is practically non-existent, but her excitement and pride didn't really require translation. It was a wonderful train trip.

Choir practice at Kronborg Castle

There Was the Music

I have been musically cursed since birth. The good music fairy, "Terpsichore," visited my baby cradle and gave me the gift of knowing every lyric I've ever heard, but none of the tunes. That doesn't mean I can't enjoy and love music, I just can't replicate it. Musical performances have been a delight everywhere I've traveled because music is one of those universal languages that transcends boundaries and links one person to another. (Rather like shopping.) I may not speak French or Chinese or Indonesian, but their music speaks to me. And again, those musical moments are part of what makes traveling so distinctive and memorable.

Once I was walking through an outer gallery of the Louvre, that ancient Parisian palace turned museum. It was late afternoon on a winter's day, cold and dark and a little haunted. Then I heard the pipes. Following the swirl of the music around a corner, there was a kilted, tartan-clad piper standing in an arcade, adding his own mystery to the lilt of the evening.

One night I sat near a bonfire in a Balinese jungle and watched the "Kecak," or monkey dance. Fifty or more bare-chested men came out of the jungle surrounding us, and the music they danced to in the darkness was made only by their chanting and the beat of palms on chests and thighs.

Once I got lost in Salzburg and found Mr. Mozart's house quite by accident. One of his melodies was playing as we walked through the rooms at "No. 9 Getreidegasse" where he was born and his childhood violin and clavichord are still kept. It was a lovely and golden afternoon. Then there was the Renaissance lute music playing at Chenonceau waiting for Mary, Queen of Scots to come home. On another trip, I listened to Vivaldi by candlelight at London's St. Martin-in-the-Fields.

Music lifts the soul, captures the mood and heightens the memory. The photo you see was taken at Kronborg in Elsinore, Denmark (think Hamlet), and it was travel serendipity that I was there at all.

Kronborg Castle, a World Heritage Site, is a unique and magnificent Renaissance castle built originally as a fortress in the 15th century to control the narrow waterway between Denmark and Sweden. Sitting on the point of the Oresund (the narrowest part of the strait), its ramparts made it stern, impregnable and lucrative. There's a lot of money to be made controlling shipping. But across the moats, through the drawbridge and inside the harsh and formidable stronghold, a jewel is hidden.

We had taken a tour of the castle which ended with a visit to the 16th century chapel. Saved from a disastrous fire in the 17th century by the strength of its arches, the gold-trimmed chapel includes a beautifully carved gallery pew reserved for the royal family and a magnificent Baroque organ. Some churches become dusty with disuse or decline into museums, but not this one, it was vibrant and alive, full of light and music. When we visited, the choir was practicing an elaborate hymn. Arranged in choir stalls around the altar, their music swelled up toward the church's stone arches, and the light coming through the stained glassed windows blessed them with a benediction as they practiced.

The light streamed in, the enormous and magnificent gold-rimmed arches soared, the red robes of the chorale shone in the sun, the choir master waived and pleaded and cajoled and the voices went straight up to heaven. I don't speak Danish, but it didn't matter. The music stays.

And Then There Were the Children

*"Children are the brightest treasures
we bring forth into this world."*
Charles de Lint

I have been asked where I live, how I am feeling and how old I am by children in Bali and Egypt, Turkey and India, Ireland and Thailand. Those questions seem to be the universal opening conversation for every beginning English speaker. Surrounded by fresh eager faces looking up at me, I used to answer sincerely and truthfully, "I am fine, thank you." "I am 35 or 40 or 45, etc. years old." "I am from Arizona in the United States of America."

I've lightened up since those early, serious travel days. Now I squat down to 7-year-old eye level and answer, "I am lost." (Unfortunately, this is often the case.) "I am 120 years old." "I live on the moon."

It takes a minute to register, and sometimes the home I have picked for myself needs to be gravely considered, but what follows is always the same worldwide. They look down at the ground and giggle. Then they poke each other and grin. Then they look at me and laugh out loud. And I have gone from being a foreigner giving them a chance to practice their English to a real person, albeit a silly one. Then they begin to talk to me.

I was clambering over fallen columns on the backside of the Acropolis hill. (If you'll remember, I got lost and had to come in the back door.) Down by the theater of Dionysus, I met a group of Greek school children who were in Athens on a field trip from a little town in the country. After we had gotten through the ritual questions regarding health and age, I knelt down, and one little girl shyly put out her finger and touched my hair. "Baruka?" she asked. I looked up at their teacher, and he explained. "She asked if you are wearing a wig." "No," I said, "I been stuck with red curly hair all my life." He told the children, and then I got to sit down patiently on a fallen column while each little one came and gravely, skeptically, tugged my hair.

My red hair wasn't quite so unusual in Ireland. In fact, that's the one place I've been asked for directions. But being from Arizona was unique. I picnicked in the grass

The little ones of Turkey,

Norway,

Denmark,

178

Bali

Arizona

and England

outside an open air museum in Ulster and shared sandwiches and stories one afternoon with a gaggle of 2nd graders. They told me all about ponies and soccer and pixies. I told them all about cowboys and Indians. I think I probably stretched the truth just a tad, but then, so did they. I told them my Indian name was Princess Summer-Fall-Winter-Spring, and they told me that pixies lived in the bottom of their gardens.

Do you remember my story about riding the little train up the mountains in the high Himalayas? There were children out that day too. Laughing and running beside the train like so many bright butterflies, they would jump on as we slowed down around the corners and jump off again at the next slow-down. We were all part of a great childhood game of racing and keep-away and catch.

In Turkish Konya, at the 13th century shrine of Mevlana, the Anatolian poet and mystic, a little boy offered to take me home with him. He was there with his father to visit the splendid museum, and after we had been introduced and I had explained that I lived on the moon and was 145 years old, he asked me home to meet his mother. We had to get on to Cappadocia that afternoon or I would have gone in a minute. So I had to settle for a hug instead.

The children of Bali told me that they were on their way home from school. Two sisters and a friend, they were 8 and 9 years old. They liked their school, loved their teacher and thought English was very difficult. I agreed. We shared tic-tacs and smiles, and I bought all the bananas they had.

Reflections on Travel – Opinions from Seat 43C

If you've read James Joyce's *Ulysses*, you're a better man than I am. I've tried to slog my way through it, but truthfully the only part I really like or remember is Molly Bloom's lush soliloquy, either because it is a feminine voice or because it is so blessedly short. Someone has said that a stream of consciousness monologue is like plunging into a flowing river and Joyce's success with Bloom's interior monologue is epic. Personally I just think it is soggy. At any rate, I've tried that inner consciousness technique a time or two, once on a plane, and I'm going to share it with you, although I admit I don't think I have much future in that genre.

I was flying back from London to Phoenix, and this was written on board the plane as we traveled. It is episodic and disjointed partially because of the length of the flight and partially because I was pooped.

"It's a longish flight," says the pilot as we prepare for take-off. Actually ten hours seems long until you've been to Sydney or Calcutta and then it pales in comparison. When I get stiff from sitting so long or bored by music or books or movies, I try to consider what getting from London to Phoenix was like even 100 years ago. Boats and trains and months of worry and aggravation. Lugging your belongings, what little you could take with you and just hoping you would make it before disease or Indians or mischance befell. With that in mind, today's current flight doesn't seem quite so bad. Although like the flight of the bumblebee, I never quite understand how the airplane gets off the ground.

Ice in your ginger ale and cashews in your hand at 34,000 feet. At this altitude, even the act of washing your hands becomes something of a miracle. The first time I was on a plane I looked for miracles too. I was hunting for castles in the clouds, couldn't find any and cried halfway to Nebraska,

Flying over Londonderry and Donegal in Northern Ireland, I began to read the flight map in Spanish. It's amazing what you will do to entertain yourself when ten hours of inactivity stretch out in front of you. Barriers began to break down on these long trips. The lady across from me is very pregnant, and I have been keeping a wary eye on her since we took off. Now bored and lonely, she is anxious for conversation, and I'm happy she wants to chat. She's British and married to an American doctor. This is her third baby, and she is only six weeks away from delivery. (I begin to wonder if the cabin crew know how to birth a baby.)

She and her husband lived in Virginia, handling a wealthy practice, when he decided he wanted to do something more. Now they live in the middle of the Navajo reservation in northern Arizona, and he takes care of people who truly need him. What stories her children will have to tell!

Past the tip of Greenland with sun-covered, snow-crusted mountains, beautiful and harsh in the light. Godthab and Angmagssalik, unpronounceable Viking names. Now North Labrador and Thunder Bay. Small things begin to take on significance. Why are some of the crew clutching blankets and pillows and hurrying to the back of the plane? A medical problem on board? Will we have to land in Montreal? At least it's not the pregnant woman across from me; she is sleeping peacefully if not comfortably. Thinking perhaps I'll be asked to perform open heart surgery, remove a brain tumor or fly the plane, I stop a stewardess. She laughs at me. No, they were just on break and were rushing to make the most of their time.

You know that the flight is beginning to wear when a sort of somnolence overtakes you. The books that you brought don't attract. The movie is ignored, and you are lulled into passive Zen detachment. I have visions of the Flying Dutchman, ever sailing, never landing. Finally, we fly over the Valley, and I am home. Getting away is good. Coming home is even better.

I like to remember the example of Montaigne, who found that when he was not at home, he could forget his illnesses and age. "Always in good spirits," says Bates, "always interested in everything and ready for a talk with the first man he met," wishing to avoid only those places "where he had been before or where he had to stop" for fear of coming upon the last page "of some delightful tale."

Leslie's Axioms of Travel

- *The farther south you are, the warmer the people become.*
- *It is possible to exist in Thailand for two weeks without mascara,*
- *but it ain't pretty.*
- *The longest plane change and the dullest book always coincide.*
- *Children will grin back if you smile. Grown-ups aren't so easy.*
- *Everyone will pity the poor stranger.*
- *The difficulty of locating items lost in a suitcase is always in inverse relationship to their importance.*
- *The more you need it, the farther away the restroom.*
- *If you are on a long bus ride, the people immediately behind you will be idiots who talk loudly.*
- *No other country ever carries your lipstick color.*
- *Taking only one pair of comfortable shoes is the best way of proving they aren't.*
- *It is possible to stand up in front of rare and wonderful things,*
- *fall asleep from exhaustion – and not care.*
- *Clean clothes are an unappreciated blessing.*
- *The best restaurants are available only when your tummy isn't happy.*
- *The toilet paper sold in 3rd world countries is always scratchy.*
- *No one can ever resist comparing photos of his children.*
- *When brushing your teeth, orange soda can sometimes be preferable to local tap water.*
- *Camera batteries only give out when there is a chance of a splendid shot.*
- *On an airplane, your lost shoe will always be found as far under the seat as far possible.*
- *Wine always tastes best in the region where the grapes were grown.*
- *It is possible to function without sleep for 36 hours.*
- *Every country's best food is its freshly baked bread.*
- *Extra pens always come in handy.*
- *The best thing about any trip is coming home to your own bed.... and ice cubes.*
- *The amount of wine drunk is in direct proportion to the distance from home.*
- *A bath tub plug can be a valuable commodity.*
- *The quirky experiences are always the best remembered.*

- *Dirty clothes at the bottom of a suitcase do not become cleaner through pressure.....but it is a nice thought.*
- *Nothing ever sounds as good as a call home.*
- *Only pack cheap sunglasses, umbrellas and pens. You will lose them.*
- *You always need to get more foreign currency just before you leave to go back home.*
- *Take curiosity and patience. Everything else (except lipstick and curling irons) can be purchased.*
- *Strangers will always prefer to tell you about their life rather than hear about yours.*
- *Danish television really does offer a man who plays his cheeks with a spoon.*
- *Humor rarely translates well.*
- *Everyone – in every country – has a cousin who lives in Chicago.*
- *Athens doesn't have traffic "rules"; they have traffic "suggestions".*
- *People prefer not to be told that their customs are "interesting folk rituals."*
- *Your camera will always wait to break until you are far from home and surrounded by beauty.*
- *It is possible to survive an oncoming tsunami of tourists by standing completely still and – as a rock in a stream - divide the current.*
- *Ideas captured on a plane are never as clever once you touch down.*
- *Always assume that everyone around you speaks English and is listening to you, and behave accordingly.*
- *The one belt that you brought to wear with everything will eventually be found – as you are unpacking at home.*
- *No other country is as beautiful or varied or as noble an experiment as ours, but it is not necessary to say so. Nonetheless, never pass up an opportunity to proudly declare, "I am an American."*
- *Pens always run out of ink just prior to a brilliant idea.*
- *When you come home, your dog will be thrilled; your cat will be irritated that you left at all.*
- *And finally, in the words of the indefatigable Queen Mum, "Never ignore an opportunity to eat, smile or use the loo."*

Michelangelo and the Snowstorm

Bruce Chatwin was a traveler addicted to seeing what was over the horizon and down the untraveled road. He believed that the urge to wander was a natural part of primitive man. "We are travelers from birth," he wrote. He felt that we are descended from hunter-gathers, but we have, over the millennia, allowed ourselves to crush this. The settlers have defeated the nomads. But not completely.

There are still nomads left, people for whom travel is as much a part of life as breathing. Robert Louis Stevenson was such a traveler, and he put it like this, "For my part, I travel not to go anywhere, but to go. I travel for travel's sake. The great affair is to move, to feel the needs and hitches of our life more nearly, to come down off this featherbed of civilization and find the globe granite underfoot and strewn with cutting flints."

When you are upset that the legroom in coach is not what it should be or that the lasagna served on the flight is cold, remember what travel used to be. Sir Ernest Shackleton, in his 1914 trans-Arctic expedition, advertised for fellow adventurers this way, "Men wanted for hazardous journey. Small wages, bitter cold, long months of complete darkness, constant danger, safe return doubtful. Honor and recognition in case of success."

Travel is not something you can get your hands around. You can't take it home with you, hang it on the living room wall, invite the family in and the neighbors over to admire your new acquisition. It is transitory and fleeting, as quick as a glance, as wispy as a bit of cloud. The harder you try to grab it, the more elusive it becomes.

Once, after a rare winter storm in Florence, Pietro de Medici is said to have asked Michelangelo to create a sculpture in the snow. Legend has it that it was the artist's greatest work. More beautiful than the *Pieta,* more awe-inspiring than the *David*, it was conceived, created and existed for only a few brief days. And then it was gone forever.

Travel is like Michelangelo's snowman; it cannot be replicated. It is an ephemeral experience and melts quickly away. It is irreplaceable, unrepeatable and priceless and lives only in the memory which makes it all the more precious.

May the road rise up to greet you.

32331538R00112

Made in the USA
Lexington, KY
15 May 2014